PRIDE
AND
PREJUDICE
II

The Sequel

VICTORIA PARK

Order this book online at www.trafford.com
or email orders@trafford.com

Most Trafford titles are also available at major online book retailers.

Printed in the United States of America.

ISBN: 978-1-4669-4135-9 (sc)
ISBN: 978-1-4669-4137-3 (hc)
ISBN: 978-1-4669-4136-6 (e)

Library of Congress Control Number: 2012909914

Trafford rev. 10/02/2012

 www.trafford.com

North America & international
toll-free: 1 888 232 4444 (USA & Canada)
phone: 250 383 6864 ♦ fax: 812 355 4082

Author's Acknowledgements

While writing a technical thesis, the Pride and Prejudice II occurred to me from somewhere called the ether. I started typing, hoping to do justice to Jane Austen's classic work, Pride and Prejudice.

Pride and Prejudice II unrolled before me as I typed. Many other writers have experienced this phenomenon. The problem was not the writing of it but the stopping of the work. I could easily complete another three volumes. I have my technical work to complete so that I have set aside Jane Austen just for now. However, I shall return to finish the third book of Pride and Prejudice.

I dedicate this work to Martyn, Penelope, Nigel and Samantha who I hold in the highest esteem.

I would like to offer thanks to Bob and Joy. They assured me that they do not mind making a debut in the story for all eternity. I do hope you both enjoy the read.

Bob and Joy own three cats, two black and one ginger cat called Fred.

More thanks to Mary, a class mate for five years of the Alpha stream of our grammar school. Mary owns a dachshund named William.

Robin Chandley, my dear, charming nephew has been a real practical help with my life while I busied myself writing these volumes. So more grateful thanks there.

My apologies to all my French friends who I regard highly and not any are as ghastly as during the Napoleonic Age as I have portrayed

Many of the places mentioned in Pride and Prejudice II are real and make for interesting visits their atmosphere breaths life into the story and will enhance the readers' enjoyment.

Pride and Prejudice II, The Sequel is an inspiration that I put on paper mainly for the pleasure of writing for me and the entertainment for my dear readers. However, there is some educational value to enjoy on many pages of the book.

Happy reading to all!

The Main Characters of Pride & Prejudice

Mr. Bennet
Mrs Bennet
Jane Bennet - Eldest daughter
Elizabeth Bennet - 2nd daughter
Mary Bennet - 3rd daughter
Kitty Bennet - 4th daughter
Lydia Bennet - 5th and youngest daughter

Sir William Lucas - relatives of the Bennet family
Lady Lucas - wife to Sir William Lucas
Charlotte Lucas -Eldest daughter of Sir William
Lucas - friend and cousin to Elizabeth
Maria Lucas - younger sister to Charlotte

Mr. Gardiner - London family, brother to Mrs Bennet.
Mrs Gardiner - Sister-in-law to Mrs Bennet

Mr. Darcy Landlord of Pemberley House and estates
Georgiana Darcy - sister of Mr. Darcy
House keeper to Pemberley House
Mr. Wickham - Son of the late steward of
Pemberley - boyhood friend of Mr. Darcy.

Mr. Charles Bingley - Gentleman of substance
five thousand a year and Darcy's friend

Mrs Louisa Hurst - Sister to Mr. Bingley
and married to Mr. Hurst
Mr. Hurst - Husband of Mrs Hurst
Miss Caroline Bingley - Mr. Bingley's second sister

Lady Catherine de Bourgh - Aunt to Mr. Darcy
Anne de Bourgh - daughter of Lady Catherine
Mrs Jenkinson - attendant and companion to Lady Catherine
Mr. Collins - Cousin to Bennet family heir to Bennet
estates. Parson to the Parish, which includes Rosings
Park, the residence of Lady Catherine.

Colonel Fitzwilliam - Cousin and friend to Mr. Darcy
Colonel Forster - Colonel to the Infantry Regiment
Mrs Forster - Wife to Colonel Forster

Résumé of Pride & Prejudice by Jane Austen

The story begins with the arrival on the local scene of Mr. Bingley. He is accompanied by his good friend, Mr. Darcy who has a large estate in Derbyshire and ten thousand a year—twice that of Bingley.

Bingley takes a lease of a local estate insisting that he must live somewhere.

A dance at the local Assembly Rooms is attended by the local ladies and gentlemen of any consequence and their families. Darcy proves to be unsociable and his pride and his prejudices are publicly aired to the distaste of Elizabeth and many others. Darcy has established his reputation so that Elizabeth rules out any romantic notions.

In contrast, Mr. Bingley demonstrates his attraction to Jane Bennet. In subsequent dances and social events, Mr. Bingley continues his admiration for Jane. While this was expected, Darcy falling for Elizabeth was not. Elizabeth ignores his attentions. Charlotte heeds Elizabeth to consider the advantages of Darcy's interest of her. During visits to Rosings Darcy proposes to Elizabeth but she makes emphatically clear that she dislikes him. "You are the last person on earth that I could ever marry."

Mr. and Mrs Gardiner invite Elizabeth to join them on an excursion around the country. While stopping over at an inn at Lambton where Mrs Gardiner grew up, Elizabeth is persuaded to join them for a visit to Pemberley. Being assured that the master of that great house would be absent they visit the house and grounds only to discover Darcy returning a day earlier than expected. The two parties encounter each other but everything goes off well. Bingley and his two sisters join with the Gardiners, Elizabeth and Darcy for a social evening which proves to be successful.

The following day Elizabeth receives a letter to explain that Lydia has eloped with Wickham. This news changes everything and Elizabeth's party are obliged to terminate the excursion to return home in disgrace.

Mr. Darcy steps in to resolve all the problems, pays all the expenses so the good name of Bennet is untarnished. Girl impressed, falls madly in love with her hero, so marries him at a double wedding, which included Bingley and Miss Jane Bennet.

Pride & Prejudice II follows on from that wedding.

Main Additional Characters in
Pride & Prejudice II

Mr. Robert Dubery - Landlord of the Two Black Cats Inn

Mrs Joyce Dubery - Landlady of the Two Black Cats Inn

Fred the ward of Mr. & Mrs Dubery

King George the Third

Barney - Leader of the gypsy family

Sacha - Son of Barney

Contents

Volume One

Chapter One

The Engagement and Wedding

Mr. and Mrs Bennet had announced in the newspapers the engagement of their daughter, Miss Elizabeth Bennet to Mr. Darcy. The bride's father felt great pride in next announcing that the double wedding of his daughter and Mr. Darcy and his eldest daughter, Miss Jane Bennet to Mr. Bingley will take place at the church at Meryton. Family, friends, acquaintances and the country all around received the announcement with great alacrity.

— o —

INVITATION

The double wedding
(by special license)

of

Miss Elizabeth Bennet and Mr. Darcy

and

Miss Jane Bennet and Mr. Bingley

The Service

The wedding service will be conducted at the Parish Church of Meryton on the 10th day of January in this New Year.

— o —

Following the completion of the ceremonies, Mr. and Mrs Bingley returned to Netherfield Park to find the staff waiting to greet them. Everyone was eager to offer their congratulations to the young couple. No greater greeting was surely ever seen between servant and master? The villagers made the ceremonies of the double wedding an excuse for much festivities and merrymaking.

The first party of the double wedding, now Mr. and Mrs Darcy, took their coach to London. After an overnight delay, they continued their travels. From London, their road led directly to the East Coast of Kent to find the ancient town of Dover. The road proved to be of good metal and their journey swift and comfortable.

Chapter Two

Mr. and Mrs Darcy Journey Home

Mr. and Mrs Darcy, the newly wed couple, had sojourned for a month at the beautiful Port of Dover. From Dover, they had spent much of their time exploring the places of interest even as far as the City of Canterbury. They were captivated with its grand cathedral, the ancient buildings and sightings of the Pilgrim routes of medieval times. This month had seemed to pass too quickly for them, for they became accustomed to the style of living that included pure self-indulgence and leisure. The sojourn had offered Mr. and Mrs Darcy the opportunity to explore also each other more intimately. The experience did not disappoint either party. One might even observe that they had moved closer together, even more consolidating their intimacy and harmony.

With their honeymoon spent, they made good preparations for departure. Now they would journey homeward but also, along the way, pay their respects to their friends and family before finally moving on to Pemberley.

Elizabeth was in high expectation of returning to Pemberley. The house that she believed to be, "the most pleasantly situated." Pemberley was now her home of which she was the absent mistress.

This, the last breakfast before leaving, was in progress even before Elizabeth arrived at the table with her customary polite but cheerful morning greeting. Over her husband's shoulder, as he sat at the table, Elizabeth leaned forward to start their day with a kiss on his cheek. Then she enquired if any post had arrived. Mr Darcy was already anticipating her, in return offering letters and smiling at his new wife saying in good humour,

"Only three for you today, Mrs Elizabeth Darcy."

Delighted both for the mail and the address of her new married status she exclaimed,

"Three, but from whom?"

Taking them eagerly, Elizabeth shuffled through the letters, "One from Charlotte.

This letter is from dear Kitty and this one? Oh! How grand this one appears. Do you recognise the seal, sir?

Mr. Darcy had already marked the letter but knew nothing of its contents. He was, of course, aware that this was their first married correspondence from his Aunt, the Lady Catherine de Bourgh.

"Why", He thought, "should my aunt write to Elizabeth and not to me in the customary fashion?"

Mr. Darcy addressed Elizabeth, "My dear Elizabeth, why not save your letters to read while we are on the road? You will, no doubt, be glad of the diversion."

Disappointed but in agreement with her husband's sensible submission, Elizabeth carefully placed her correspondence into her pouch. She looked forward so much to the news from Charlotte and from home. The third letter was less certain. Was this a dark foreboding or an elevated greeting from what was now a distinguished relative by marriage?

Preparations all made, the luggage loaded, Elizabeth and Mr. Darcy mounted the coach to take their seats for the journey that should eventually lead them home. As they quitted the town, Elizabeth could not but look back and remember all the happy events that she and her husband had enjoyed over those precious days of the last month. Across the coach, Elizabeth looked at her most handsome husband to inform him, "I am so very happy Mr. Darcy."

Then Elizabeth asked, "Will it always be like this?"

Mr. Darcy beamed a smile as broad as his face and took Elizabeth's hand to reassure her,

"I am told it improves with the years."

Mr. and Mrs Darcy smiled broadly and at length to each other until Mr. Darcy reminded Elizabeth of the contents of her purse.

It was after a few miles, upon the prompting of her husband; Elizabeth retrieved her correspondence from her pouch. The initial problem for Elizabeth was which piece of news to read first. As the coach continued onwards, her thoughts meandered back to her former life with her mother and father and four sisters. How she would miss all her family. All the memories she recalled, including the fiasco with Mr. Collins' proposal and then Charlotte marrying him. Latterly, her visits to Rosings and the overpowering Lady Catherine de Bourgh did not make her decision easier. At length, Elizabeth took the letter that was from her sister Kitty. It read,

— o —

Longbourne March 1ˢᵗ. May

Dearest Elizabeth,

My mother and father and Mary too, desire that I should send you their very best wishes. All the family knew that I was about to write to you again. Our home seems so empty now without our three lately married sisters.

Maria is visiting often because she too must miss the company of her elder sister.

We have not heard from Lydia yet but I understand that Wickham has sent a note to father to say that they shall be in the country while they travel south. He gives no reason for their move but seeks an invitation from our father for a visit. I know no more than that. I am sure we will learn more in due course.

I have had more news from Charlotte but she says that she will write to you. She will tell you her news but I must add that by the time you reach her Charlotte will be in confinement. She asked me to beg you not to prevent that from visiting her. We are planning a family outing to visit Charlotte immediately after the birth or as soon as she is ready to receive us.

Dear Jane and Mr. Bingley have travelled north to choose a house for their future life together. I understand that they may not be too far distant from Pemberley. It is not yet decided.

I will write again as soon as I am able to learn of the missing pieces of information.

Your most affectionate sister,
Kitty.

— o —

Elizabeth contemplated the contents of the letter. It was quite short and precise, as she would expect from Kitty. The news that Jane may not be too far from Pemberley pleased her immensely. Elizabeth could imagine many visits to Jane and Mr. Bingley and their return visits to Pemberley for many happy distractions. The news from Wickham was no less interesting but intriguing. Why should he and Lydia be travelling southwards? Was all well with the regiment? Were Lydia and Wickham still in favourable circumstances? With so many questions running through her mind, Elizabeth wanted so much to know more. The answers must wait as she and they endure the passage of time. Elizabeth carefully refolded the letter to replace it in her purse. As the coach rumbled and tumbled on its way, her thoughts dwelt on Charlotte, her cousin and best friend. As Charlotte now is to become a mother, so she, Elizabeth, will become an aunt. The thoughts provoked the feelings of a sense of really being adult and important now in some way. The thoughts of her importance naturally led her to the tasks and adventures awaiting her as Mistress of Pemberley. Pemberley, her home and her responsibility is waiting for her so patiently in Derbyshire. Until Elizabeth returned to Pemberley, she felt that she could never be a complete person.

These thoughts were galloping through her mind as she automatically withdrew the next letter from her purse. Slowly breaking the seal and unfolding the letter from her Cousin Charlotte as though, deep in her thoughts as she was, Elizabeth was far distant in spirit.

Mr. Darcy invaded her contemplations to explain, "We are making good progress. Already we have passed the little village of Bonham Marshes. The next place of interest is Dagenbury and we could stop to refresh ourselves and rest the horses awhile if it would please you? There is a wholesome inn called The Two Black Cats, which boasts an excellent fare and good stables for the animals."

This interjection drew Elizabeth's thoughts back to the present moment and place.

"Why, yes that would be an excellent diversion indeed and good for the horses too. Thank you, Mr Darcy, and thank you from the horses."

They smiled again at each other until her eyes were distracted and rested on the unread letter.

"I will sit here quietly while you read your letter." Darcy assured Elizabeth with a broad smile, which she returned.

Elizabeth unfolded, the letter to reveal the hand of Charlotte. She read on . . .

— o —

The Parsonage, Hunsford   Friday

My Dearest Cousin Elizabeth,

I do hope that you are well and that you have enjoyed your stay at Dover with Mr. Darcy.

I have heard some news regarding Lady Catherine de Bourgh who is still unashamedly opposed to your marriage with her nephew. Her objections seem to be your family connections, which are bad enough in her opinion. Also, that you have little otherwise to recommend yourself as the wife of her closest nephew. I tell you this so that you can be on your guard when you arrive here.

As you must know, I am in confinement waiting the birth of our baby. I am so apprehensive and to make things the worse everyone is trying to reassure me that there is nothing to give concern. If there is indeed nothing to give concern, why do they say so and so often? I shall be so pleased to see you and I shall be pleased when this uncomfortable event is over. Make all haste, dear Elizabeth; I so need your company even more at this time.

Mr Collins keeps to himself but busy and apart from me, mainly because he has no comprehension of this situation. So that I am really alone.

I have more news of Lady Catherine but I cannot set it on paper. It will do until you come.

Writing is so very uncomfortable. I cannot find a position that does not give me some pain so.

I apologise for being so short. Come with haste and I will tell you all.

God bless you.

Your affectionate friend and cousin,
Charlotte

—o—

This was unlike Charlotte, to be so self-indulgent. Charlotte's anticipation of the birth of her baby must be the reason.

"I agree, Charlotte." Elizabeth thought to herself. "Let us pray that all will go well for you and your baby."

Folding the letter, she carefully returned it to her purse.

The thoughts of Pemberley were ever with Elizabeth. "Later today, just hours away, I shall be mistress of the house and all that surrounds it. There will be so much to do and learn. So many tasks for me to attend. So many new people to meet."

These thoughts became more detailed, made her feel even more excited for the new life waiting for her in Derbyshire.

Chapter Three

Mrs Darcy meets Mr. and Mrs Dubery

Elizabeth was pleasantly surprised as the coach reached the very pretty town of Dagenbury. As they passed the houses and places of trade and business, all seemed much like any other little market town with all the accompanying noises and voices crying their wares. The hustle and bustle of market day was now in full swing. The excitement it caused took Elizabeth's attentions away from the correspondence and Pemberley even.

The party arrived at The Inn of the Two Black Cats. Ostlers were there at once. They attended to the horses even before they had descended the coach. Elizabeth was thinking this to be strange because Mr. Darcy had not yet settled with the office.

From the coach, Elizabeth was at Mr. Darcy's side as they approached the entrance to The Inn of the Two Black Cats.

Mr. Darcy took Elizabeth's hand as they walked forwards to the doors to say; "This will prove to be a pleasant breaking stage for us, Elizabeth. Our hosts Mr. and Mrs Dubery are very attentive and will be even more so where you are concerned. They have been looking forward to meeting you for some time."

These words surprised Elizabeth. She felt like something small bobbing in some vast ocean. She had lost control of her normal sense of decorum. She did not know nor had she ever heard of a Mr. and Mrs Dubery.

There were questions running through her head. "Why should this be so? Why attentive to me so specially?" Before Elizabeth could dwell longer on the puzzle, she was inside the inn and before Mr. and Mrs Dubery, their hosts for the short break of their journey.

Mr. Darcy with his broad smile spoke first to announce proudly, "Mr. and Mrs Dubery, my wife, Mrs Elizabeth Darcy."

This, he followed with a polite bow.

Mr. Dubery was a tallish man of full figure. Smiling pleasantly almost constantly, he presented a picture of an altogether very agreeable gentleman. Mrs Dubery looked very pleasant and appeared to be an ideal match to her husband. Less than him physically but having the appearance that suggested a more practical turn of mind.

Mr. Dubery took a generously low bow, "I am indeed enchanted, Mrs Darcy. On behalf of my family, I would like to greet you to our establishment and offer you all assistance to satisfy you and Mr. Darcy during your stay here now and at any time. We are at your service Mrs Darcy."

Mrs Dubery curtsied and politely suggested to Elizabeth, "Dear Mrs Darcy, if you would like to refresh yourself and inspect the services I should be pleased to be of assistance and show you the way."

Grateful for Mrs Dubery's few words Elizabeth followed her through rooms and passages to the rear of the establishment to the private apartments. There she could refresh herself from the dust and trials of her journey. All the while though, Elizabeth's thoughts were racing to make sense of this situation.

"Why should their hosts be so warm and so generous? Mr. Darcy must have arranged this staging off to break for some refreshments." She was thinking, "But this did not explain the extraordinary behaviour and why me personally? We have never been acquainted."

Elizabeth once more recomposed, accepted Mrs Dubery's invitation to a seat in the private dining room. The table displayed much fine fare. All appeared very inviting, more than she had seldom ever enjoyed. As she was making herself comfortable at the table, Mr. Darcy and Mr. Dubery entered the room while talking and exchanging words in a most informal manner. Mrs Dubery arranged the gentlemen's seating and in a moment, they were ready to eat. Mr. Dubery made a motion to Mrs Dubery and to Mr. Darcy. They then bowed their heads to give thanks to the Almighty for the food on their table adding that Mr. and Mrs Darcy should enjoy a pleasant and uneventful journey as they travel to Rosings.

Elizabeth joined them in the "Amen."

"Now," Mr. Dubery pronounced the statement with some emphasis to gain everybody's attention, "We can be quite informal here, so I will introduce you, Elizabeth, to our names. Mrs Dubery, my dear wife, is Joyce or Joy to her friends and family and I am simply Bob to you."

Elizabeth looked enquiringly to Mr. Darcy. Shocked, surprised, completely bewildered at this strange announcement, especially the friends and family claim. "But what is all this, Mr. Dubery, who are you?"

Mr. Dubery replied straight away but not exactly as Elizabeth expected. "Bob please, Elizabeth, we have so much to talk about so let us be friendly and informal."

Mr. Darcy interjected to rescue them, "Dear Elizabeth, please allow me to explain. Bob and Joy are actually part of your extended family now. Bob and Joy are close cousins to Lady Catherine de Bourgh and this means that we are all related. Wickham, Bob and I were all at college together. These two vagabonds inherited Dagenbury including the inn, amongst other things, and took to the trade. They discovered that they enjoyed the inn so much that it is now their life. Bob is a gentleman innkeeper. This is what they want to do. Naturally, my aunt, Lady Catherine de Bourgh, was not overjoyed at hearing the news of her cousins voluntarily involving themselves in trade. She is therefore very careful to guard the secret from the world. It would be most indecorous of you to give any hint of your knowledge of her secret. Although I know you will not utter a word on the subject to anyone else."

Elizabeth tried not to imagine the detrimental effect of this knowledge becoming widely known. The possible damage to Lady Catherine's status threatened to undermine her position of authority.

She could not help but recall the question by Lady Catherine, "But what of your connections?"

Elizabeth looked down at her plate for a moment or two, and then straightened herself up to say, "Bob and Joy, I came here today expecting service and civility. Instead I find friendship and kinship and an excellent lunch altogether. So, please forgive me if I appeared somewhat bewildered."

"Oh! Bravo! Cried the hosts who hardly expected quite such an adjustment to what might have been impossible to some, like Lady Catherine de Bourgh for example.

They were all looking at her, smiling, delighted at her reaction to the news and all three waiting as though expecting some other response from her.

Elizabeth hesitated. She did not know what to do or what was required of her. Elizabeth was well aware of the importance and the implications of this new and unexpected knowledge.

"So this," Elizabeth thought to herself, "Is why Mr. Darcy came this way and to this inn in particular. I must not mention it to anyone else because if I do, I shall lose the power it has if this relationship became common knowledge. The power is in the secrecy."

Her attention came back to the present company. Elizabeth measured her words while toying with her cutlery then looked up at her hosts, "I understand wholeheartedly, Bob and Joy, the wisdom of your choice of lifestyle because I too have found my dream, my happiness."

She leaned across to take Mr. Darcy's hand to squeeze it firmly to indicate her meaning. They could not help but smile at each other and feel so much more relaxed as they should at a family meeting.

Mr. Dubery joined into the spirit of the occasion to add, "And all imaginable happiness and joy to you both in your new life together, . . . Mr. and Mrs Darcy."

Mrs Dubery raised her glass to announce, "Happiness and joy to you both!"

Together they raised their glasses to drain them of the excellent wine, thus sealing the equally excellent sentiments.

The generous repast continued in jovial style. At length the food eaten, the party rested, it became time to make the farewells and to make promises to return and often.

However, for now it was, "Onward to Rosings! Then all haste to Pemberley."

Reluctantly, the travellers made their way to the carriage, which was waiting and ready for them. To Elizabeth's astonishment, this was not the same coach in which they had arrived. This was a Landau carriage bearing the liveries of Lady Catherine de Bourgh.

Elizabeth was not mistaken. The livery of the retinue and the coat of arms on the door of the carriage were all too familiar to her by now.

Mr. Darcy, anticipating her reaction, felt it timely to explain. "Lady Catherine's carriage was sent yesterday. I imagine, in the hope that you would not delay your journey by visiting the inn and contacting Bob and Joy. If you say nothing of the visit, my aunt will be in high suspense for evermore."

"But the top is down and it looks like it could rain Mr. Darcy."

On overhearing this, the retinue looked at Mr. Darcy who nodded to them. Thus, the men proceeded to put the top in position. The luggage was already loaded and once again, the couple were mounting their carriage, this time in order to complete their next stage of their journey to Rosings before going on to Pemberley.

All the time Elizabeth was mentally dwelling on this new turn of events. How this secret must haunt Lady Catherine. Elizabeth did not want to hurt anyone but the protection of her own interests may at sometime lie in the secret at the inn. As the carriage moved away, both her newly found relatives and allies were waving a farewell to which she and Mr. Darcy responded enthusiastically.

It was after some distance and some time Elizabeth thought of her letters. There was one more still unread. The most intriguing letter in view of her new found relatives and the contents of Charlotte's letter. She felt a new confidence now through the experiences of this day. Elizabeth felt in her purse for her letters. It was, at first, with complete disbelief that she could not feel her letters in her purse. With growing concern, her hand fumbled more for the letters but there were none. Mr. Darcy could see the look of concern on the face of his wife and enquired as to the reason for such apparent alarm.

Elizabeth responded, "My letters, my letters, where are they? They should be in my purse but are no longer. My letters are missing, Mr. Darcy."

Her husband, more calm but still concerned for Elizabeth and the letters, responded, "They must still be at the inn, Elizabeth. You may have left them somewhere or perhaps, dropped them. I am confident that Bob or Joy will find them and forward them on to you expeditiously."

"The problem is that I shall not be able to read Lady Catherine's letter before we arrive at Rosings." Replied Elizabeth.

She tried to picture in her mind what terrible faux pas she might commit without knowing the contents of Lady Catherine's letter.

As Elizabeth spoke, it began to rain. For some miles, the rain persisted but becoming heavier and again heavier before it settled to a steady rate. Apart from the noise of the rain beating on the outside all was quiet inside the carriage. The silence was, perhaps, partly due to the concern of the problems that the rain could make to their journey. Fate was not in the mood to disappoint their concerns as the carriage slewed, slowed, and then came to a halt with a judder.

Mr. Darcy leaned out of the window and through the rain shouted, "Driver, what is the hold up?"

The coachman retorted, "We are stuck in a quagmire of mud sir. We shall have to ease the carriage out by turning the wheels at their spokes by hand until we can free her, sir."

Darcy, "Can we not solicit help?"

Driver, "I am afraid we are in an isolated spot just here. The two coachmen will manage I am sure sir. It shouldn't take long and we will be on our way again"

The two liveried men jumped down from the carriage to find themselves already ankle deep in mud. They looked at each other with disconcertion. The men stepped warily through the mud until they reached the carriage wheels. Each took a rear wheel and prepared to grasp the spokes in readiness, then called to the driver to pull with the horses. The men were floundering deeper into the mud but after several tries without making any headway they stopped to rest themselves.

With the rain still incessant, one of the men shouted to the driver, "It won't work, the carriage won't move, not even with the horses pulling."

Cursing under his breath, Mr. Darcy jumped from the carriage into the mud to give more muscle to the job.

Mr. Darcy gave the order and all three men shouted together, "Heave! Heave! Heave!"

With the horses straining and the men heaving, the carriage was nearly moving up and forward. The party only needed one more man. The three men stopped for breath, so exhausted now, they cared little for the constant rain. It was a blessing by way of being cooling to the hot and exhausted men.

They stayed in the rain to cool down. They were recovering from their efforts, leaning over with their hands resting on their legs while trying to recover their breath.

Their attempts had taken a deal of time and effort. Even Darcy was not inclined to take shelter from the rain. A distant sound of horse's hooves was breaking through the noise of the continuous downpour.

"A rider, listen, a rider approaches." Called out one man.

Further down the way, riding at some speed, a horseman was making good headway through the rain. He was coming from the direction of Dagenbury. The men and Darcy all laughed with relief upon realising that God-sent help was approaching nearer by the minute.

"Soon," Each man thought, "We shall be on our way again."

The rider came nearer. He was well covered and protected against the rain. As he brought his horse alongside the carriage he called out, "Are you in difficulties? Are you stuck in ser quagmire?" The man spoke in a slight foreign accent.

Mr. Darcy came forward to ask if the gentleman would help.

Again, the rider spoke, "Can you not move zur?"

Mr. Darcy only just recovering from the physical exertion was in little mood to answer the question or deny the obvious.

He asked the rider, "Can you help us sir? Can you lend a hand to turning our wheels so to free us out of the mud?"

Whereupon the rider produced two fine matching pistols at such a dash that it took Mr. Darcy aback.

The rider called out, "Your money zur, or your life."

Chapter Four

Problems for Mr. and Mrs Darcy
on the Road

Mr. Darcy stepped forward to plead with the rider, "If you help us now I will give you more than the earnings from a night's work such as yours . . . ."

Before Mr Darcy could finish his sentence, the horseman deliberately aimed at Mr. Darcy and fired off one pistol. The report of the firearm disturbed the horse. The force of the ball into his body threw Mr. Darcy violently back against the carriage.

Elizabeth, having witnessed these events, then upon being frightened by the report of the pistol, rented the evening sky with a scream. Thereupon the rider's horse reared with fear that caused the highwayman to inadvertently fire off his remaining pistol but wildly. The second ball smashed into the woodwork of the carriage to disappear harmlessly into the interior. The horseman immediately took flight and at such speed so that he was soon out of sight in the fading light.

Elizabeth fell from the carriage door onto the muddy road and was instantly kneeling beside her husband. Not one of the retinue of the three liverymen could move. The speed of the life threatening events transfixed the men out of their senses.

Elizabeth screamed, "Help me with my husband."

The retinue immediately attended to Mr. Darcy, picking him up with all the utmost heedfulness that their charge deserved. By a great number of various contrivances, the four of them managed to move the body into the carriage from the muddy ground and pouring rain. In the dry, they had some light from the interior carriage lamp. The sudden sight of the gash, and the blood and the wound in Mr Darcy's body caused Elizabeth to lose her senses and collapse onto the floor of the carriage.

The rain was beating down incessantly. The retinue were now without an authority to give them orders. Two were standing in the rain and the third stood inside the carriage. He looked down at the collapsed Elizabeth and then at the bloody body of Mr. Darcy.

Through the dark and the beating, pounding rain, the noise of a rider, again coming from the direction of Dagenbury, began to make itself heard. The sound of the hoof beats seemed to come and go but gradually as the hoof beats drew nearer they grew louder and became more consistent. The rider approached in the darkness and in the incessant pouring rain. He had no idea what lay ahead of him and might have passed the carriage by had the servants not called out. The horseman pulled over and sighted the carriage lamp. He drew nearer and peered through the carriage window. Searching with his eyes, he could see a prostrate man with a serious open wound. He could see much blood. He could see a woman prostrate on the floor.

A servant now called to him, "Will you help us sir? We have a mortally injured gentleman and the carriage is stuck in the mire."

The horsemen called out, "What villain did this?"

"It was a highwayman sir, a robber. Will you help us?"

"I am after that villain." The horseman tugged on the reins to ride off at a great haste into the night, the darkness and the rain.

The carriage, its contents and the servants were once more alone.

The servants took what shelter they could. In the rain and cold, they waited. The men had no idea how long they would have to wait, but waiting was all they could do. At that time of night, there seemed little hope of any new company before the morning light.

Through the noise of the whipping rain, the distant sounds of hoof beats heralded the approach of a number of horsemen. One of the servants moved quickly to take a carriage lamp to light it from the interior carriage lamp. He then stepped out again in the rain and stood in the middle of the road waving his lamp to and fro. As he did so, he called out for the riders to stop.

Thinking quickly meanwhile, the driver had moved swiftly to mount the coach to the driver's seat. Under the seat was a very business-like small arm by way of a blunderbuss. There was no time to check anything but simply to wait as the sound of speeding hoofs advanced towards them from the direction of Dagenbury. Four horsemen arrived, all military men. From their appearance, they had ridden their horses hard.

The driver shouted to the soldiers, "There are three of us here, gentlemen, and we are all armed. One of the horsemen gently urged his mount forward to show himself so that they could see that he was an officer then calmly asked the driver, "You have a problem with the coach sir?"

The driver explained to the officer that they had a mortally injured man in the carriage.

He continued, "We're stuck in a gutter in the quagmire and we're not able to move the coach back'ards or for'ards, sir."

The officer gave instant orders for two of his men to lend their shoulders to the wheels. Within seconds, the two coachmen and the two soldiers were pressing on the spokes of the wheels. With barely two minutes but of a great deal of exertion the coach lifted up as it moved forward onto firmer ground. The driver with much needed effort restrained the horses.

The officer shouted up to the driver, "Have two villains passed you by this way, sir?"

Meanwhile, inside the carriage, Elizabeth was recovering. Then, upon hearing a familiar voice, appeared at the window of the carriage to scream out, "Wickham! Wickham!"

At the moment of this sudden noise that disturbed the horses Wickham quickly pulled alongside the window and could not but show astonishment and pleasure to discover his favourite sister-in-law.

"Wickham, Mr. Darcy has been shot. Look here!"

Wickham dismounted his horse and was inside the carriage in a moment. The carriage lantern revealed an unexpected scene of Mr Darcy and blood all over. It was beginning to smell putrid. Upon discovering the serious condition of the wound, he turned to Elizabeth to say gravely, "There is an army surgeon in the next village. You may have passed it by, called Dagenbury."

Giving her instructions on the best way to find the surgeon, Wickham continued, "I will leave one man to escort you and another will ride ahead to warn the surgeon of the situation. Meanwhile, keep your husband as comfortable as possible. During the journey, he may come round. If he does, keep talking to him all the time. Prepare yourself for the very worst possible situation, my dear sister."

Turning his attention to his soldiers, Wickham gave orders to one of his men to escort the carriage to the army surgeon at Dagenbury. He ordered another soldier to ride off in the direction of Dagenbury to warn the surgeon of the arrival of their charge. He ordered the remaining soldier to accompany him to continue their pursuit of the villains. After the briefest of courtesies, Wickham and his man soon disappeared into the darkness.

Through the dark and the rain Elizabeth could hear the sound of their hoof beats gradually lessen, leaving her with a feeling of loneliness.

It seemed strange that in the depth of her despair that Wickham should arrive take full control of the situation and then disappear again so suddenly leaving her abandoned with Mr Darcy. It was now just as though nothing had happened and nobody had been.

Elizabeth thoughts echoed, "The worst possibility."

Suddenly she felt very cold and lonely. Life without Darcy gave her an intense feeling of emptiness. Her deepest emotions of love swept through her, which made her stronger, to think that she would not let him down. Elizabeth called out to the driver to return to Dagenbury with all haste.

The coach started, turned slowly to face Dagenbury then gradually gained momentum to proceed at such a pace that allowed the maximum speed without compromising the comfort of their wounded passenger. The road surface improved gradually the nearer to Dagenbury they approached.

The army surgeon was already in the street with a torchbearer at his side waiting for the arrival of the carriage and his patient. After the briefest formalities, the two soldiers transferred Mr. Darcy into the surgeon's offices for immediate attention. Working as quickly as possible the doctor applied the best medical attention. This was routine work for the army doctor who had conjured the same surgery many times on the open battlefield. He removed the ball, cleaned the wound and bound bandages across his arm and shoulder. It was only then that the doctor invited Mrs Darcy to see her husband. His patient was still unconscious.

The doctor advised her not to do anything to awaken her husband because he will be in considerable pain for some time, "The more he sleeps it off the better he will be. When he awakens, give him nourishment and drink. In my experience, if he can keep it down, he may live. Otherwise, forearm yourself for the worst expectations . . . . Be prepared Mrs Darcy."

"What are the chances for my husband to live sir?"

The surgeon was unable to be more exacting than, "I will give you no false hope Mrs Darcy. I have seen men die of lesser wounds and I have seen men live through worse injuries. He is now in God's hands. Further than that, I cannot honestly answer your question."

Elizabeth called for the soldier who was now waiting in the doctor's house trying to dry himself from the saturation of the day's weather. He attended to Elizabeth immediately while still halfway through his attempts of removing his overcoat. She could now see his stripe and understood his rank. Elizabeth realised now just how wet she was. If she did not do something soon, she too would contract something serious. Elizabeth addressed the soldier,

"Corporal, please guard my husband while I am gone. I shall be but half an hour at the most. Do you know in what direction the local inn would be? I particularly wanted to meet some people at The Two Black Cats?"

From his reaction and his precise directions, she understood that he was well acquainted with the establishment.

"If my husband becomes conscious while I am gone it is important that you talk to him continuously. I will return with food and drink for you both."

"Very good ma'am and thank you ma'am. Your other soldier has returned to duty with the Captain. It was orders m'am."

The corporal sank into an easy chair beside Mr Darcy. Obviously, the day's exceptional activities had drained the soldier of all his physical resources. The patient was lying on the doctor's bed.

Elizabeth approached her husband. She looked down at him. His familiar, handsome features relaxed in a deep suspending sleep. Her impulse was to bend over to kiss his cheek. The doctor's words echoed through her mind to restrain her.

Outside the doctor's office, the carriage was still waiting for instructions from their mistress. As she left the doctor's surgery to make her way to the Inn of the Two Black Cats, Elizabeth realised that she had the carriage still. She mounted the carriage and ordered the driver to the inn. On arrival, Mrs Dubery greeted Elizabeth with much surprise and concern for her dishevelled appearance. Seeing Elizabeth's condition, Mrs Dubery immediately ushered her to a fire.

All the time Elizabeth was protesting about the three man retinue of the carriage, "Please bring them in to the warm and feed them." Pleaded Elizabeth. "I have dreadful news for you but the men outside, they *must* be attended to. In addition, please, there is a soldier guarding Mr. Darcy who has nothing to cheer him. Can you send to him something, hot victuals and some ale for the poor man?"

Immediately, Joy called to the kitchen for help. She gave full instructions to prepare hot food and to bring the men on the carriage into the house for food and refreshments. She made good Elizabeth's promise to the corporal and dispatched a man with hot victuals and a beverage to sustain him in his lonely vigil. The inn staff then supplied clean, dry, warm clothing for Elizabeth.

Only when the staff had accomplished this did Elizabeth then relate of the events that occurred that same evening on the way to Rosings, Lady Catherine de Bourgh's residence.

Finally she said "You must now excuse me, Joy."

This respite from all the emergencies made Elizabeth conscious of her own state of exhaustion. She could not help but mentally collapse in on herself. She reclined into a voluminous armchair. There, the exhausted lady fell into a well-earned repose to sink into a deep slumber.

The following morning Elizabeth woke early. The subdued sounds of some morning activity of the staff in the kitchens disturbed Elizabeth's sleep, for which she was grateful. Awakened and much refreshed she could think of nothing else but her husband's condition and to be beside him. With no thought at all for anything or anyone else, Elizabeth vacated her comfortable chair and left the inn to make her way towards the doctor's surgery.

Upon arriving at the doctor's house, she was surprised to discover the front door wide open. Without any sense of caution, Elizabeth walked straight into the doctor's surgery. The sight of blood on the floor and walls made her go weak at the knees. The sight of the mutilated body of the corporal, whom she had left in good stead, if tired and hungry, caused her to stagger. Then turned towards the bed where she had left her husband. With her senses reeling, it was difficult for her to take in the absence of her husband. He was not in the room nor was there any sign of his ever being present there.

Chapter Five

Elizabeth Travels to Rosings

It was Mrs Joyce Dubery who took care of the removal of Darcy from the surgery during the night. Then his subsequent transfer to a coach on the inn yard during the early hours of the morning. She arranged for hot breakfasts for everyone of the party for Rosings and plenty of porter to counter the early morning cold air. With the three men of the retinue made ready, two men were inside to attend their wounded master, Elizabeth mounted the coach. The driver, exposed to the elements but well wrapped up, braved the journey on top. This was not Lady Catherine de Bourgh's grand carriage but a more modest equipage, adequate, comfortable and drawn by a fresh team of the inn.

As dawn was beginning its usual magical routine of shedding light and warmth on the world, the party made off towards Rosings. Elizabeth's hosts had said their adieus inside the inn to limit their departure from hidden prying eyes.

Neither Mr. and Mrs Dubery nor Elizabeth had any knowledge of three men leaving Rosings Park for Dagenbury on that same morning to search for the missing party of Mr. Darcy and Elizabeth. As Elizabeth's party moved towards Rosings, so the party from Rosings moved northwards to Dagenbury.

Elizabeth was very attentive to her husband while the two-man retinue served her as though she was Lady Catherine herself. The men were glad to be inside the carriage because the cold outside was severe. Little time had passed before they reached the place where the party experienced so much trouble only the night before. Everyone went quiet and no one a spoke a word. Only Elizabeth shed a tear or two silently as she reflected on their problems and the disasters in its wake. She was not aware of the fate of her brother, Wickham, later that day. He too would receive a ball from the very same pistol as Darcy.

The distance from the inn grew greater and the journey onward was making good time. The passage over varying road surfaces and through tolls was a classic example of what good travelling on English roads should be. Elizabeth recalled that Mr. Darcy had once said to her, "Precisely, what is 50 miles of good road?" It echoed through her mind as she remembered it and the following day his first proposal. She had been so wrong about Mr. Darcy then. She might always have feelings of some shame of the way in which she refused his first proposal. As she reflected on these memories, Elizabeth thought of how much her rejection of Mr. Darcy's declarations of love and later his offer of marriage had served to prove his sincerity. Elizabeth's rejection of him served to prove her integrity also. Of course, this was all unintentional on her part. How romantic it seemed now, seeing it in this new light. How well things had turned out except now, Darcy's life was hanging on a fine thread.

Little by little, the company began to relax more and their confidence renewed. As the light grew stronger the temperature rose and so did the hope in their hearts that the horrors of yesterday were really now just history. Elizabeth was talking, sometimes reciting poetry or prose, to Darcy who was still unconscious. Once or twice Darcy made an incoherent noise and stirred. Each time she thought he was about to wake up. She was glad the he did not. He would be better sleeping through the journey but to wake in a warm comfortable bed at Rosings Park.

Above the noise of the wheels on the road, the party heard the driver blowing his horn to give advance notice to the residents of Rosings of their approach. Everyone in the carriage reflected the same relief of suspense. Smiles and sighs of tension release completely changed the atmosphere.

Elizabeth whispered, "Sleep on, sleep on Mr. Darcy, sleep on."

The carriage turned off the road then into the grounds of Rosings. As they approached nearer, they could see Lady Catherine de Bourgh and Miss Anne de Bourgh waiting to welcome their arrival. At reaching the company, servants came forward to open the coach door. They were much surprised to find the retinue of two men inside the carriage. Then surprised again but concerned for Mr. Darcy in such a distressed state.

Elizabeth addressed the servants to say, "Very quietly, help me with my husband but try not to wake him. He has been wounded by a ball from a hand gun."

Elizabeth then addressed Lady Catherine de Bourgh without ceremony, "I will require the best doctor to come immediately. My husband will be in need of some hot soup and a good fire in our room."

Lady Catherine felt affronted. She was not accustomed to this mode of address.

Lady Catherine thought, "In the circumstances what else can I do?"

She reflected for a moment on her interview at the Bennet's house. She recalled how Elizabeth was so headstrong. Lady Catherine felt a shiver going down her spine at the recollection of the experience. Never before or since had she met her equal, nor indeed her better, in firmness of purpose. As the servants carried Mr. Darcy still unconscious, they passed by Miss Anne de Bourgh. She espied the bloody bandages and the extent of the wound and immediately fainted on the steps at Rosings. Lady Catherine herself called for more servants. A messenger rode hard to the local physician to summon him with all immediacy.

Lady Catherine de Bourgh continued to reflect on this new insight into her nephew's choice of partner. Elizabeth was busily yet calmly giving orders to the staff and arranging everything. Two servants carried her unconscious daughter, Anne, into the house.

"Perhaps." she thought, "Just perhaps I may have misjudged Elizabeth. Her connections may have been low but as now my niece by marriage the quality of her connections are without question."

However, her thoughts were not likely to impinge too quickly or too deeply on her opinion of her nephew's choice of partner. Lady Catherine still cherished the life long wish for her daughter's marriage to her nephew. This was an insurmountable obstacle against the acceptance of this Miss Bennet in her mind still. So much did the thoughts of Elizabeth's roots still trouble Lady Catherine that her attitude to Elizabeth was less than warm. The fact that she was a gentleman's daughter was not enough. Miss Elizabeth Bennet was not a Miss Anne de Bourgh!

In his customary chambers reserved for him at Rosings and settled in his warm bed, Darcy lay unconscious even now. Motionless, he was, apparently, lifeless but for an occasional utterance of a groan.

Elizabeth whispered close to his ear, "Wake up Mr. Darcy, wake up Mr. Darcy."

This she repeated many times. She continued without a thought of discouragement until she saw a flicker from his eyelids. Then one sign after another signalled the return of her man to this world. Elizabeth leaned over so that the first thing he would see would be her face. Then it happened.

Darcy opened his eyes and indeed the only thing he could see was the face of Elizabeth. She was smiling at him. It was this smile, on this face, with which he fell in love. The smile triggered the recall of all their enjoyable times together. The pleasant evenings they shared, the music and the songs, the long talks about everything. How they discovered each other and their shared dreams. It was all there, in that face, in that smile. Mr.

Darcy returned the smile, broadly. The sight of her smiling face was by far the finest medication. He could wish for no more; he would want nothing less.

Then he winced from the pain coming from somewhere on his body.

He croaked, "Where am I?"

Chapter Six

The Waiting Family at Rosings

It was a cool fresh day on the occasion of the expected arrival of Mr. and Mrs Darcy to Rosings Park. Towards evening, the weather turned to rain. It was not until the evening at Rosings Park that Lady Catherine de Bourgh and her nephew, Colonel Fitzwilliam, began to feel any serious concern for the welfare of their family members on the road from Dagenbury.

The household was trying to continue the normal routine. Lady Catherine de Bourgh did not look upon the Darcy's marriage with any great joy. Lady Catherine had wanted and indeed expected that her nephew would marry her daughter, Anne. Lady Catherine had not solicited either party upon their wishes. She completely ignored the fact that neither Anne nor Darcy had any intention of uniting themselves in marriage. Lady Catherine became most displeased with the events as they unfolded. Her displeasure she mainly targeted at Elizabeth Bennet as she used to be. Even now, as she awaited the arrival of the party, Lady Catherine could not help but be something less than warm in her thoughts towards Elizabeth.

Colonel Fitzwilliam on the other hand was very happy to have this occasion to meet his friend and cousin and Elizabeth again, but now married.

The later than normal dinner was a source of irritation to Lady Catherine de Bourgh who held formal routine and dignity to be in keeping with her status. During the evening meal discussions naturally polarised around the absent party. Lady Catherine was not at all in favour of taking any direct action. Colonel Fitzwilliam on the other hand was for pursuing a positive course on horseback by searching the road with the help of two servants.

Mrs Jenkinson advised against such a reaction pointing out the problems of getting lost in the dark and perhaps encountering villains of the night. The general conclusion was therefore to enjoy a good night's sleep and to start refreshed early next morning.

While the party at Dagenbury was breakfasting before daybreak, at Rosings Park, two trusted servants and Colonel Fitzwilliam breakfasted and took to the road. They began to investigate the route that the colonel was sure their missing party would follow. The road towards Dagenbury was direct enough and easy to search but there were neither sign nor word from the good folk in the villages along their way. There was no hint of any event that might give them the smallest clue to help the colonel resolve the mystery of his missing relatives. The conclusion he drew from the lack of evidence was that Elizabeth and Darcy had not travelled along this road the night before. As the three men moved slowly forward making their way towards the Inn of the Two Black Cats, they had no apprehension of the messenger sent from that same inn during the early hours that morning. His task had been to convey the news of the previous night's events to Lady Catherine de Bourgh at Rosings Park. Nor had the search party any knowledge that Darcy and Elizabeth left in a coach of the inn two hours later than the messenger and before the colonel's party arrived at the inn.

Elizabeth's party travelled in a coach, which Colonel Fitzwilliam or his party would not have recognised. Nor would they have associated such a coach with Darcy, as it passed them on the road.

The messenger from the inn could be forgiven for the tardiness in the delivery of his charge, not accustomed to the road at night and consequently the difficulty he experienced in finding Rosings Park. The messenger, having found Rosings Park, made good his task of verbally detailing the message from Mr. Dubery to a member of the staff, who in turn relayed the information as best he could to a senior member of the household. Eventually, the housekeeper then passed on the final version to Lady Catherine de Bourgh. For the rest of the day the lady pondered, "Who had shot two black cats but were still alive?"

This did little to inspire the good lady to respond favourably to the request, "Come at once."

Colonel Fitzwilliam with his two menservants of Lady Catherine eventually arrived at the Inn of the Two Black Cats. Lady Catherine de Bourgh had kept the secret of the inn and the proprietors from her nephew, Colonel Fitzwilliam. He therefore had no knowledge of the real status of Mr. and Mrs Dubery.

The colonel consequently took Mr. and Mrs Dubery as just their hosts. Mr. and Mrs Dubery knew of the colonel and that he was a cousin in an extended family circle. Although the hosts knew of the existence of the Colonel, they would have no way of recognising him in person.

When the colonel arrived at the inn with his two attendants, he made enquiries about the whereabouts of a Mr. Darcy. Mrs Dubery overheard their questioning of her serving staff and immediately informed her husband.

Mr. Dubery quickly gathered a party of five stablemen, well armed and fully instructed them to surprise the three strangers at the inn. They set about to apprehend Colonel Fitzwilliam and his "two cohorts". The stablemen outnumbered their quarry and together with the advantage of surprise, quickly overcame the colonel and his men. With less physical resistance but more verbal protestations from their prisoners, the five ostlers marched their captives to the stables. They were ushered each into separate stable apartments.

Having safely secured and locked up their charge, the leader returned to Mr. Dubery to tell him and boast of their success. Mr. Dubery then dispatched his trusted young ward, Fred, to inform the doctor who in turn would pass on the message to the military.

While the three prisoners were writhing in utter desperation and indignity, a party of three soldiers were making their way across country towards a military surgeon at a village called Dagenbury. The military assemblage consisted of three soldiers, being an officer and two men. The officer, a certain Captain Wickham, was critically wounded. One of the soldiers was dead. The third soldier was the sole man able to deliver his two comrades to the military surgeon at Dagenbury. A squad of soldiers had ventured out on a heroic cause the day before. Their return journey was now slow and arduous. The squad originally consisted of three men and their officer. They arrived at Dagenbury as three men, one alive and well but exhausted, one gravely wounded, the third mortally slain and the fourth, slaughtered in the doctor's surgery the night before.

Chapter Seven

All Will Go Well In The End

Elizabeth flinched on seeing her husband respond to his painful wound.

"We have arrived at Rosings at last." She replied. "Will you try to eat something now? Lady Catherine wants to see you. First, you must think of your strength and recovery."

Mr. Darcy complied and ate in a manner uncustomary to his normal habits. With his constitution refuelled, he felt better but still with some discomfort. Elizabeth suggested a glass of wine to reduce the pain.

"Yes, a glass of wine will help very much I think." Mr. Darcy replied.

Elizabeth sent for wine.

Darcy was soon sampling a fine glass of claret with great satisfaction. All the time Elizabeth was personally attending to his physical needs such as wiping the perspiration from his brow and whatever else to be done.

The time had arrived to explain that Lady Catherine would like to speak to him, "She wants to know how you are, quite naturally." Elizabeth added almost apologetically.

"Oh yes! Let my aunt come in please." Mr. Darcy Insisted.

Lady Catherine de Bourgh sailed into Darcy's room with all the majesty that the occasion would allow.

Her first question was, "How are you my dear, dear nephew?"

As Lady Catherine drew nearer to his bedside and without waiting for an answer to her question, continued, "You must be feeling very down just now so I will . . ."

A disturbance outside the chamber door interrupted her conversation.

The doctor exploded into his patient's room and demanded loudly, "Everyone out of the room, *if* you please."

His intention was to have a clear room in which to work, save one servant. With much objecting and much protesting, the willing servants all wanting to help the injured Darcy, withdrew. The doctor thus cleared the room of everyone except one servant and Mrs Elizabeth Darcy. The doctor looked at her and demanded, "Who are you?"

Elizabeth looked straight into his eyes and announced calmly and politely, "I am Mrs Darcy, your patient's wife, doctor."

"Oh, very well." The doctor replied, "But do not get in my way."

Lady Catherine thought of this as something that she could not even have imagined. The Lady Catherine de Bourgh ordered by a physician out of one of her own rooms, in her own house? At the same time, "Miss Elizabeth Bennet" remained with the physician. The affront was felt the more so, as it occurred before the staff. This was indignity indeed. This was indignity before the servants even. Lady Catherine resolved to have her way regardless of the consequences. Lady Catherine opened the door and walked into the bedroom. This was partially to have her own way and partially to demonstrate before her staff the full dignity of her authority.

The doctor was leaning over his patient grossly intent on a delicate operation on the wound. The doctor continued his work but said calmly to Elizabeth, "Please tell Lady Catherine to leave the room."

Elizabeth addressed Lady Catherine with the uttermost dignity and politeness that she was able to summon, "Lady Catherine, please, would you be kind enough to respect the doctor's wishes and leave immediately?"

In return, the lady reacted with a verbal violence that one is always on the edge of expecting from Lady Catherine de Bourgh but rarely ever actually happens. "This is my nephew and I am entitled to witness anything going on."

She would say more but on the impulse of the instant, it was the best she could manage.

"I understand completely how you feel, Lady Catherine, but we must try to think of the patient before our own interests at a time like this. Mr. Darcy is your nephew but my husband and just now it is my husband's life which is in the doctor's hands."

The doctor stood up from his intense inspection of his workings on the wound to add to Elizabeth's statement, "Lady Catherine, I am trying to save this man's life. I have to caution you to the discharge from his wound. It could be putrid. It could infect anyone. Disease is no respecter of rank and I do not need another patient on my hands. So milady, if you would kindly attend to Mrs Darcy's request I will be able to continue my operation."

With that, he dismissed Lady Catherine by simply turning his back on her to continue with his work.

Lady Catherine was not quite sure of her situation but the sound of; "Putrid infection" was enough to hasten her from the chamber. As she left, she was surprised to discover the staff scurrying away to their posts and back to their work. Lady Catherine returned to her salon in high dudgeon. It was unthinkable that she should tolerate such demeaning disrespect from people of no breeding whatsoever. This was by that uncouth doctor in the presence of her servants and Elizabeth Bennet as she once was. Her mind dwelt on nothing else for the rest of the morning. Unfortunately, she could not resolve any satisfactory solution to the problems.

Meanwhile at the bedside of Mr. Darcy the doctor was just completing his work. Elizabeth, seizing the opportunity asked the doctor, "Can you tell me of his condition, sir?"

The doctor straightened himself to reply to Elizabeth "Well, yes and no." The doctor hesitated a little, "The wound is serious but the condition appears to be improving. The progress if any will depend on his stamina and rheum. The wound does appear to be healing but after applying medication, we fall back on God's good will, which is paramount. However, in these cases I have observed that in the early stages much rest appears to be the most efficacious, no excitements or too seriousness of situations. I hope he does fully recover for you madam."

"I thank you for that doctor and also for coming so promptly and the work you have done."

The doctor nodded and added, "I must leave you now but I will return tomorrow. I now have to go to the vicarage to Mrs Collins who has just presented Mr. Collins with . . ."

Elizabeth interjected, "Oh! Doctor, please say no more. Mrs Collins, Charlotte, is my cousin and it was my wish to see her on this occasion. I must to hear from my cousin herself whether I am an aunt to a boy or a girl. Please say no more, sir."

"I understand you perfectly Mrs Darcy." If you wish to visit your cousin now, allow me to offer you the convenience of my humble transport to take you there."

"Well, thank you sir that is thoughtful of you. This will save me some time and much inconvenience. We may take the opportunity to discuss more of your patient. I must first inform my husband of my intentions so that he will know that I will not be long from his presence."

The doctor, already gathering his instruments and medical effects together said with a slight bow, "I will wait for you at my carriage, madam."

Elizabeth made her husband comfortable first and then explained of her expedition to see her cousin. He raised a smile for her. Elizabeth felt some concern for his lack of interest and the distant look in his eyes. The doctors words repeated in her head, "Much rest . . . no excitements or too seriousness of situations. She left him in the care of a servant and made her way to the doctor and his carriage.

The doctor greeted Elizabeth at her arrival. First assisting her to mount onto the front seat, he sat alongside her to drive the horse.

As the doctor guided the carriage along the driveway of Rosings, Elizabeth posed the question to the doctor, "Doctor, if you cautioned Lady Catherine to the exposure of infection, why did you not so caution me?

"Mrs Darcy, would you have left the room had I warned you of the most terrible dangers?

"I should not. No, not at all." Elizabeth replied with emphasis.

The doctor continued to speak but in measured terms about his patient, Mrs Charlotte Collins.

"You will learn soon enough, Mrs Darcy that your cousin is experiencing some discomfort. Your presence will surely prove a pleasant distraction to take her mind away from any pain." He explained that she had an exceptional confinement followed by a difficult birth.

"There was some great pain and with complications for which modern medical science has not yet found the answers. These conditions are by no means uncommon and after a brief rest, mother and baby soon recover from these idiosyncrasies of nature. I tell you this, Mrs Darcy so that you will not feel too despondent on your visit. Mrs Collins is a strong healthy woman with an equally healthy baby."

"Thank you, doctor, for your reassurance. I am confident that all will go well in the end." Elizabeth replied.

In a short while, they were entering the familiar forecourt of the vicarage.

✢

Chapter Eight

A Matter of Urgency

The message, "Come at once." delivered to Lady Catherine by word of mouth at Rosings gave her much unrest. Further, Lady Catherine suffered greatly the indignations showered on her by the doctor attending to her nephew, Mr. Darcy. She felt the need to escape also to satisfy her curiosity of the message from the inn.

Lady Catherine de Bourgh ordered the carriage of the inn to be prepared in all haste. Her intention was two fold; firstly, to call on her cousins at their inn at Dagenbury to satisfy the summons, "To come at once."

Secondly, she wished to collect her own carriage to return to Rosings. The journey was swift and comfortable but her disposition was less than agreeable. She had been unable to find any salve for the mental wounds caused by the doctor's impertinence. In this mood, she arrived at the inn. Her curt manner was always expected but on this occasion, she made the extra effort to be particularly cutting.

Following the briefest of pleasantries, Lady Catherine would learn of her carriage, horses and nephew, Colonel Fitzwilliam. With his conversation with Lady Catherine, Mr. Dubery now understood the significance of his prisoners. There was one protesting to be a Colonel Fitzwilliam. This man was accompanied by two accomplices who could well be staff employed by Lady

Catherine. These men he had mistaken for French spies seeking to finish off Mr. Darcy.

Suspecting that he may have made a serious error, Mr. Dubery excused himself. He then gave instructions to Mrs Dubery to entertain Lady Catherine. It was important to re-assure Lady Catherine that everything was well and that she could take her leave to return to Rosings where, he said, "She will surely be missed."

With three stout staff of the inn, he hastened to the stables to find his prisoners. Young Fred was trying to torment the occupant of one of the stables. Mr. Dubery, guessing that his ward had selected the most apparently noteworthy prisoner, made good his way to the man.

Calling the prisoner to attract his attention, Mr. Dubery demanded to know his name, "Your name Sir, and be quick about it and truthfully or your life!"

Mr. Dubery then drew his prisoner's attention to a large handgun levelled at the colonel, his finger on the trigger.

Taken very much by surprise, this serious and urgent change in temper from the young boy's teasing to mature threatening brought hope and a sensible frame of mind to Colonel Fitzwilliam. He emerged from the shadows of the stable to join willingly with the innkeeper in any inquisition to establish his credentials.

"Colonel Fitzwilliam sir, an officer in the service of his majesty King George." Fitzwilliam replied.

"Come with me colonel." Mr. Dubery Responded.

He signalled to his three men to accompany him with the prisoner. They marched the colonel into the private quarters of the inn. Still brandishing his small arm across a large table, Mr. Dubery sat opposite the colonel. Mr. Dubery thought with certainty that he need ask the colonel one question only, which would verify his prisoner's claims.

"Where did you come from this morning?"

"From a house named Rosings."

"What hour did you leave to come here?"

"It was ten minutes past the hour of five o'clock."

This satisfied Mr. Dubery because Lady Catherine had told him that her nephew made his departure at about five o'clock. Only the colonel would know such detail. Further, this was a true military man. Precise and accurate and he delivered his answers in a soldierly fashion.

"Welcome to the Inn of the Two Black Cats, colonel. I must apologize for your wrongful arrest but we must be careful in these dangerous times. Our very lives are at risk. Please, now accept my hospitality and good intentions."

He indicated to a variety of alimentations and wines arranged on the table purposely for his guest.

"We will also attend to your men; I believe to be Lady Catherine's servants?"

The colonel nodded in reply.

Mr. Dubery continued, "Now I am obliged arrange for Lady Catherine's departure for Rosings. I have further news to share with you when I return in a few minutes."

Mr. Dubery rose from the table. As he did, the colonel stammered out, "Lady Catherine here? Surely not!"

This put Mr. Dubery out much. With haste, he left the colonel with a single servant girl of the inn. The innkeeper found Lady Catherine by the stables, inspecting her carriage, now cleaned sufficiently for her to enjoy a comfortable journey to Rosings Park but still in need of repairs.

"We are pleased to see you Catherine whenever you are in the country. When I meet with Colonel Fitzwilliam, I will give him your compliments and remind him of his commitment to Rosings Park."

"Thank you, Dubery but I find this all most disconcerting. One nephew has been shot, the other has disappeared and my carriage is all but destroyed. I will have your fastest equipage to leave immediately for my return to Rosings Park. In my absence here, you would please me to oversee the repairs to my own carriage as soon as possible. I will enquire further of the whereabouts of my nephew. The world, it seems, falls apart when I am not present to take management of its affairs."

"Feel free, Catherine, to enjoy every facility of the inn and my staff. I am sure you will find everyone keen to help you whenever they can. We do have a new curricle in the stables. A carriage that is capable of passing by anything. Please excuse me now I must leave you. Duties of a host, you understand."

He smiled and took his leave of Lady Catherine to return to the colonel and his servants.

Dubery found the men relishing their refreshments and celebrating their freedom. He then made his way to the colonel.

"Fitzwilliam of Matlock Park? That is so, is it not?" Dubery questioned Fitzwilliam.

"Matlock Towers, why, er, yes. You know of me, Mr. Dubery?"

"I have a special reason for asking. We have never met, but through our mutual cousin, Lady Catherine, I believe that we are related."

"How can you substantiate such a claim, sir? My aunt has never spoken of you."

"We would not expect it otherwise but we are cousins with Darcy. He has known this for many years. Perhaps, there has been no occasion to make it widely known?"

"That may be so, Dubery"

They fell quiet for a moment.

They heard a disturbance, a noise on the outside.

Fred put his head around the door, "Please sir, the surjun wants Mr. Kurnel ever so quickly."

"Thank you young Fred. What is the problem?"

"I don't know sir but he had dead soldiers all over his 'ouse."

Mr. Dubery and Fitzwilliam exchanged looks of alarm.

"I will find another weapon for you. Wait and we will go together."

"No, no. This sounds to be a military matter Dubery. Give me your gun and follow me when it is safe to do so."

They left by a side door to avoid being noticed. As he walked past the stables, Dubery saw his fastest carriage, the curricle, which was returning Lady Catherine to Rosings Park at some speed. "One person less to worry about." He mused.

Fitzwilliam the while, made his way expeditiously to the doctor's house. As he passed through the surgery door, he could hear the low moaning of a man in pain. The doctor had his back to him but turned to face his visitor to announce, "This is Captain Wickham colonel. He said that you would be at Rosings Park but you are obviously not."

Wickham summoned enough strength to speak, "Fitzwilliam! Thank God, you're here. Come closer and listen carefully I have the most top secret intelligence for you."

The colonel glanced at the men guarding Wickham. He gave a sideways nod of his head to indicate that meant that their presence was no longer required. He then turned to give his attentions to the wounded man.

"I'm listening." The colonel assured his confidant while the men were leaving the room.

"I have information regarding a French agent we call Marcel."

In being able to convey the information to the Colonel there appeared to be a great burden lifted from his shoulders. Wickham continued further, "You must swear to keep this to yourselves and impart it to no-one else, only you, Colonel Fitzwilliam and to my wife."

He then relayed his intelligence. Upon completion, any last vestiges of reason for hanging on to a spent life gave the relief, which visibly drained the tension from his countenance.

The colonel summoned the landlord and informed him of the demise of Captain Wickham. The landlord was visibly disturbed at the news of the loss of a cousin and a good soldier who obviously commanded great respect from his men.

Colonel Fitzwilliam called the soldiers back for them to pay their respects to the sinking soul they had been guarding and on whom so much had depended. Standing at the foot of the bed with sadness written on his face, Mr. Dubery crossed himself in the traditional manner.

The esteem of the Captain was all the more evident as when his sole surviving comrade was informed of Wickham's "demise", the battle-hardened but weary soldier broke unashamedly into tears.

Now was the time for the landlord to make amends to Colonel Fitzwilliam. Returning to the inn, all sentiments of enmity were resolved with a profusion of apologies from Mr. and Mrs Dubery and of course very ashamedly from Fred.

The colonel enjoyed a meal with his hosts. It was conversation during the meal that the colonel and Mr. and Mrs Dubery became acquainted with their relationship through Lady Catherine de Bourgh. Captain Wickham's reference to being able to find the colonel at Rosings Park had raised Mr. Dubery's curiosity. The company continued to delve and exchange each other's knowledge of their connections. They included the discovery of a tenuous relationship to the "fated" Captain Wickham, bringing an even deeper sense of regret.

The recounting of the details of their adventures of the last few days revealed the unity of the families of Fitzwilliam and Dubery and Darcy, the Bennets and Lady Catherine de Bourgh. The party became acquainted with the marriage of Elizabeth's sister to Wickham. The men and the lady discovered that the marriage of Lydia and Wickham forged the relationship of the whole party. They now understood the full degree of their "loss" in the apparent fate of Captain Wickham. In this humour, the family realised the full extent of their connections. In this room at the inn, this family bonded.

Breaking the mood, the colonel spoke of his reason for being in the country. "I came from Rosings searching after Darcy and Elizabeth. They were overly late with their arrival. I now have to continue the search for them."

Mrs Dubery interrupted, "Colonel I have yet to tell you of the circumstances that has led to this final situation. You must know by now that a highwayman accosted Mr. Darcy's carriage and demanded money?"

"I have no knowledge of this, Mrs Dubery."

Mr. Dubery intervened, "Then I must explain it all to you, Fitzwilliam. When Darcy tried to reason with him, the highwayman fired one of his pistols and wounded poor Darcy. It was only through the intervention of Elizabeth that the scoundrel was distracted and missed with the second fire. With no loaded firearm left, the highwayman made off his escape. A short while later another rider, who had ascertained himself of the circumstances, rode off in pursuit of the highwayman. We have not seen or heard of that rider since except, Wickham informs me that he dealt with him."

Mr. Dubery continued, "A short while later after the second rider left, who should arrive at Darcy's carriage but our man Wickham with three soldiers? He left two of his men with Darcy and Elizabeth with instructions to return to Dagenbury to seek medical help from the army surgeon based here. He then took the other soldier with him in pursuit of the so called highwayman."

Mrs Dubery intervened, "Elizabeth managed to deliver Darcy to the surgeon. Then one soldier returned to duty with his Captain while a corporal stayed to guard Darcy. Elizabeth then made her way to the inn where we sat her next to a blazing fire and provided dry clothes. She would not accept any nourishment until we had first taken some to Darcy. When we arrived at the surgery with some vitals, we could see the serious state of our cousin and I insisted on transporting him here to the inn. The poor soldier guarding Darcy was already fast asleep in the chair at the surgery and we saw no reason to wake him. We decided to take him some comforts early the following morning."

The colonel interrupted with impatience, "But where is Darcy now? And Elizabeth?"

Mrs Dubery replied, "Well, in the early hours, sometime past midnight, we returned with some lads to collect Darcy. As Mr. Dubery said, we left the soldier being still fast asleep, poor soul. We brought Darcy back to the inn and took him upstairs to a comfortable bed."

Once again, the colonel intervened to enquire anxiously after Darcy, "So Darcy is upstairs?"

"No, no," Mr. Dubery edged in. "We thought it better to take him away out of the country to Rosings as quickly as possible. There he would be safe and receive continuous support and medical attention. To that end, we provided another coach to dispatch Elizabeth and Darcy to Lady Catherine at Rosings. The three-man retinue from Lady Catherine's carriage went with them for support. We fed and cleaned them and gave them a night's sleep so they were quite fresh even for the early start. "And, God willing, they will all be safe at Rosings by now."

"Mr. Dubery, I must tell you that Darcy will never be safe." Colonel Fitzwilliam said. "For as long as that highwayman, as you call him, lives. I will remind you that he is not a highwayman. Darcy's would be assassin is a French agent. We do not know his name. For two years, he has harassed our military. We consider him to be a very devious enemy. We do not even know what he looks like. The only two people in the world who can identify him are Darcy and Wickham. While our cousin lives his life is under threat."

For a few moments there was an utter silence while Mr. and Mrs Dubery took in these revelations. Mrs Dubery broke the peace, "So it was the French agent who killed or should I say, slaughtered the poor soldier at the surgery?"

Mr. Dubery then wanted further enlightenment, "Who was it then, who Wickham killed?"

The colonel explained further, "Wickham believes he killed the second rider who is or was the French agent's aide.

"The French agent pretends to be a highwayman in the hope that he is not suspected then his aide followed after him on the pretence of chasing him but in reality is just checking to see if the killing was complete?"

The colonel nodded.

"But why should anyone want to kill our much loved Mr. Darcy?" Mrs Dubery asked of the colonel.

"As far as I know, until now, nobody wanted to harm our cousin. The French agent must have mistaken the exceptionally fine carriage travelling along the road towards the South Coast and Portsmouth as belonging to Admiral Brooks. He was to make a journey from Greenwich to Portsmouth by coach on the Dagenbury road. This, we pretended to be a great secret, which was deliberately leaked. The admiral was to take a different route in fact. Somehow, that slippery French fish must have obtained the leaked information or perchance, by accident. Then he came by the information of the exceptionally fine carriage on the Portsmouth Road.

In due course, he will know he was mistaken and that he did not kill his intended quarry. I imagine he will then be trying to learn exactly who he encountered on the road that evening."

They all leaned back from their intense listening to take it all in.

Then the colonel continued, "The admiral is to liaise with the military with regard to the defence of the South Coast. We have information that the French are showing interest in our coastal defences though much in particular, those of the South. The perceived threat is the reason for moving Wickham's regiment from the North, down to Brighton. We thought of the possibility that the French agent might be in the country, so Wickham was detached with three men to try to hunt him down. They were obviously doing a good job except that Darcy and Elizabeth were in the wrong place at that time."

The colonel then reflected, "Lydia must be informed through the military immediately. You will excuse me now; I have so much important business that will not wait?"

Therefore, with much great parting sentiments reflecting on their recent experiences and their united family the colonel took his leave. His immediate concern was to find the army surgeon.

In order to relay his important intelligence it was necessary for the colonel to gain access to communication with the regiment. The army surgeon will have express horsemen for the purpose. The regiment was now making its way Southwards.

His second task was to inform Lydia of her husband's condition. A task he did not relish though must be done and quickly.

Thirdly, there was the safety and condition of his cousins, Darcy and Elizabeth, which was much on his mind.

At the surgery, the colonel requested of the doctor for a private room to complete his reports and correspondence. The doctor readily agreed to the request.

First, he must dispatch a letter to Darcy to warn him of his danger. This letter he dispatched by way of Mr. Dubery's messenger who had long returned from his first mission to Rosings. On his first very hasty visit to Rosings, the messenger delivered his information verbally. Fortunately, this time he was acting as postman but with a much more serious and very important communication.

Next, the colonel completed his report including the secret intelligence given to him by Wickham. This he followed with a request to the colonel of the regiment to inform Lydia officially of the "fate" of her husband. Lydia had accompanied her husband on his visit to her mother and father. Wickham planned to leave Lydia with her parents while he pursued his real purpose that detached him from his regiment. That real purpose was to track down to capture or kill the French agent they called, Marcel.

Chapter Nine

Charlotte, Elizabeth, and Baby

Mr. Collins himself came to welcome Elizabeth and the physician. He showed surprise and much pleasure to see Elizabeth and extended a special greeting.

The doctor proceeded without ceremony to his patient, while Mr. Collins detained Elizabeth and drew her to one side.

"My dear Elizabeth, I have to tell you that Charlotte has had a very difficult time. The doctor has much concern for her. I am sure everything will turn out happily in the end but for now, there is, according to the doctor, some cause for concern."

"Oh! I am so sorry to learn of this. Let me see her immediately. I hope I can give comfort and cheer during this difficult time, Mr. Collins."

Elizabeth was more pleased than surprised that Mr. Collins did not mention if he was the father of a boy or girl. Her main interest now though was to see her much loved Charlotte. With the minimum of the conventional courtesies, Elizabeth hastened up the staircase to Charlotte's room. She knocked gently before entering, and then put her head round the door to address the doctor,

"May I come in now?"

The doctor readily agreed and with a smile he added, "I am sure you will prove better medicine than any I can prescribe."

He then left them.

Elizabeth approached Charlotte's bed where she lay with her baby beside her. The baby looked beautiful, as perfect as any babe she could remember ever seeing.

Elizabeth was cooing with the baby when the face of Charlotte attracted her attention. She was quite shocked to notice the strain and concern of her cousin's countenance. It would seem to Elizabeth that her cousin was in some not inconsiderable pain. She dared not inquire from Charlotte of her state but remarked most enthusiastically on her beautiful baby beside her.

"My dear Charlotte, you must have the most handsomest baby in the country! Please tell me now, have I a niece or a nephew?"

Charlotte's face seemed to soften for a few moments before she replied, "Can you not guess, Elizabeth? Can you not know by looking?"

Charlotte was teasing Elizabeth.

They were both enjoying the moment but the mood changed violently as charlotte winced for some duration. Gathering herself again but with much less cheerfulness pronounced in an undertone, "A niece, you have a niece Aunt Eliza. Leave me now for a while and summon the doctor again please."

Elizabeth naturally fulfilled her cousin's request. She then hastened back to her husband but all the time feeling greatly disturbed from her experience.

Darcy was asleep but Elizabeth always the comforter did what she could to improve his situation. She then collapsed in a chaise-longue. It was only then she realized just how tired and how hungry she was. Elizabeth ordered the attending servant to bring some food for her and some clean towels for her patient. After a satisfying repast, Elizabeth fell into a deep sleep on her chaise-longue alongside the bed of her husband.

Upon awakening the following morning, Elizabeth breakfasted and made good a list of tasks she needed to complete that day.

First, she must write to her aunt and uncle to inform them of the birth of the baby girl and Charlotte's unhappy condition with a plea for them to visit as soon as possible.

Secondly, she must send Mr. Dubery's carriage back to the inn and Lady Catherine's carriage collected and returned. Elizabeth thought to send three Servants with two horses with Mr. Dubery's carriage. Remembering her recent experience, she had doubts then thought again, "2 men should suffice. Elizabeth at this time was not aware that Lady Catherine had journeyed to the Inn of the Two Black Cats in the inn's coach and horses."

The most demanding problem was the division of her time between the two patients, Charlotte and her own husband. One other task that she considered very important indeed was for her to make good her acquaintance with Miss Anne de Bourgh. Making friends with her might help to make Lady Catherine more ready to accept the situation of Elizabeth and Mr. Darcy. By the time she had written the letter, to Sir William, dispatched it and sent instructions to the stables for the coach and horses to be returned to the inn, then for the men to collect Lady Catherine's carriage, it would be time for the doctor's visit. As she wished to include Lady Catherine to visit Mr. Darcy this time, Elizabeth sent a servant to inform Lady Catherine of the opportunity.

The servant returned accompanied by Miss Anne de Bourgh only.

Anne said, "My mother can't be found anywhere. She must have made errands without telling anyone."

"But you would like to see Mr. Darcy would you not?"

"Oh! Yes, I have much to say to him and to you. It is not easy with my mother so omnipresent and demanding. I have long hoped to talk to you and to make your better acquaintance, Elizabeth."

"My dear Anne, I should be honoured indeed if we could become acquainted."

"The honour would be mine."

"Well, let us visit Mr. Darcy and then we can talk. Perhaps you would like to come with me to see my cousin, Charlotte, and her new baby after we have seen my husband?"

"Oh! I should like that most of all, I think. I have never seen a new-born baby."

This exclamation took Elizabeth by surprise and astonished her. She thought that Miss Anne de Bourgh must have led a very sheltered life indeed. She looked at Anne and she could see a girl almost grown up in years but not in experience.

By the time they reached Mr. Darcy's chamber, the doctor had already arrived. He welcomed the two ladies and addressed Elizabeth, "I think we can say that the conditions have stabilized. I hope we can look forward to signs of definite improvements shortly."

This was good news and bad news for Elizabeth. So much did she want her husband well again and to be at Pemberley. Just now though, Elizabeth wanted greatly to make her acquaintance with her new friend at Rosings. Then her mind would be happier to see her cousin, Charlotte, to full recovery along with Mr. Darcy. Otherwise, however, Elizabeth had paramount in her mind, quite naturally, her dreams of Derbyshire and of Pemberley.

On their return, Mr. Darcy appeared to have improved. He was more awake and aware. He had indeed made progress. When Anne explained that she and Elizabeth were making each other's acquaintances, Mr. Darcy was very surprised so that he could not take it in for some time.

She said to Mr. Darcy, "I am going to ask Eliza if she will teach me how to play the pianoforte. I have heard her play and I would very much like to do the same."

Elizabeth could not help but laugh at this innocence. Her laughter was infectious and soon all three were laughing helplessly and with much abandon. The visit concluded with more merriment and good humour.

Elizabeth said to Mr. Darcy, "If one glass of wine can make so much improvement, next time I will have fetched the bottle!"

Laughing still as they were leaving, the two friends made their exits. The next visit was to take them to the vicarage to see Charlotte.

As the two visitors entered Charlotte's room, the first thing Elizabeth noticed was how much improved Charlotte was looking. Now glowing and smiling with her baby cradled in her arms, she welcomed her two guests. Charlotte being very surprised but pleased to see Miss Anne de Bourgh had accompanied Elizabeth.

"How nice of you to come." She addressed Miss Anne de Bourgh, "Would you like to see a brand new baby girl?"

The most amazing sight presented itself before Charlotte and Elizabeth.

Anne was looking intently at the baby girl with evidence of great pleasure. She was obviously completely enthralled but with tears running unashamedly down on both her cheeks. Anne kneeled beside the bed and spoke so softly they could barely discern her words, "This is . . . she is . . . the most handsomest thing ever, in all the world."

For several minutes, she continued in this fashion while the company just looked on.

Elizabeth was the first to speak, "Soon you will be thinking of a name for her. She must be christened as soon as possible so that we know who she is."

The company greeted this statement with glee and total agreement. They offered to Charlotte, names and names and their meanings until they were completely exhausted of all sensible names for the young thing. There seemed no hope of resolving the issue. They agreed to consult the father, which led to further discussion of the most probable choice he would make. Anne and Elizabeth stayed to enjoy some small repast with Charlotte before leaving her to the nurse once more. With excellent good humour the party broke up to allow mother and baby to attend to their routine and to rest but promising to pursue the matter of naming the new arrival the following day.

On their return walk to Rosings, the cousins discussed much of just about everything. Anne was waking up to a realisation. She had been starved of young female companionship. For so long, it seemed, for all her life, until now. Elizabeth raised to the status of a married woman, she stood as something of an authority of female matters. She was happy to confide with Anne and talk about personal problems and on some things, even to offer advice and suggestions. Too soon, they arrived at Rosings. Anne thought that she could talk endlessly and learn so much from her cousin Elizabeth.

"I wish we were sisters." Anne said while looking straight at Elizabeth.

"Under the skin, we are." Elizabeth smiled broadly back at her. They held hands as they continued the return walk to Rosings.

Two sisters under the skin had forged a bond of friendship at that moment on that day that would carry them through a lifetime.

Chapter Ten

Shocked Elizabeth

Arriving at Rosings, the two young women parted company, Anne to continue her search for her mother, Elizabeth to see her husband.

At Mr. Darcy's bedside, Elizabeth felt overcome with compassion for her wounded husband. He looked up at her and smiled his broad smile that he seemed to keep just for her.

"Can I get you anything?" Elizabeth asked of him. Mr. Darcy replied in the negative.

"How are you feeling now?" She asked.

"I am feeling better all the time. The doctor said that I could expect to improve rapidly as from tomorrow. I do believe him to be an excellent doctor indeed. But, how are you Elizabeth, how are you managing?"

Elizabeth reminded him that she was making friends with Miss Anne de Bourgh also visiting her cousin Charlotte who had just presented us with a new baby cousin. If that was not enough burdens for one visit to Rosings, she had to attend to a wounded fellow who refuses to get well soon enough! They both laughed until tears of joy ran down her cheek. They continued to talk for some time until Elizabeth remembered the post had arrived.

"Have you had post this morning?" She asked.

He shook his head to demonstrate a negative. Elizabeth nodded to the nurse who dispatched herself to recover any possible post. She returned to tell them that there was only one letter for Mr. Darcy.

"A youth had just delivered the message letter by hand from Dagenbury, milady."

"Oh! Please ask him to wait." Elizabeth pleaded anxiously. "Give him refreshments and I will come shortly"

"Very good ma'am." She curtsied, handed Elizabeth the message and disappeared to attend her mission.

Elizabeth then turned to Mr. Darcy to ask him, "Shall I bring him to you or shall I make my enquiries alone downstairs, sir?"

Mr. Darcy said, "Oh, bring him up and let us all hear what he has to say. What news he can bring us."

The nurse, now gone, Elizabeth felt reluctant to leave the patient by himself. She called for help. A servant duly arrived and Elizabeth gave instructions that they wished to receive the messenger but to come upstairs.

Elizabeth opened the letter. It was from the Inn of the Two Black Cats. She explained that it was from Lady Catherine and read, "I have returned to Dagenbury to collect my carriage and find it in a dreadful condition." The letter continued in this vein as one might expect from the author. She described the condition of the carriage in detail and complained of the hole caused by the ball discharged from a pistol. Lady Catherine described how the inside smelt of mud and much blood. The letter continued to relate of news but in a general rather than in any specific sense. A faint knock at the door suggested timidity though it was enough to interrupt their deliberations on the contents of the letter.

A boy was ushered into the chamber. It was Fred the ginger-headed ward of Mr. and Mrs Dubery. He appeared a little shy and nervous.

Elizabeth wanted to put him at his ease, "Have you had plenty to eat and drink, Fred?

"Yes lady they give it me down stairs."

"Good, and did you enjoy it?

"As good as 'home, lady." He assured her and with a big grin.

"I am happy to hear you say so. Please sit here, Fred, and tell us all you can of Lady Catherine's visit to your inn."

"Lady Catherine? She came in our carriage and our 'orses and she walked about as though she owned the place. My mum and dad both laughed at her antics. They said there was no pleasing her. When they told 'er how the soldier was shot, she went white. I thought she was going to faint, you know, pass out as my mom says. Then . . . ."

Elizabeth interrupted him, "What soldier was this Fred?"

"Er . . . er . . . soldier . . . but there was more . . . and more killed." Young Fred added.

"What more killed, Fred?"

"Yes, more killed but there was more soldiers and they were alright."

Elizabeth was becoming more concerned with each drip of information coming from her messenger. Darcy was alerted and somewhat alarmed on hearing this news.

"Would you have any names of these soldiers? The names of the soldiers who were not alright?" She was almost afraid to ask the question.

"The important one was the captain. He was an officer. A good man and a good soldier, they say ma'am. I am not really sure of his name but it sounded like, er, it sounded like er . . . Capern W'kum, ma'am. Yes, that's it Capern W'kum."

Before passing out, Elizabeth felt her head reel and her mind not able to cope with that which she had heard. This must be the worst possible news to come from Dagenbury. A servant ran forward to attend to Elizabeth and called for more help from downstairs. Mr. Darcy felt confused and helpless to give assistance in any way. He was concerned for Elizabeth but the news of Wickham was dreadful indeed. Lying so low in the bed, he could not even see her on the floor. The nurse brought her back to consciousness but into a state of high mental pain of grief, which culminated in a howl and scream. It was more than Mr. Darcy could bear. He struggled to raise himself. Against the pain, he gained an upright position while still remaining in his bed. He was beginning to feel dizzy. Two servants ran towards him to help Darcy but the effort proved too much and he fell back helplessly onto the pillows. He felt as though he was no longer the man he was, no longer a protector but the subdued shadow of manhood.

Chapter Eleven

Wickham's Demise?

Servants found smelling salts to bring consciousness back to the mistress. The nurse revived Elizabeth but she was still without even a little sensibility. She sat up, erect though still on the floor. She was trying to confront in her mind to that which she had heard from her little friend.

She burst, almost exploded, "No! It cannot be possible!"

She began to speak her thoughts loudly. They had achieved a great amount since those early days, while so much affection had built up between him and the family. Even Mr Darcy had reconciled his feelings to accepting that they were more than just boyhood friends. The fact being that they were now cousins he could not but feel the loss of a close relative. Her thoughts went to Lydia whose sparse letters were often full of her love for her husband. Elizabeth's own mother and father had taken to him with great affection as a very worthy son-in-law.

"How can this be? How can this happen?" Her thoughts revolved round in her head with no answers, "It cannot be so. Say that there is some great error here."

Slowly her mind began to take in the awful news until she exploded into tears. Unashamedly, tears ran down the cheeks of Mr. Darcy. Fred burst into tears at the realisation of the distress he had caused by the telling of his news. The entirety in the chamber felt and displayed individually and collectively the unhappiness of their master and mistress.

Through his distress and tears, young Fred attempted to mitigate the offensive news for which he was and felt responsible. "They say he died bravely at the sword of a Frenchman who he killed before dying. A very nasty piece of work my dad says. My dad says he was a French spy and deserved to die."

This did something to temper the distress felt by Elizabeth and Mr. Darcy. "What more can you tell us Fred?" Elizabeth asked of the boy.

"The other two were brave soldiers as 'im, I mean, the Captain, ma'am."

So far, Mr. Darcy had not joined in the interview. He was content for Elizabeth to deal with the young messenger. Now even Darcy looked uncomfortable enough to enquire.

"Can you give us any names, boy?"

Fred answered apologetically; "No I don't think so. I am sorry sir."

"Think Fred, think. Cannot you remember any more names, anything at all?" Elizabeth pressed him.

"There were so many of them."

Fred was speaking his thoughts as his memories appeared in his mind of the events of yesterday.

"Dad locked them up in the stables. French spies all of them. I saw them all. I riled them up right properly when they were locked up, I did."

"Whatever happened to them? Did your mother and father call the military?"

Mr. Darcy questioned him almost afraid of what was to come next.

"Well, there was one, I think, Dad it might have been, called him Fitsy something." Fred spoke as he was trying so hard to recall the details. "They all went. They all disappeared except Fitsy . . ."

Mr Darcy interjected. "Fits . . . Fitzwilliam? Is that what you heard Fred?"

"Fitswillum! Yes, that was it, Fitswillum sir." Fred felt pleased that he had at last recalled the name correctly.

"Oh, it wer'nt long but he soon disappeared 'long with the rest of 'em sir. You know. He drew his digit finger across the front of his throat while displaying a broad grin on his face.

Elizabeth fainted.

Simultaneously Mr Darcy became distraught at the news.

"But this cannot be so, this cannot be so. You must be mistaken young man."

Immediately, two servants lifted Elizabeth onto the bed to lie alongside her husband. She lay on top of the bed unconscious and without any wit at all. Mr Darcy looked at her whitened face, gazed upon it, to see the beauty that he adored so much. He was struggling to think, to imagine anything, any reason why all these calamities should befall them. He was struggling with these thoughts as a servant interrupted his train, announcing that Mr Collins was asking for admittance to speak to him. While his hosts received the parson, young Fred, seeing that he had caused much distress for Mr. and Mrs Darcy, made good his exit surreptitiously.

Mr Collins, ever the clergyman, hat in hand while nervously fumbling it by the brim, advanced reverently to the bedside and was surprised to see Elizabeth apparently asleep on the bed. He fidgeted continuously with his hat as he struggled to find his words.

"I hope I find you a little better this morning Mr. Darcy?"

He glanced again at the unconscious body of Elizabeth.

He wondered, "Had she heard the news already?"

Mr Collins looked about him at all the servants in attendance. Even they appeared disturbed. The staff at Rosings had held Colonel Fitzwilliam in much affection.

"A superfluous number for any normal occasion and all in sombre mood." He thought to himself.

He noted that Elizabeth was breathing deeply and Mr Darcy was obviously recovering.

His thoughts continued, "What otherwise can it be? The family must have heard by now and the servants too."

Mr Darcy waited patiently for Mr Collins to continue. Mr. Darcy was also of a similar train of thought that Mr. Collins must have heard of the calamities that had befallen the household at the inn. Darcy assumed that Mr. Collins had come to offer his condolences. He must have heard via the servants. "You are welcome Mr Collins. It is very kind of you to visit us on this sad occasion."

Mr Collins did continue. "The Good Lord giveth and the Good Lord taketh away."

At which point Mr Collins could not speak more but broke into tears of extreme grief. The look of torture apparent on his face spoke of a soul in torment. He could do no more than turn around and walk from the room. Mr. Darcy was surprised to see for himself how hard Mr. Collins was apparently taking their news.

Elizabeth began to stir and the nurse came forward to lend assistance to her. While Elizabeth was reviving, the memory of the scene with young Fred returned to her.

She could but say, "The dear, dear Colonel is lost. But why, why can this be so? Is this not the most deleterious visitation?"

Two of the servants were showing signs of extreme distress. They were obliged to leave the room. Colonel Fitzwilliam, a universally liked gentleman among his peers as well as the servants, would be missed by many houses in England. The servants mourned his loss for they too suffered the shock and anguish of the news from Fred.

Her husband interrupted Elizabeth's grieving thoughts as she was sitting up. He suggested that she should go to visit Charlotte. He explained that Mr. Collins had just paid a visit and showed great distress at our loss. The distraction may cheer him and Charlotte a little and you also. Even while he spoke, tears were running down his face. It was not easy to be so distressed while encouraging his wife to revive her spirits. His thoughts were for her happiness as always.

Elizabeth was reluctant at first to leave her husband at this time of shared double loss of the Colonel and Wickham. However, by persuasion, Mr. Darcy was able to convince Elizabeth of the kindness it would be to her cousin and together they would lend mutual support. Swayed by his arguments, Elizabeth left her husband to visit Charlotte.

Outside, in the light of day, with fresh air and a broader outlook Elizabeth found it a little easier to cope with her losses. She reflected in her mind how things seemed to be deteriorating. The course of events often goes in that manner.

"Now is the time for our happiness to appear." She thought. "Now we can put bad experiences behind us and count what blessings we have."

With this encouraging inspiration in her mind, Elizabeth stepped out a little more boldly towards the vicarage. Elizabeth took the longer, prettier walk to help wash away the recent events. Her thoughts laid so heavily on her every introspection. She was eager to present a cheerful countenance to her dear cousin and her new, oh so pretty, little niece. Everything of the earth was waking up. Nature was renovating herself, being born again. In this way, her walk through the lane presented Elizabeth with all the reminders of nature in the act of regenerating anew. Mrs Darcy drew comfort from these meditations.

She thought, "It will always be like this but I shall miss my brother Wickham and my cousin Colonel Fitzwilliam. I trust to God that nothing can hurt my dear Mr. Darcy in any way.

She continued in this theme as she made her progress towards the parsonage.

⁜

Chapter Twelve

Elizabeth Searches for the Key

There was little to suggest anything untoward as Elizabeth approached the vicarage except perhaps the curtains appeared drawn, as was sometimes the case, to counter the effect of the sun. It was not odd on this March day, even mid-day, that this should be so. The heavy winter curtains excluded the sun while retaining warmth inside while expressing respect for lost lives.

"This is the high mark of respect for their cousin, Colonel Fitzwilliam or Mr. Wickham or both perhaps?" As she approached the door, a servant girl opened it wide for her. Elizabeth could not help but notice how red her eyes appeared to be, as though she had been crying, much. She held her head bowed and there was no sign either of pleasantries spoken or on her countenance. Elizabeth was beginning to doubt her own judgement. This was too incredulous to expect that a serving girl should be so indisposed at the loss of someone she had probably seen but rarely. Alternatively, had she? Her thoughts hunted for a better explanation. Elizabeth asked of the girl if the baby was all right and continuing to do well. The girl allowed tears of grief to inch silently down her cheeks. She was unable to speak at first.

Eventually, she replied, "Oh, yes she is alright ma'am." The girl emphasised the "she" pronoun.

The girl led Elizabeth to Mr. Collins's salon.

She announced, "Mrs Elizabeth Darcy.", Curtsied and left.

Elizabeth was still not familiar with her new name. Being announced this way stirred something inside her. Elizabeth felt very proud. This was a source of pleasure. It helped to raise her depressed spirits. Elizabeth walked into a darkened room lit by two candles. At first her eyes being unaccustomed to the dark could not distinguish her cousin, Mr. Collins. He was seated bent over a davenport with his elbows on the top and his head rested in his hands creating a silent picture of complete despair. Elizabeth stretched out a hand and rested it on his back for a moment or two as a token as to express her empathy with him.

Her gaze turned towards the two candles and became aware of the view before her in utter disbelief. She could not trust her own eyes. For a few minutes, she was in personal and total denial of the truth before her. The coffin contained the body of Charlotte, her cousin and life-long friend. Charlotte, her confidant and her confessor for all her life, was now no more nor ever will be again. This was the mother of the newly born baby girl. Elizabeth realised that she was feeling unsteady on her feet. She felt her legs might give way or pass out as she had done before. She struggled to keep her senses but needed to steady herself by holding onto the desk. All the time she could not take her eyes away from the scene before her. Elizabeth had already cried herself out from her late experiences so that she had no more tears to offer. After much time had passed in this distressed state, the thoughts of the baby led her to enquire of Mr. Collins as to her welfare. Mr. Collins assured her that the doctor had arranged for a wet nurse of a woman in the parish. Elizabeth, at last, advanced to the coffin. Charlotte looked peaceful as though she had had no suffering at all.

"At least all that is passed now. Who could have guessed of such a tragedy?" She was thinking. "And such a waste of a lovely human being."

For several minutes neither of them spoke.

Elizabeth could but muse, "What could one say? It was a difficult happening for both Elizabeth and her cousin to take in. There was happiness here at this parsonage for Charlotte. Then even more pleasure in the happiness she brought to Mr. Collins. Now a huge gap in our affairs by such a loss."

Elizabeth turned her attentions to Mr. Collins. "Who will look after your baby daughter now? She will need a proper mother to raise her in a good Christian environment. A wet nurse in the village is all very well to sustain her for now but her future must be considered."

The doctor arrived and entered the room as they were talking. The servant announcing him had difficulty with her task. The doctor's countenance was solemn.

"I just cannot understand this." While shaking his head he said, "Charlotte was making such excellent progress. Nothing else was in my mind except a quick and complete recovery. God moves in such mysterious ways that we are so confounded indeed."

Mr. Collins broke in, "Elizabeth, my most practical cousin, has just reminded me that my duty must now be to find a guardian or at least a nurse to look after my daughter. This will not be an easy task. My resources are limited and my present household must suffer if I am to take on another."

The doctor had already made his acquaintance with Elizabeth and naturally, the question he addressed to her. "Have you no-one in mind that could fulfil the situation, Mrs Darcy?"

Initially, she could not imagine anyone at all. The course of events had numbed her thinking. After some quiet deliberation while the two gentlemen were looking directly at her in expectation, she mustered her thoughts to say, "My sister, your cousin Mr. Collins, Kitty, will be thrilled to help you to look after the baby. Kitty is a very sensible young lady and about the right age. It would certainly be an excellent experience for her. If I may, Mr. Collins, I will write a letter here, which I can send directly by special delivery?"

The doctor and Mr. Collins greeted this information with a united approval. Mr. Collins suggested that she should make full use of his study. "Everything you will need you will find there."

Elizabeth asked the gentlemen to excuse her in order to carry out her writing task.

The gentlemen continued their conversations.

In the study, while Elizabeth busied herself with the completion of her letter, a carriage arrived on the forecourt. Mr. Collins made haste to meet the new arrivals. Espying from the office windows, Elizabeth identified the visitors. They proved to be Sir William and his family. Mr. Collins' first duty now was to explain that his wife, their daughter, had not recovered from childbirth. Elizabeth was very well aware of the clumsy way that Mr. Collins often expressed himself that she felt it better to melt away secretly then return at a time when it would be more suitable. She made for the French windows in order to exit the house discretely. Elizabeth found the French windows locked. Elizabeth searched the desk for the keys without success. She looked around the room and in the draws of a bookcase. Mr. Collins was very security conscious and she understood his cautious attitude. Nobody could obtain access from without. Unfortunately, Elizabeth could not exit from within without a key, except through the door that would entail encountering the visiting company. She felt trapped.

In great haste, she searched around the room. She could not help but notice the quantity of wasted paper in Mr. Collins' waste paper box. With some apprehension but mixed with overwhelming curiosity, Elizabeth picked up the topmost piece of discarded waste paper. Upon examination, it appeared to be Mr. Collins' attempt at a composition of a sermon. A further inspection proved much or all of the paper was of this topic. It must be that Mr. Collins has felt deeply, the distraction of the coming of the new baby, so has had difficulties with concentrating on his work. Elizabeth felt some great sympathy for the man of whom she could never have done so in the past. She was genuinely sorry for him. Sympathy was all she could offer. There was nothing else in her power. Just now though, she must think of her escape.

Elizabeth could hear voices quite distinctly on the other side of the door of the room.

She thought, "They must be only a few feet distant from me but without. What to do?"

A closet presented itself as a possible solution. She opened it but to her dismay, it was not practical for her to occupy it. There were too many shelves installed inside the closet, empty though they were. Feeling the urgency greatly now but determined to remain calm, Elizabeth tried to think of a solution. Nothing in the room would provide an answer to her problem. She rang for a servant.

A young girl entered the room. Elizabeth enquired of her if she knew the present whereabouts of Mr. Collins and his visitors. The girl volunteered the information; they were gone with the doctor into the gardens admiring the plants.

"Do they not want to come into the house to see Charlotte?"

The mention of her deceased mistress brought an emotional response, which Elizabeth well understood.

The girl offered; "We don't think they knows yet."

This intelligence shocked Elizabeth but it did not surprised her. She thanked the young girl. Purposefully Elizabeth made her way straight to the gardens and Sir William and Lady Lucas. If the information was not yet conveyed it must be done so at once and if necessary by herself, whatever the consequences.

Chapter Thirteen

The Meeting with Sir William and Family

Mr. Collins, the doctor and Sir William and Lady Lucas with their daughter, Maria, were engaged in the distractions of the garden. There were many distractions indeed. The gardening parson had toiled much to make the floral displays so beautiful and in the cultivation of the fruit and vegetables. Many flowers were blooming in their prime. The fruit was in various stages, apple and cherry blossoms showing at their very best, while much soft fruit was well on the way to early ripening. There was an abundance and wide variety of large vegetables that would be much to the credit of a professional gardener. Amazed and interested as they were, the guests wished to see the mother and their new grandchild. For some time they had engaged their indulgence with their host though with gentle hints of the primary reason for their visit. In the ignorance of the course of events as they were, they could never guess what tragedy lay behind the reason for Mr. Collins' procrastination.

Elizabeth understood, even without being in their company, that Mr. Collins would not, indeed could not, have broached the taboo subject of the demise of Charlotte. For want of courage for the pain it would cause, not just to himself again but also for Sir William and Lady Lucas. Elizabeth was none the less sensitive but more capable with such delicate matters. She understood her duty to Charlotte, likewise to her aunt and uncle.

When Elizabeth arrived on the scene, it was natural that the company turned all eyes towards her. Their attentions diverted if not only for a break in the horticultural discourses but for the courtesy of Elizabeth also. With initial pleasantries completed, Elizabeth lost no time but proceeded to bear the burden of communicating the fate of their daughter. Elizabeth knew it would not be right to withhold the sad news from them any longer. They had come from Meryton expecting to see their daughter and their granddaughter but alive and well. This should be a day of celebration of shared joy of the united families. Heaven knows, she had more reasons for mourning on the heart rendering news of her brother and cousin, the Colonel Fitzwilliam, on this same day. This seemed to give her some sort of moral strength and greater altitude.

While a convenient garden seat was close by, Elizabeth suggested to Sir William and Lady Lucas that they might like to take advantage of the seat because she had direful news to impart. With puzzled looks and to each other Sir William and Lady Lucas made fast their occupation of the garden seat. Showing that Elizabeth had their full attentions by concentrating their eyes on her, they prepared themselves for this new intelligence.

Without delay, Elizabeth made good her resolution by opening the subject to suggest to Sir William and Lady Lucas that they should make themselves comfortable. Maria continued to entertain herself with the novelties of the garden. This was the moment Elizabeth was dreading. She was in great fear of not handling it with sufficient care.

"Sir William, Lady Lucas and of course Maria, I have the most dreadful task to relay the news of my cousin, your daughter, Charlotte. It is of the worst possible kind. I loved her dearly, just like a sister. She was my best friend. Charlotte had a difficult time these past few days and it was beyond her physical capabilities to recover and in the early hours of this morning, I am told, she passed from this life into the hands of our Lord at about 3.00 am."

Sir William and Lady Lucas sat quite still. For some minutes they remained, keeping their silence. Gradually, they began to register the facts. They became conscious of the tragedy. They continued to sit stock-still not knowing what to do next.

At last, it was Lady Lucas who broke the silence, "Where is Charlotte now?"

Mr. Collins responded, "We must go quickly or we may not be in time. They are to take her away. We must hurry now."

The party in all haste made their way to enter the parsonage. The company congregated in the salon. They approached the coffin, standing together to regard the grim scene lit by two wax candles now nearly ending their lives also. Filling the coffin were the remains of Charlotte. She seemed asleep. Charlotte was sleeping as if in life. Now Charlotte called away to greater things but a priceless loss to her family. In the subdued lighting, in the silence, a feeling of great overpowering reverence fell on the mourners. Without a word spoken but one by one, they filed out to find Mr. Collins now in his study.

The Parson related the details of the service and the burial to the Lucas's and Elizabeth. He invited his guests to stay over at the parsonage for the funeral.

Following this invitation, there was a knock at the door.

A girl presented herself and spoke, "If it pleases you Sir William," She curtsied, "We have the baby brought to you for you to see."

Another girl with a white apron and carrying in her arms the most beautiful child that any mother would be proud to call her own. The girl presented the baby to Lady Lucas.

Mr. Collins spoke at this point to assure his in-laws of the concern he has for the welfare of the baby. He continued with, "With Mrs Darcy's help I am hoping to obtain the services of Miss Kitty Bennet, who I am certain, will provide all the necessaries. Elizabeth warmed to this hidden depth of caring he was outwardly showing now. Any doubts Elizabeth had regarding Kitty's engagement to nurse the infant, Mr Collins had now dispelled.

Chapter Fourteen

A Last Farewell

This Saturday morning at Rosings, Elizabeth prepared herself for the day to experience the worst part of being alive. In her short life, she had never attended a funeral. "The colour black," Mrs Bennet assured Elizabeth, "Suited her admirably. Much better than dear Jane." Her mother insisted for her comfort. Such compliments did little to lift her spirits. However, her mother's observation did remind her of Jane. Such a sister as Jane must be feeling the same depression of spirits as Elizabeth.

As she finished the main part of her dressing, Elizabeth was beginning to feel very acutely the reality of the loss of Charlotte. She decided to seek out Jane. Lady Catherine had invited Jane together with her husband, Mr. Bingley, to stay as guests for the occasion of the funeral. With the aid of a cleaning girl, Mr. and Mrs Bingley's chamber was located. Bingley and Jane, now dressed for the service, were ready to go to the breakfast room. Their attendant maid announced Elizabeth's presence. In the grand style in which they now found themselves, the two sisters would normally have displayed acts and expressions of ecstasy upon meeting. This day brought a deep sombre mourning for the loss of their cousin and friend Charlotte. They felt it more acutely, being conscious of the circumstances. That a mother should leave the world and her newly born child must be amongst the cruellest acts of nature. There seemed to be no reason from above, no logic, and no mercy. It gave the feeling that no one was safe from such apparently enigmatic purposes of Heaven: to give life to one and take away what that new life needed most of all, its mother.

Upon meeting, Elizabeth and Jane embraced as comforting sisters. Their mutual expressions of loss culminated in tears. One making the other feel more deeply as the other made the one feel also more deeply. Their plaintive laments disturbed Bingley so that he made a quiet departure to the breakfast room where he hoped to meet his good friend, Darcy.

He left the two sisters to indulge their feelings and mutual support of mourning. This gave them the precious moments as sisters to talk and try to lend reason to the unhappy course of events. They gave little thought to sustenance but only of their shared sorrows of this most unexpected passing of their friend and cousin. Wickham and the colonel too, were in their thoughts, deepening their mutual grief. By joining their feelings by this means, they were finding it easier to cope with the enormous emotion that was building up. Gradually their conversation rounded on the more practical. Thinking and talking through the problems helped them both to deal with everything more logically.

Therefore, the subject of Charlotte's baby and her guardian rose to be the subject of conversation. Everyone of whom they could think was too old or too young or inappropriate or something missing from their qualifications with the exception of their sister, Kitty.

This conclusion supported Elizabeth's first thoughts. She had not explained so far that she had written for Kitty to come to help their cousin through this difficult time. Elizabeth had written in the most urgent sentiments. So far, Elizabeth had received no reply from Kitty to confirm her intentions but Elizabeth assumed that she would come with the family party to attend the funeral.

The sisters' debated thus on their family concerns for some time. At length a servant sent by Lady Catherine interrupted the sisters to remind them of the urgency to attend to the purpose of the day. Their response was immediate. They sought out the party to find everyone in the grand reception area. It was a dismal sight of black attire and sombre faces. The party consisted of the guests of the Lady Catherine and her family, Mrs Jenkinson, Elizabeth and Jane along with their husbands. Lady Catherine had several carriages: on this occasion three were commissioned. Two carriages for the mourning party with a third to carry the servants that might be required.

As they sought out their respective husbands to join them in a carriage another conveyance arrived. This proved to be the family of Mr. Bennet and his daughter, Mary. They made their way to meet Sir and Lady Lucas. It was not difficult to understand their obvious expressions of loss. It appeared so strong in poor Maria, who had lost her close, only dear sister. She had never known life without her elder sister. Being a novice in life's hard tests of character Maria showed extreme distress but Mary comforted her with unlimited forbearance all the time.

Elizabeth took the initiative to approach Sir William and his family to offer her deepest sympathies. She continued thus with his family until they were soon all shedding tears over their shared loss. The mourners and servants began to mount their respective carriages to follow Sir William Lucas and his party who were already making good their way to the service.

It was a cold cheerless day and threatening rain. This was weather most suited for such events as funerals. The carriages approached the church. It was here, the rest of their fellow mourners were assembling. It was with much surprise that they noticed the crowd of so many mourners in and around the grounds of the church. Among them, as the most affected person of this unhappy event, was Mr. Collins. He displayed a face contorted with grief.

At the arrival of Sir William, the congregation gradually drifted towards and into the church as though it had been spoken to do so but was never said.

Inside, the silence of the church, the people continued their conversations but in muffled whispers. The service engaged so many grieving devotees that they filled the church far beyond its normal capacity. Rarely, had the building been so well attended. Many were obliged to stand for want of seating. More still, engaged themselves with the proceedings from without but none the less, mourners. These were men and women almost all from the staff of the various households. Mr. Collins on this occasion would not conduct the service but was central in importance amongst the congregation. Mr. Collins sat at the front on Charlotte's own pew with Sir William and his family and Mary alongside. This attachment went unnoticed by everyone. Mary's natural fidelity would normally be with Mr. and Mrs Bennet but in their grief, no one gave the strictest heed to considerations of such convention. Mr. and Mrs Bennet sat close behind Sir William. Being that Sir William was the most grieving party, nobody could judge Mary but to be in respectable proximity to her own family. The preacher arrived to stand before the congregation to conduct the service. Silence prevailed following a meaningful cough from him. In the sacred silence all thoughts of the judgement that came to everyone regardless of name or rank washed through the assembled congregation. Then the peace and silence was shattered but suddenly and unexpectedly.

Mary cried out, "Where is the baby? Where is the baby? She must be at her mother's funeral service!"

This exclamation caught the breath of everyone present. The locum preacher stood his ground though confused. The congregation found itself equally confounded by Mary's outburst.

"Please delay the service while we go to the parsonage for the baby." Mary called out.

Then turned to her young friend Maria, "Come with me for the baby, Maria?"

She readily agreed but unsaid, just taking Mary's hand. The two cousins walked up the aisle with all the eyes of the congregation following their every step. This proved to be a very self-conscious experience for the two young ladies. Their journey to the church door seemed endless but with the momentum under way, there was no thought but to continue until a voice rang out. The voice carried a tone of high authority and insistence.

"Stop!" The command of Lady Catherine halted their progress.

The congregation fell silent and all eyes were concentrated on the lady.

"Take my carriage it will be quicker than going by foot."

Mr. Collins turned to Sir William; "Is this not condescension indeed? Is that not affability?"

To which Sir William and Lady Lucas readily agreed.

The two young ladies mounted the carriage and the driver obeyed their instructions.

Their return was as immediate as the circumstances permitted. Proudly, Mary nursing the baby with Maria by her side, walked down the aisle to regain the position they had left. All the time the congregation joined in subdued clapping, respectfully for the thoughtfulness of the young ladies. Mr. Collins was exuberant with words of gratitude to Mary. This pleased Mary more than anything in the world, even to her very core.

The service continued and the mournful burial rites completed to the satisfaction of all. The family and congregation returned to the parsonage for light refreshments. Much conversation included the subject of the welfare of the infant. However, it was not a time to make firm plans or immediate decisions. Whatever was to be done must be acceptable by the parson. It was universally agreed that a man on his own was no person to appreciate the needs of a baby and later, a girl and then a young woman.

✤

Chapter Fifteen

A Surprise for Elizabeth

Elizabeth felt the need to be alone with her thoughts. She decided to detach herself from the mourning company; to isolate herself and to return to Rosings.

Once more, Elizabeth found herself walking the prettiest walk to Rosings. This is the walk so much loved by Charlotte. Almost everyday Charlotte had strolled along the walnut grove and now, with the early display of daffodils that she had waited all winter to see again. Elizabeth thought that she could even sense Charlotte's presence here amongst the beautiful show of nature. Even with these thoughts, it was still not a reality in her own mind that she would never see her cousin again.

Arriving at Rosings, she decided to return to her husband and talk to him of this new tragedy. It was while she climbed the steps she became aware that tears upon tears were flowing down her face onto her clothes. Now she broke down. As Elizabeth approached the front door and in this distressed state, a servant drew near to inform her that she had a visitor.

Elizabeth could do no more than take advantage of the distraction by running to the stairs to ascend to Darcy's room in the greatest of haste.

Mr. Darcy was still in bed but was now sitting up and even smiling. How, she wondered, would he take the news of Charlotte's demise? Mr. Darcy did not know Charlotte very well but still an acquaintance. Elizabeth recalled how Charlotte and Darcy enjoyed the dances at Netherfield. How Charlotte scolded her but pleasantly for misjudging Mr Darcy and the memories came tumbling back.

She scanned the room with her tearful eyes but could see no visitor. Mr Darcy understood the situation, smiled at her and said, "Your visitor is down stairs in the morning room my dear."

Elizabeth hurried down the stairs in eager anticipation. Her mind was searching for a face, or perhaps a name. Who but who could give rise to an unexpected surprise? Who in this country could it be? Elizabeth swept into the room unannounced and fainted. A servant went immediately in search of the nurse attending to Darcy. Following a brief examination, the nurse applied smelling salts. The patient, recovering, looked around the room in her recumbent position.

She whispered silently to herself. "Did I really see him or was it a ghost, an apparition?"

He was looking down at her with that wonderful unique smile of his, "Elizabeth, are you well enough to stand? Come and sit in a comfortable chair."

A servant lifted her to her feet into an upright situation and Colonel Fitzwilliam helped his sister and guided her to a chaise-longue.

"I fear you are not well. Will you try a glass of wine? The doctor has been called."

"You are alive? Colonel, you are alive and well?" She asked of him.

To which he laughingly gave a very positive reply. The colonel then explained how Fred had made the mistake and misinformed everyone.

"He is, a most repentant young man. Will you forgive him, Elizabeth?"

She replied with a broad smile. "At this moment, dear Colonel Fitzwilliam, I think I could forgive anybody anything."

Elizabeth hugged the glass of wine to her chest as she spoke. "I have, or perhaps I should say, that we have had, of late, so much misfortune that I was beginning to think that nothing good could be ever again. My dear Mr. Darcy nearly killed by a pistol shot . . . ."

The Colonel interrupted, "Perhaps you did not know that he was shot by a French spy? The notorious Marcel no less. At least, that is the name we have given him. He mistook Darcy for an Admiral on the way to Portsmouth. Must have had orders to kill him, to kill the Admiral not our Darcy. Thank Heaven he did neither."

This reminded Elizabeth of the tragedy concerning her brother, Wickham."

"So we should be safe travelling on the road to Derbyshire, Colonel?" Elizabeth asked for reassurance.

"Safer than staying here with my aunt always on the warpath." He whispered to reassure her.

They had a secret laugh together.

"Anyway, I shall be accompanying you so that you will virtually have a military escort all the way to Pemberley. Miss Anne de Bourgh has expressed a wish to visit Pemberley. As you are mistress of that particular house I have no doubt that she will soon seek your permission for a visit. That is if she can catch you between faints."

Again, they laughed though ringing out with more confidence this time.

He continued, "You see, I have been kept up to date with events."

They talked further of Charlotte and Wickham. Elizabeth was trying hard to come to terms with so much by way of personal loss and distress in so short a time.

Chapter Sixteen

The Journey from Rosings

Early preparations made by Mr. Darcy were near to completion for a hasty departure from Rosings for the drive to Pemberley. The party of travellers was busily engaged packing trunks and boxes the evening before the journey. Men and boys busily loaded the luggage onto the carriage while the travellers enjoyed their final breakfast at Rosings.

Mr. Darcy had ordered a personal carriage for his bride-to-be in their early engagement days, as a special surprise for this occasion. The carriage was still in the course of completion before they left for Dover. Darcy had hoped that it would be ready for her for the final journey to her new home, Pemberley. When designing this gift for her, little did Mr. Darcy imagine that he too would be travelling in the carriage alongside Elizabeth as her patient.

The party for Pemberley consisted of Mr. Darcy and Elizabeth, Miss Anne de Bourgh and the Colonel Fitzwilliam. The Colonel would ride while the rest of the party would travel in the carriage. The liverymen consisted of the driver and two attendants.

It was a fortunate situation, for the journey could easily accommodate a brief visit to a certain manor house in Hertfordshire very close to a small village by the name of Meryton. Elizabeth was unaware of this arrangement. Mr. Darcy and his good friend Colonel Fitzwilliam and of course Mr. and Mrs. Bennet together secretly contrived to make this happy meeting. Thus, the family hoped for a pleasant surprise for Elizabeth and a welcome distraction from the journey. The added bonus would be much fine fare and convivial company consisting of the household of and including her dear father, Mr. Bennet and her sister Kitty who remained still unattached.

Descending the steps at Rosings, they began to move towards the carriage, with great expectations of their journey and the thoughts of their destination. Elizabeth and Colonel Fitzwilliam were helping a cautious Mr. Darcy to negotiate a step at the time.

Therefore, it was that Elizabeth, engrossed as she was with the task of helping her husband, did not realize the significance of the carriage. The magnificence of the new conveyance before them drew her attention once they had gained level ground. The glossy navy-blue new coachwork boasted the scripted initials E.D. in gold leaf. A contrast in colour, the four white horses could have been two pairs of identical brothers.

Mr. Darcy whispered to his wife, "My gift to you for being such a wonderful person. May I ride with you in your carriage for the journey home my lady?"

Elizabeth could but stand and stare at her new carriage. The entourage, liverymen and the party of travellers watched while she continued to admire the beautiful equipage motionlessly and in apparent disbelief. Unable to release her support of her wounded husband she could do little else. However, an attentive manservant noticed her predicament.

He immediately stepped forward to say to Elizabeth, "Allow me take the master's arm milady?"

She thanked the servant for thinking so. Then Elizabeth alone advanced to the new carriage. She then studied every nook and cranny, every nail and escutcheon then finally talked to each of the horses in turn while stroking their foreheads and tickling behind their ears. The assembled company gazed upon the prospect. They watched patiently, totally absorbed at the display of emotion being acted out by Elizabeth. This was Mrs Elizabeth Darcy, appreciative, thoughtful, and considerate. It was to the credit of the driver to advance towards Elizabeth to remind her of the journey ahead and that her horses were eager to be going.

"But yes! Of course! We must be starting early so as not to press the horses."

Elizabeth returned to her duties of helping her husband to the coach where a liveryman then took Mr. Darcy's arm to help him carefully into the carriage. The two ladies mounted the coach. The colonel took his steed apace to encourage the carriage horses and they were off to the country.

As Elizabeth's carriage drew away from the waving party of her family and their domestics, the two ladies in the carriage waved enthusiastically in return. The attendants and servants waived until the carriage was out of sight. They had formed a favourable opinion of these gentlepeople, who they may not see again for some time.

The carriage sped easily and smoothly over the metalled roadway. Elizabeth turned from waving to the standing crowd and looked towards her husband.

"He has quickly fallen asleep." Elizabeth mused.

She was thinking that he must be very exhausted while his body is coping with the healing processes of his wound. Even the perambulation from his room to the carriage must have taken much effort. She wanted to thank him for the carriage. She felt bad about not being able to express her appreciation for the surprise, for the most thoughtful gift. Anne looked at her and smiled. She viewed Elizabeth's countenance and understood that Elizabeth was distracted. In reply to Anne's questioning, Elizabeth explained that she was uncomfortable that she was unable to thank Mr. Darcy because he was asleep.

"No I am not." Mr. Darcy opened his eyes and smiled at the ladies. "But you are correct in thinking that I am very tired. I feel exhausted. I may have dozed off for a moment or two."

"Then try to relax." Encouraged Elizabeth, "We can talk later when you feel more able."

The journey continued through towns and villages, through woodlands and farming lands. The carriage ran so smoothly and with so little noise, without the customary rumble so that both Elizabeth and Anne knew that this must be the very latest and the last word in modern carriages. The two friends talked much of most things until at length one fell into a shallow sleep and then the other. During moments between naps, Elizabeth reminisced of the events leading to this drive. She remembered the wonderful month in Dover with her new husband. Thinking back, she recalled the arrival at the inn at Dagenbury to meet her new beautiful cousins, Bob and Joy and their ginger-haired charge, Fred. It all seemed so idyllic and everything agreeable. So too, was the food and the wine.

All had seemed good and pleasing until Lady Catherine's carriage wheel became embedded in a rut in the muddy road. She remembered the relentless rain; the darkness, the highwayman, the gunshot and her husband falling back wounded against the coach before collapsing into the mud. The fate of poor Charlotte came to her mind. She continued to dwell on these events until she fell asleep again.

Elizabeth's slumbers were suddenly disturbed. The carriage lurched and jerked to the discomfort of the passengers.

Mr. Darcy called out to the driver, "Have a care Jacobs!"

The carriage finally came to a halt. The sounds of much jostling and shouting made themselves heard. Elizabeth lowered the carriage window and looked out, forwards.

In front of the leading horses was a crowd of ragamuffins, small boys and girls. The children, jostling and shouting, were gathering around Colonel Fitzwilliam who was holding a limp child in his arms. Hastily, Elizabeth opened the carriage door and descended with the intention of obtaining a closer inspection. She walked towards the colonel. The children, upon seeing such a gentlewoman so finely dressed and with much gracious demeanour, became immediately silent. Elizabeth continued her walk towards the colonel. The horde of children parted seemingly spontaneously to make a path for her as she advanced through their company.

"What has happened sir?" Elizabeth inquired of her friend.

The colonel was studying the child's head. He looked up at Elizabeth. With much concern in his voice, he spoke to her, "The boy fell before the coach. He must have been hit on the head by one of the horse's hoofs."

There was indeed a mark of a blow on one side of his forehead. The colonel stroked the poor boy's head and talked gently to him. The boy opened his eyes but seeing the colonel, broke with a cry. The boy struggled, afraid of his captor, and fell from the colonel's arms. He landed roughly but was up and away, running for his life, making good his escape, perhaps afraid of what might happen to him if he stayed.

Elizabeth looked at the little waifs. They were young boys and girls dressed in dirty rags, playing in the dusty street not even a shoe between them. The children were now cautiously retreating away from the two gentlefolk. They backed away as much in fear as in awe following the escape of their wounded friend.

The colonel looked at Elizabeth's concerned face. "This may be the first time that this gentlewoman had encountered such extreme poverty."

He thought and said, "This is the way with these people. They know nothing else but what can you do?"

Elizabeth asked, "Do you have a purse on your person Colonel?"

"Why, yes indeed." He replied.

Elizabeth held out her hand and the colonel unhesitatingly produced a money pouch and placed it on her outstretched hand.

Anne was watching and studying the proceedings. She admired the confidence of Elizabeth. How generous of the colonel to give her his purse. This held him high in Anne's esteem.

Elizabeth thanked him.

Then she called out to the children, "I would like to know where your wounded friend lives because I want to find out if he is badly hurt or not. If you tell me, here is some money for you to share."

It produced the required result from the hungry little faces, "He comes from cottage next t'mill down by t'river."

The reply emanated from a cheeky little urchin who was pointing to a path that the injured boy had indeed followed.

Elizabeth picked out a coin, held it up between her fingers and smiled at the boy, "Come here young man and receive your prize."

The young urchin collected his coin while all the others looked on with gaping mouths.

Then Elizabeth ostentatiously emptied a quantity of coins onto the palm of her hand and shouted out, "One, two, and three!"

She then threw the coins to scatter them over the children. Diverted with this distraction the children did not hinder the progress of the two gentlepeople as they moved quickly away to find the cottage. One of the retinue of the servants who felt concern for the safety of his master and mistress followed Elizabeth and the colonel along the path.

The mill was a large building with a poor but tidy cottage leaning against it. As they approached the cottage, a ragged woman came to the door. She had obviously seen their approach. The woman stood legs apart with her arms crossed and expecting the need to counter incivility.

"Good morning madam, we have come to inquire after your little boy. Your son fell before our horses. Is he much injured?"

The boy appeared from the cottage and scampered to hang on tightly to his mother's skirts. She confirmed that he was all right but very frightened. Elizabeth took a few coins from the remains in the purse to proceed through the routine of offering the money and the woman refusing. With much rationalizing on both sides, Elizabeth finally persuaded the woman to accept with grace if only to purchase the services of a physician. The woman curtsied and thanked this fine lady. Elizabeth said to the woman that she hoped that the boy was not too hurt and that he will fully recover and very quickly. She inquired after the little boy's name. "David, ma'am is his name."

Elizabeth and her entourage made haste to return to the carriage. Both Anne and Darcy had descended from the coach and were now looking anxiously in their direction. With waving and smiles as they spotted each other, Elizabeth and the colonel continued their advance to the carriage. The children had all gone with their prizes. Darcy and the ladies returned to the comfort of carriage while the colonel recovered his seat. Elizabeth spilled a few coins more from the pouch into her hand. She threw the money through the open window towards the same place were she had thrown the other coins. Then with a careful aim threw the pouch back to its owner. The colonel made humorous gestures demonstrating that he no longer had much money left. Following this, he laughed while he urged his horse forwards to encourage the coach to do likewise.

The journey thus continued through the peripheral of the suburban villages while the party was in high discussion of the events that had just taken place. Eventually they reached the open country once more. Here they made good headway again. The passengers in the coach dozed and woke alternately as the hours and miles passed by.

Chapter Seventeen

An Unexpected Visit

This special gift carriage ran smoothly over the roads making much good headway towards their next stop. Their journey skirted London Town through the southern suburbs. The villages they passed through were delightful. Each different in its own way but held forth their very English character.

As the party approached Chiddingfold, Mr. Darcy said that he had a mind to stop for refreshment. The universal cry rose against Darcy's suggestion. Even the thought of a minor delay was totally out of the question. Mr. Darcy continued his insistence that a stop at the next inn would break the journey.

"It is certainly a very old inn, very old indeed and it does boast of royal connections."

Anne spoke up. "No! No! Mr. Darcy, we cannot countenance even one hour's delay."

She surprised her travelling companions with her unyielding determination to have her way. They had never heard her speak out so: never to countermand anything spoken, even in jest.

In their surprise, the party became silent to the eventual embarrassment of Anne. She visibly reddened before her travelling companions.

Elizabeth regarded Anne's sudden change with some curiosity. Her thoughts were searching for answers, "Why was Anne so insistent to be at Pemberley and with such immediacy?" Elizabeth understood her own reasons well enough though Anne did not share Elizabeth's yearnings.

Elizabeth developed from an early age to become an excellent proponent of human behaviour. Reared with four sisters of varying characters and an eccentric mother, she had an abundance of material to study. Elizabeth was well aware that nobody did anything without a reason. The questions in her mind remained unanswered. She thought it politic to demonstrate her empathy with Anne and to mitigate her unease.

"We all feel the same, Anne it is just Mr. Darcy's little tease. Please do not pay any heed to him when he is in a playful mood."

After which Elizabeth added, "No one wants delay less than I. The sooner we arrive at Pemberley the fresher we will all be when we are introduced to the staff."

Without any more thoughts or words of stopping, even in humour, the journey yielded to time and distance. The miles had passed. The carriage fell silent as the travellers dozed recumbent on their comfortable seats.

Anne was shaking her cousin gently, "Wake up Elizabeth! Wake up! We have arrived at Longbourn. Look, your mother and father. And there, your sister Kitty!"

With a spontaneous whoop of joy by Elizabeth that even her waiting family heard, she startled the exhausted husband from his slumbers. The carriage glided along the drive to halt at the assemblage of delighted family.

There was just sufficient time for Elizabeth to thank Mr. Darcy, "My dear husband, you have made this come about for my pleasure. You are the most considerate, kindest husband in the country and I thank you so."

She leaned forward to kiss him but the carriage door flew open so that the party spilled out of the carriage into the arms and love of their relatives. Without sufficient time for Elizabeth to say more, much was left unsaid but for another occasion.

Mr. Bennet had a special welcome for his favourite daughter, Jane not withstanding.

They were engaged in much conversation. Elizabeth formerly introduced her cousin Anne to the family. Questions galloping backwards and forwards too fast and too many to be answered all before they ate their welcomed repast. One concern in particular occurred to Elizabeth. It was a surprise for her to see Kitty in the welcoming party. She had written to her mother for the express purpose for Kitty to go to the parsonage to nurse Mr. Collin's new baby. At the same time, Mrs Bennet was eulogizing over her daughter Eliza's new carriage and of the beautiful horses.

"They will be well cared for and rested for your journey home, you can be sure Elizabeth." Her mother said to demonstrate her continuing mother's concern in her daughter's interests.

"And the dear Colonel's horse also, of course. He will be well stabled and refreshed with great care. That is the horse of course not the, well . . . but the Colonel will be well fed also!"

Elizabeth did hear clearly up to, "Your journey home." Then her mind wandered off to what her mother referred to as, "Home." The rest of her mother's words were lost in a bottomless sea of irrelevance. Something deep inside her stirred. It drew her mind away from the ordinary. "Was it really possible that at last, today, she would actually reside in her new home to become the mistress of Pemberley; her own home?"

Elizabeth's first concern would be the complete recovery of her husband's physical state. Only then could she enjoy the rewards. There was so much to see and to learn, to discover of her Pemberley, her own Pemberley. As a young woman, as a new bride, Elizabeth was conscious that she was on the threshold of her married life. These thoughts filled Elizabeth's heart with a thrill of happiness and high expectation. What life adventures lay before her? She could only wonder and dream in excited anticipation. So many things she was planning in her mind and with the recollections of the events of her journey this day there would be further considerations.

Elizabeth had wandered off in her own mind away from her companions who were now sitting silently at the dining table with all eyes turned on her in expectation.

"I said, did you reconcile your relations with Lady Catherine de Bourgh, Elizabeth?" her father repeated the inquiry again, a little louder this time.

Her father's voice brought Elizabeth's attention to the present company. "Oh! No, we lost her."

"You lost Lady Catherine de Bourgh? I thought one day you might try, but so soon?"

The whole party including Miss Anne de Bourgh and Mr. Darcy exploded spontaneously into a chaos of laughter. Such excessive merriment and on a full stomach disarmed Kitty into an indisposition. She left the company and the room hastily with her napkin held to her mouth. This event at the table somewhat tempered the excessive gaiety of the company remaining at the table.

This was the opportunity that Elizabeth needed.

"I wrote asking for Kitty to go to the Parsonage to nurse Charlotte's baby. Who is attending this issue? Surely you cannot expect Mary to cope with a new born child?"

Elizabeth had noted the absence of her sister and had concluded this possibility.

Mrs Bennet rose to the occasion. "Dear Mary will cope very well. She will be a mother one-day herself so I thought that this was a good opportunity for her to gain experience. She will manage quite well I am sure."

Mrs Bennet continued, reflecting, "There is the nurse from the village and enough staff at the parsonage to support her during those early months that can be so trying."

Still in good humour, Mr. Bennet pressed his question, "But what of Lady Catherine, Elizabeth? Has Mr. Darcy still got an Aunt at Rosings?"

Mr. Darcy assured Mr. Bennet that his aunt was, as far as he knew, in good health and as imperious as ever."

Mr. Darcy continued, "As for being lost, that was only our error. We heard from the Inn of the Two Black Cats that Lady Catherine was overseeing the repairs to her damaged carriage. I understand that she is actually enjoying some convivial company."

Mrs Bennet interjected, "Perhaps there may be romance in the air, Mr. Darcy?"

Mr. Darcy smiled, "Perhaps, Mrs Bennet. I do not know but it is a thought and it is always possible. We shall just have to wait and see."

Miss Anne de Bourgh had not contributed anything to the family conversation. Anne remained attentive and studied the ways of her relations at this, an informal gathering. She was surprised at the banter, the good humour and the total disregard for strict decorum.

Now Miss Anne de Bourgh wished to join in, she wished to establish her credentials and become one of these people, to qualify as one of the family, "I want to say that I do not believe my mother has any plans along matrimonial lines at all."

She blushed so deeply it could not escape the notice of the company. For a moment, it seemed that the conviviality had been broken.

Colonel Fitzwilliam noted the situation and spoke; "You may be right Miss de Bourgh but in my experience this is an area where making plans is irrelevant."

The colonel then leaned forward as to address mainly Anne with a smile and added, "Uncertainty and not knowing . . . , that is half the excitement of romance you know."

This personal attention from such a man as Colonel Fitzwilliam especially on such a subject caused Anne to blush again but so much more so. Anne could not say or do anything under such powerful an influence on her emotions. Her own introspection found it impossible to reconcile the experience with anything she could rationalise. Elizabeth being as expert as ever in observing human behaviour studied the events with a keen interest.

The season of the year at this time being halfway between solstices, the evening light would fade all too soon to make travelling inconvenient if not dangerous. The horses had remained in the Bennet stables while the men awaited their orders. The carriage had been carefully stored for safekeeping until it was required. The daylight faded but no orders came.

Hill and a girl entered the dining room ostensibly to clear away the used dishes.

Hill went immediately to Mrs Bennet to ask in an undertone, "Will you be requiring that sleeping arrangements be made for the guests madam?"

Elizabeth leapt to her feet, "Oh! No, we must be on our way. We are on our way to Pemberley and the light is fading. No! No! We cannot stay."

"Nonsense girl!" Mrs Bennet responded so sharply as though Mrs Darcy was still her little prodigy, "Kitty can share her room with Miss Anne de Bourgh. The Colonel can have Mary's Room and you, Elizabeth, can have your old room for the night. I am sure we shall all be very warm and comfortable."

Mr. Bennet supported his wife's opinion, "You are quite right my dear. The light is fading and there may be highwaymen abroad. You cannot countenance any more holes in Mr. Darcy or Hill will want to use him in the kitchen as a colander."

Following which, Mr. Darcy and all the company continued in this humour with much merriment.

Hill, accompanied by helpers set about to make the arrangements. The hosts and the guests all protested that the meal so excellent and the company so good that they had not noticed the hours passing and the darkness coming. Elizabeth collapsed back onto her seat and wanted to cry. She had, of course, intended to be sleeping at Pemberley this night. All the time there had been delays and problems. Now, so close, her excitement was brewing up inside her only to be confounded again.

"Would she ever be the mistress of Pemberley?" Elizabeth asked herself.

Darcy could read the disappointment in her face and in her eyes. Ever the understanding husband Darcy knew that no comforting could match her continuing disappointments. He reached out with his good arm and gently squeezed her forearm,

"Patience my dear one. Tomorrow we will arrive at Pemberley and then all will be well and all will be yours."

Elizabeth turned and looked at him. He smiled as she felt the bittersweet tears of disappointment now but of tomorrow, what joys would abound? The two faces focused on their counterparts, one with a smile, and the other with salty droplets falling down her handsome cheeks. She wiped away the woeful tears to smile back at him, "Yes, you are right and of course you are never wrong, my dear Mr. Darcy."

The company spent the evening pleasantly with cards and some excellent wine.

Chapter Eighteen

An Unexpected Encounter

Mr. Darcy and Mrs Darcy with Miss Anne de Bourgh and Colonel Fitzwilliam breakfasted early before sunrise. They ate mainly in silence except for the customary morning greetings. Hill had provided an excellent meal in spite of the short notice.

Men were organising the carriage and horses on this dark morning. The air was cold and fresh. The horses' breath was like steam and they were eager to get on the road. The whole family and the retinue were engaged in loading the luggage and making last minute preparations. The ritual good byes caused numerous delays. The good people of The Manor House of Longbourn suffered the departure of their family guests so that it would leave an emptiness in their lives.

Elizabeth felt that she so wanted to talk to her horses before their work. That was a minor delay but all agreed as they watched her, a good one. The party mounted the carriage while the colonel sat astride his horse, then they were off.

The carriage party waved in return to the Bennet family and their retinue as the horses weaved their way along the drive and out onto the open road. At this time, the travellers fell back in their seats. Their faces reflected the pleasures of their visit to Longbourn but tempered somehow by the sadness of leaving such wholesome company.

Elizabeth jested, "Where are we going?"

This innocent question dismissed the prevailing mood and turned it into something more jocular.

Mr. Darcy and Anne spoke in unison, "*Pemberley* of course, *Elizabeth*!"

She smiled and replied, "I cannot believe that at last we are on the road to Pemberley."

"We shall be there by this afternoon if all goes well." Darcy assured her.

"If all goes well." Elizabeth repeated, "If all goes well."

"And why should it not?" Anne inquired.

The carriage reached a toll road and was soon speeding along towards the North. The only thoughts in Elizabeth's head were of Pemberley. It now seemed unbelievable that she was actually on the way and it was only a matter of a little time and some short distance of the final leg of their journey. She struggled to dismiss her high anticipation mingled with her excitement of going home at last.

They passed by country churches and city cathedrals. Darcy knew each one and when not dozing, he would give a commentary. His detailed knowledge of the country seemed without bounds. Well versed as he was with the ecclesiastical establishments, Mr. Darcy could deliver excellent commentaries even on the secular buildings of any particular note.

"Oh, Mr. Darcy tell us more!" Miss Anne de Bourgh demanded.

Darcy smiled at her enthusiasm. "If that is your wish, then I shall tell you of the time the young king Edward the Sixth stopped at The Crown Inn for His royal needs. It was in the year of 1552, a year before he died . . ."

Elizabeth interrupted, "Is this a legend of ghosts and ghouls crying out in the night, Sir?"

"Not at all madam, my story is historical."

Anne intervened with good humour, "We would rather the ghosts . . . but if you must historical, so be it!"

Mr. Darcy expounded the tale as the carriage sped on over hills and down dales. In time, they arrived at a small village with a particularly pleasant looking hotel.

"We shall stop here for refreshments. It will give your horses a rest also Elizabeth."

Mr. Darcy knew that would gain favour with Elizabeth even if the stop irked her.

"Very well." Said Elizabeth, "But I knew there would be some event to impede our journey. This time tell me, are there any relatives inside the establishment, perhaps anybody I know or should know? Are there any kings or queens inside?"

The company laughed at both of Elizabeth's remark and her questions as they entered the hostelry but in good humour. Inside they found a large room set with round tables covered by white linen with flower displays. The blazing log fire was very much appreciated. The subdued light prevented them from fully appreciating the fine interior. A gentleman alone seated at a table away from the window was barely visible at all. Mr. Darcy called for service while the rest jostled round the fire to take best advantage of the warmth.

Within a few minutes, a serving girl walked in to attend to the needs of the travellers. After giving their orders and for the liverymen, the ladies and the colonel took advantage of the refreshing facilities available.

Mr. Darcy alone remained to select a suitable table and at once seated himself waiting for the fare to arrive and his party to return. The other solitary occupant of the room rose from his chair and made his way slowly to the exit. There was no acknowledgement or passing the time of day but Darcy was transfixed. He could do nothing else but wait for his party. The food and drink arrived and then the ladies followed by the colonel. Fitzwilliam caught a glimpse of Darcy's face and even in the subdued light could tell that he was ill at ease to an extreme.

"Darcy, are you all right?" The colonel asked with great consternation.

Darcy's countenance was extremely disturbed and the ladies too could see that something was wrong. They knew of nothing that could have deranged him so.

"Colonel, it was him."

"Who?" The colonel asked.

"I could neither apprehend him nor defend myself. If he had looked at me . . . had he recognized me I should have been helpless."

Understanding Darcy's unspoken meaning, the colonel was eager to put his cousin at ease, "You have been very lucky then but consider I was just a moment away. From now on, we shall be on our guard. In addition, he did not look at you and did not recognize you and perhaps he would not even know you again if he did see your face. Remember your last meeting? It was very dark with extreme inclement conditions."

The colonel began to realize the seriousness of the situation. "Attend to the ladies and I shall be just a moment, Darcy."

Colonel Fitzwilliam did not wait for any protestations from his cousin. He left the room to make inquires of the Landlord as to the identity of his guest. The Landlord explained that he arrived late last night and was not acquainted with the man. He came down within this hour for breakfast, paid his bill and left.

Colonel Fitzwilliam asked, "Has he visited on a prior occasion?"

The landlord continued, "I have never seen him before. The man said little, he hardly spoke a word. I believe that he did have a secretive air about him."

"Your guest was alone then?' The Colonel enquired

"He had no-one with him as far as I know sir."

"In which direction would he go from here, Landlord?" Colonel Fitzwilliam asked of him.

"Oh, I saw him leave, sir, by way of the Ashbourne Road but he will not pass because the river is flooded. I told 'im so. He could go by way of Rocester or perhaps, . . . or perhaps the other way to Derby. Anyway he has gone now."

"A pursuit would prove fruitless I think." The colonel mused. To which the landlord agreed.

The colonel returned to his party.

He waded into the victuals. Anne and Elizabeth were very inquisitive regarding his temporary disappearance. The two ladies were discussing the colonel's withdrawal more from a romantic point of view. By this time, Elizabeth had communicated to Anne of her observations of Colonel Fitzwilliam's attentions to her and the possible implications. The possible implications were in no way offensive to Anne. Their deliberations completed, Elizabeth made a hint of their departure for Pemberley.

"Pemberley and home." Thought Elizabeth. "So close now. Surely nothing can impede our progress so that this afternoon, as Darcy promised, we shall be at Pemberley, and we shall be at home."

The duties attended all completed; the party stepped out of the inn to discover that it had started to rain. Elizabeth attentive as always to the gentlemen's welfare suggested that the colonel should ride inside the carriage. At this the colonel protested by opining that it would prove to be a short shower.

"Inside would keep you dry and make the going easier for your horse." Elizabeth offered the recommendation to justify her advice.

Inside the carriage, Elizabeth arranged Mr. Darcy and herself on one side of the carriage while Miss Anne de Bourgh sat alone facing towards the horses. As all the company was insisting that the colonel should try to keep dry, he capitulated and somehow soon found himself seated inside the carriage next to Miss Anne de Bourgh and facing his good friend and cousin, Mr. Darcy.

As the party and the horses had refreshed, they would make easy going to complete the final part of the journey. Elizabeth felt again the excitement of her anticipation welling up inside of her. The horses stepped out eagerly towards Ashbourne. On seeing the sign to Ashbourne at the crossroads, the colonel then recalled that the innkeeper told him that the ford was flooded. The colonel explained this to Darcy and they pondered a while trying to decide on the best action to take. Eventually they agreed to continue to the ford and make their plans according to the situation.

Upon reaching the ford, although the rain had ceased, they did indeed find the river swollen and the ford flooded. Elizabeth was imagining her dreams disappearing once more. She felt like crying but held back her feelings. The colonel descended from the carriage together with the driver and the retinue to take a closer look. This, they all agreed, was not passable and they should have to turn round and take the Rocester road and rejoin their route further north. On communicating this to the ladies, the gentlemen were overwhelmed with protestations. They agreed to take another look to see if there was a way. To which aim, the men left the carriage to examine the ford once more. This time however, a number of surly looking men had gathered and were regarding these gentlemen with a curious eye. The men were advancing slowly from both the right and left sides.

Chapter Nineteen

An Event at the Ford

Miss Anne de Bourgh recalled from her conversations with Elizabeth that the blunderbuss would be kept under the driver's seat. With the gentlemen off guard, they would be totally exposed to the mercies of the prowlers. Quickly and quietly, Anne slipped out of the carriage door and carefully mounted to the driver's position. She lifted the seat of the box containing the weapon to extract it. Miss Anne de Bourgh had never fired a gun of any sort before. In fact, this was the first time she had actually touched one. She lifted the blunderbuss cautiously being careful to conceal the weapon from both the gentlemen and the prowlers by keeping her back turned to the men. Anne took up a stance that she imagined would be a good shooting position but as she did so the horses jostled a little. The horses jostled just a little but enough to jerk the carriage just a little which was just enough to threaten Anne to loose her balance, which in turn caused her to become tense all over including her trigger finger. The blunderbuss fired. The recoil was tremendous. The recoil was unexpected by Anne. The recoil threw her backwards to fall in front of the rear horses and at the rear of the front horses. Simultaneously the report frightened the horses. They bolted forwards straight towards the ford and into the water. The party of gentlemen and their retinue who were inspecting the ford, dispersed left and right, away from the path of the bolting horses. Some of the prowling men on hearing the gun ran off. Four of them had the presence of mind to dash forwards into the water to restrain the horses. The men appeared to be very capable in their handling of the animals.

Colonel Fitzwilliam saw Miss Anne de Bourgh amongst the horse and carriage harnessing. She was slipping slowly down into the water.

The colonel cried out to the men, "Hold the horses. Hold the horses."

As he ran forward to rescue Anne, he could see that she was very much in distress. The colonel reached the horses and tried to recover Anne but she dropped down into the water and floated among the horses' legs. He could see that her body was all-limp as he reached through the horses' legs to catch hold of her to pull her from her entanglement back to safety. The colonel raised her up in his strong arms, waded back to the dry land but would not put her down.

Two of the men who proved to be gypsies ran to the colonel. "Fetch 'er to our fire, she must dry out and keep warm. Bring 'er now. Bring 'er this way zur." The gypsies urged.

The colonel needed no further persuasion but followed the two gypsies to their encampment where a fire was indeed an ideal antidote for wet and cold. The rest of the party followed the colonel and the two gypsies to the camp. Behind them came the other two gypsies who, having rescued the carriage, were now bringing it to their camp for safekeeping.

The colonel laid the limp body of Anne gently down on the grass. Her eyes were closed and there was no sign of life. The colonel rubbed her hands and wrists and then her arms but it seemed to no avail. The frail, delicate body lay motionless. In desperation, he picked her up and drew her close to the fire to get some warmth into the cold body. All the time this pleasant but battle-hardened soldier was wiping away tears that streamed down his cheeks. Elizabeth came forward to help the colonel. She felt for Anne's pulse and put her cheek to her nose. "I am sure I can feel something colonel, keep trying, please."

At this point a gypsy woman arrived, "Ere, give 'er this, it'll bring 'er round."

Spontaneously Elizabeth put the cup to Anne's lips but there was no response. She parted the lips with the rim of the cup to pour in more of the precious elixir. The rest of the party had now caught up with the colonel and were horrified to witness the ashen face of Miss Anne de Bourgh.

There was no response. In desperation, Elizabeth poured the rest of the cup into her cousin's mouth. Again, there was no response. She looked up at the Colonel. They were both crying as now Elizabeth held Anne to her bosom and rocked backwards and forwards. There came a splutter quickly followed by a cough and more coughing.

The colonel was the first to announce, "She is alright! She is alright!

Tears were flowing down his face again but this time with the happy turn of events.

Anne's eyes opened to the colonel's face then to Elizabeth and then looking about she could see that a whole encampment of gypsies surrounded them. They were watching her cough intermittently still. Their faces had been of a very serious turn. The faces now changed as the gypsies let out a cheer. Many exclamations of dubious meanings and origins rang out from her foreign audience. One of the women of the crowd came forward smiling through large gaps in her teeth. She tended a wooden bowl and spoon. She explained that it was hot and would "Bring 'er round right good. Lord luv 'er." Dutifully, Anne consumed the stew, which she found very palatable and efficacious indeed.

It was now necessary for Anne to change her clothes while the retinue attended to the horses. The four of them had had a very frightening experience by the discharge of the gun by Anne. The men loosened the horses from their harnesses to allow them to graze on the fresh green spring grass. The gypsy-men closely inspected the four horses and they all confirmed that they were as good a team of animals as they had ever seen.

The men built up the fire further. This was not only for their guests but all the family of gypsies also. The light was fading. An elderly member of the group played a violin of such a tone as none of Darcy's party had ever heard before. The tune was probably his own but was so haunting an air that nobody could speak. They could only listen and follow the air as it swept them away on a magical music carpet. Without a word spoken gypsy women passed plates of food to everyone so that soon they were all eating rabbit pie. The fire, the music, the food and some alcoholic beverage seemed like enchantment under the stars that evening. The gypsies wanted to know all about these peoples' lives and much exchange of such information passed between them.

Somehow the mood changed and the music also. The violin became alive again but with a different tempo. This was music for dancing. A harmonica and a penny flute joined the violin to make the air more of a merry tune. By now, some gypsies were dancing. Some men, by themselves, were jogging to the melody while groups of women with their arms intertwined were swaying in time with the music. A tall thin man joined the musicians to swell the volume of the harmony with his concertina giving to it a new dimension. Several men and women began dancing freely in a very primitive fashion. To the amazement of Elizabeth and Anne, Darcy and the colonel rose to their feet to join in the jogging, dancing and laughing. Much whooping and joyful gypsy cries filled the night air.

Elizabeth watched incredulously as the gentlemen fell to the spell of the magic of the night, of the gypsy's music and perhaps some drink. She recalled her first meeting with Mr. Darcy.

His words came to her mind, "Excuse me madam but I rarely dance."

Then later the same evening when Mr. Bingley was goading Darcy to dance, his reply was "I certainly shall not, in such a company as this it would be insupportable."

Mr. Darcy was now dancing with the gypsies and looked as though he had never enjoyed himself so much, ever. The pride and the prejudices have all gone and it seemed, from the look on their faces, for always. The evening spent its hours in this mingling of company and pleasures. In the course of time, the various gentlemen and gypsies began to yearn for rest more than they did for entertainment. The company thinned slowly and lessened.

In time, only the Darcy party remained around the fire. The glow from the embers or from the wine and dancing or any combination lit the complexion of each face. Tired and exhausted, their thoughts also spent, their desire was only on the idea of sleep.

Finally, it was not anyone's idea nor did anyone say anything, but Mr. and Mrs Darcy and Miss Anne de Bourgh and Colonel Fitzwilliam and the retinue, one by one, fell peacefully into a deep slumber.

Chapter Twenty

The Horses Lost

The sun had already risen on a cold morning as the first of the Darcy party began to stir. The dying embers of the fire had little cheer left in them. Mr. Darcy raised himself from the ground. While the others continued their awakening routine from a very heavy sleep, he looked around. Several things he noted. Firstly, the gypsies had up camped and apparently moved on. That is, all but a small gathering of four of the gypsies still breakfasting around a low fire and trying to find some warmth from it. Otherwise, the scene of the meadow was one of desolation.

The next thing that occurred to him which was giving him more reason for concern was that their equipage was nowhere in sight.

"There are no horses that the gypsies had admired so much." Was the thought that went through his mind."

The colonel was addressing Miss Anne de Bourgh to inquire after her condition. This might have been for the incident at the ford or it might have been because of some special concern or both.

Mr. Darcy returned to deliver the news of their new situation. The Colonel turned his concern to Mr. Darcy, "My horse too? Have they left us with nothing?"

Mr. Darcy checked his purse. It was light. They had lifted his purse while he was asleep, taken some coinage then returned the rest with the purse to his money belt.

"The scoundrels thought I would not notice." He concluded.

The colonel was pleased that they had taken nothing from his purse as he had little left after the gratuitous acts of charity at the village where the young boy was injured.

Two of the gypsies who had remained, approached while the party had been counting its losses. The gypsies stood stock-still. They stood just looking on while they waited for the party to notice them. Upon realizing their presence, the gentlemen looked their way while remaining silent. For a moment, they were not sure what to do.

"Beggin' yore pardon zur, a good mornin' to 'e all." One of the gypsies ventured showing a smile as broad as his face.

"Er, good morning to you too my good man." The colonel answered while the rest of the party followed with similar greetings but without much enthusiasm. The colonel continued, "Your friends seem to have taken my horse, do you know where they have gone?"

"Well zur I knows were they go but they wont take 'es horses. No zur not them."

Mr. Darcy doubting the veracity of the men declared, "They have stolen money from my purse, how can we believe you man?"

"Beggin' yore pardon zur, the gypsies gives t'thee theys take some payment loike. It's the gypsy way. Oi fancy y'll find your 'orse with all t'others down on t'road by t' ford Oi 'as a moin'd, zur."

From the depths of their misery, the spirits of all four of the little band lifted and all thoughts were now turning towards feelings of goodness and gratitude. Elizabeth and Anne raised themselves from the ground to run together down the embankment in search of the horses and the road. Long before they reached the carriage and their retinue, the ladies could see the carriage and the horses. As they ran down the slope towards their horses, their squeals of delight signalled to the men that the gypsy's' words were true. The men smiled at each other.

Mr. Darcy mused on his purse and said to the men, "Your friends are welcome to their money I am sure."

Mr. Darcy was feeling some warm respect for these men and their code of conduct.

Mr. Darcy lowered substantially his prejudice though his pride remained. He extended his good arm out to them. The leading gypsy took it with a smile. The gypsy stood as though he was waiting for something more. Darcy's reaction was to think, "This man is going to be a nuisance now."

Cautiously Darcy asked the man if there was something else.

"Beggin' yore pardon zur, will 'e be wontin to cross t'ford t'day?"

Darcy wondered at this enquiry and thought the man could be up to some mischief.

"Why? Is the situation improved today? Is it passable now?"

"Oh. Oi'm zorry zur, if anythin' it be worse. But we c'n 'elp 'e cross safely loik if e wishes zur."

Darcy thought for a moment. "Should we take the risk or heed to the wisdom of caution?"

He looked towards the men and said, "We may be safer going by Rocester I believe and bypass the ford?"

"Very good zur. As yur wish zur, but the Rocester road crosses the same river three toimes. It winds and turns its way 'cross the country . . . loike a serpent zur. With no-one to 'elp 'e, 'e might be worse orf . . . Ev'n if 'e do not 'ave a problem crossing further up stream it'll take 'e much longer. Thy best way zur would be crossing safely 'ere at Potter's Ford."

Darcy pondered for a moment, recalling that the ladies much prefer to cross here if it is possible. "Well, we will give it a try. You really think you can get us across safely?"

"Lord bless 'e zur, 'tis a gypsy crossing. We c'n cross when it's worse than 'tis, much worse, zur."

The gypsies and the gentlemen made their way down to the ford. They found the ladies fussing the animals while the retinue was busy generally tidying and cleaning the coach and the harnessing. As soon as Anne saw that the gentlemen were arriving, she ran towards them. She then addressed the colonel to ask if it would be safe to cross the ford.

"The gypsies seem to think it possible though we are not so convinced." The colonel replied and feeling very good that Anne should ask him and not Darcy.

This did not go unnoticed by the party.

The driver and his team harnessed the horses while all the time Elizabeth and Anne would be talking to them and caressing them.

While this activity proceeded, the gypsies gave instructions to the driver. They first had to take the carriage as far upstream as was possible. Then the practice was to cross diagonally towards the opposite bank. It was thus allowing the current to carry them along a diagonal sweep across to the bank onto the opposite side. It was essential, according to the gypsies, to keep the horses moving all the time on this plan.

With the passengers mounted inside the carriage and the retinue to their normal positions, the gypsies lead the horses upstream as far to a point where the overhanging foliage would just allow the manoeuvring of the carriage and horses. The gypsies, knee deep in the water, then slapped the rumps of the two rear horses while shouting loud gypsy noises. This had a strong motivating effect on the horses. The horses may have had doubts about the water but the gypsy cries quickly dispelled them. The team made full speed, with ears flattened back, towards the opposite bank. The two gypsies jumped onto the rear of the carriage giving more weight to the equipage. It seemed seconds only that the horses were climbing the slope of the opposite bank safely and easily. The gypsies jumped down, ran towards the front horses, one on each side to take control, to arrest the carriage.

The leading gypsy went to the side of the coach to address the gentlemen and smiling asked beaming faced, "That be safe enough for 'e zurs?"

Mr. Darcy could not help grinning, "That did indeed seem to be so simple. How much do we owe you? And what do we call you because we would like to remember you?'

"You owe us nothing zur, they took it last noight. T'was t'reason we stayed behind. T'names Barnie zur."

The occupants in the coach could not help laughing at the ease of the crossing.

Miss Anne de Bourgh lost all sense of decorum and called to the gypsy, "Allow us to give a little extra by way of showing our gratitude Barnie!"

The gypsy smiled a gypsy smile. He smiled with his mouth; he smiled with his face and with his eyes while tugging at his forelock. Anne turned to Colonel Fitzwilliam to display an empty palm. Dutifully the colonel dug deep into his money pouch and with a look of good-humoured despair retrieved a silver coin.

Darcy, smiling, added, "And here's something from me. Well done! It has been a pleasure, zur!" He mimicked, with good humour, his gypsy benefactor.

He then called to the driver and the carriage began to move forwards towards Pemberley. The ladies waved enthusiastically to Barnie and his friend then regained their seats as the gypsies slowly shrank into tiny dots. The conversation following was all about their experiences of the previous evening. They all recanted of the romantic music, the mysterious atmosphere, the food, the drink, the stars and the gypsies. Such deliciously romantic memories, unforgettable experiences, they each shared between them.

When every detail was exhausted, Elizabeth posed the question,

"Where are we going?"

Miss Anne de Bourgh, Colonel Fitzwilliam and Mr. Darcy all called out in unison,

"Pemberley of course!"

At which they all laughed.

Chapter Twenty one

Onward to Pemberley

The continuing journey took the party through more villages and even more scenery. On approaching a village signed as Rowsley, Mr. Darcy felt it his duty to remark of The Peacock Inn located there. He further expounded on its exceptional fishing facilities and its connections with Izaak Walton. As he filled in more and more detail, he sensed the interest of the party slipping away. New objects of interest were continually coming and going so that even he could not hold their interest indefinitely. Slowly, repetitive interests overwhelmed the company's passion for such study. Not even the mention of Chatsworth House, close by, stirred the curiosity of anyone in the party.

The time had passed but all the while, the horses had made good headway. Their spring grass supper was telling and the extra speed made the miles seem shorter. By now, the passengers were all in a semi-dozing attitude. They were, for the moment, without any specific highlight to inflame their passions.

Darcy knew so well the road and all its idiosyncrasies of surface, turns and sounds. So that he was the first to notice, "We are here. We have arrived!"

The astonished passengers expressed their doubts first but then demonstrated their surprise and happiness. The colonel called out to stop the carriage. He had in mind to ride the final distance.

By coincidence only, the coach had stopped at the same place on the road from where Elizabeth first saw the fine prospect of, "a house most pleasantly situated." The sun was now highlighting the Pemberley House. The building and the setting did indeed look very pleasant.

Anne was the first to notice the scene, seated as she was facing the horses in the direction of travel. She gazed at the scene then looked at Elizabeth and caught her breath, "Pemberley?"

Elizabeth leant forward with much haste to witness the scene.

"Pemberley." She whispered to confirm but hardly able to believe her eyes.

She took a deep breath. Gazing down for some moments the feeling and thoughts that came to her were quite natural and quite right. There it stood: Pemberley House. This was the Darcy home, her home, of which she was mistress.

"I am mistress of all this. I really am mistress of all this." Elizabeth spoke her thoughts but silently.

Elizabeth needed to reassure and remind herself of the fulfillment of her destiny.

She turned to her husband and took his large masculine fist into her soft feminine hands and said softly, "My dear Mr. Darcy, I shall always try to be worthy of you and of Pemberley."

"My dear Elizabeth, I hope that I and Pemberley will always be worthy of you."

Anne witnessed the private, tender scene. For a moment or two, they sat in silence. There seemed nothing more to say. They had arrived and the epic journey was now over. There was nothing more to do but to go home.

Darcy called out to the driver, "Jacobs, sound the horn to notify the staff of our arrival."

"Elizabeth, you remember the staff will parade before the house? The housekeeper will introduce you to the women first and then the men." Mr. Darcy explained.

She confirmed that she expected to shake hands with the highest and lowest and that she has every intention of knowing them each by name.

"Shall I too, shake hands with the staff also?" Inquired Anne.

"If that is your wish Anne, then you may. Then I should be glad to introduce you." Elizabeth confirmed.

Elizabeth remembered the first time she visited Pemberley. The housekeeper, Mrs Taylor, showed her and Mr. and Mrs Gardiner around the house while speaking praise on praise of the good and generous nature of her master. How surprised she had been then to learn of so much approval for his character. How much she would agree with her now.

"I wonder," thought Elizabeth. "If she would ever eulogize over her new mistress in a similar manner."

"Mr. Darcy will of course introduce me to the housekeeper. Is that not so, Mr. Darcy?"

To which Mr. Darcy readily agreed adding that it would be a pleasure to perform such a task.

The colonel now mounted on his horse, called to the driver of the carriage who knew how to respond.

The occupants heard the anticipated horn sound. They felt the carriage move forward and gather apace. They were at last arriving at Pemberley.

Elizabeth asked, "Where are we going?"

Darcy quickly responded by putting his hand across his forehead and leaning forward to say, "I could not imagine!"

Anne followed quickly, hardly able to speak for amusement it caused her, she exclaimed, "Pemberley, of course, Elizabeth!"

At which they all laughed all the way to the front of the big house they call, Pemberley.

⊹

End of Volume One

Volume Two

Chapter One

Lady Catherine Refuses Consent

Following the introductions and the customary indulgent speeches to the staff, Mr. Darcy and his party were in a single mind to refresh themselves and then to rest before dressing for dinner. Returning to civilization had its blessings and its duties. The housekeeper had informed Mr. Darcy of the presence of his aunt, Lady Catherine de Bourgh and that the lady was waiting in the salon.

He, in turn, informed Anne and Elizabeth. Mr. Darcy then spoke to Colonel Fitzwilliam. Mr. Darcy thought it his duty to do so considering the confidence he enjoyed of the conversations with Elizabeth regarding Miss Anne de Bourgh and the Colonel. By their conversation Mr. Darcy understood that the colonel was now an interested party. Their first obligation was to deal with this visitation of Lady Catherine.

The lady had made the journey, uneventfully from Dagenbury to Pemberley to recover Anne. That is to re-establish her sovereignty over her family, her own daughter. Before Anne left Rosings for Pemberley, she had written to her mother who was then visiting The Two Black Cats Inn. Anne's letter was to inform her mother of her intention of leaving with Elizabeth, Mr. Darcy and the colonel in order to spend some time at Pemberley as the guest of Mr. and Mrs Darcy.

Mr. Darcy entered the salon to welcome his aunt on this occasion of her first visit to Pemberley for many years, "Lady Catherine, you are very welcome. How good it is to see you at Pemberley. I trust we have made you comfortable?"

The lady did not respond so warmly. Mr. Darcy asked of his aunt if he could bring Anne and the colonel to see her. To this, Lady Catherine insisted that she should see her daughter immediately to make arrangements to return to Kent at the earliest possible convenience.

"My dearest aunt, would you take away . . . would you deprive *me* of my most popular guest? You are both most welcome to stay as long as it pleases you. There is one matter which may appeal and give you pleasure. I have been asked by Colonel Fitzwilliam to seek your permission for an audience with you."

In her most aloof manner Lady Catherine replied, "What can my nephew have to say to me that cannot wait until I have spoken to my own daughter, pray?"

"With respect Lady Catherine, it is not for me to say. Why not receive the colonel first while Anne refreshes herself from her journey? I imagine Anne would wish it that way. We have had the most arduous drive from Rosings. When Anne is herself again I know she will be as pleased to see you as I am." He smiled.

"Wish it would she? Oh! Very well then, I will see my nephew first but tell him to be brief." Lady Catherine emphasized brief while being as brief herself as she could contrive.

Mr. Darcy excused himself from his aunt to discover his cousin Colonel Fitzwilliam.

Mr. Darcy did not remain at the house but set about some business at the stables.

A few moments only passed but enough time for Lady Catherine to arrange herself before a servant announced, "Colonel Fitzwilliam."

Lady Catherine was standing looking through the window as though intent on admiring the view of the landscape. She was practicing the technique of not being where her visitor expected her to be upon the visitor's arrival to her presence.

It was a strategy designed to disarm her guest but a trifle. The colonel entered the room and was indeed at a loss as to his bearings until he located his aunt by the far window. With the usual greetings complete, the colonel informed his aunt that he had some important news and wished to seek her approval.

"My approval?" She asked in a haughty tone. "What important news can this be?"

"Lady Catherine, my dearest Aunt, we have been on excellent terms for so many years, all my life in fact. I do have the greatest respect, indeed love for you, and you must know that. Lady Catherine, I feel that I can be frank with you. That is to say, that I am in love with Anne and she assures me that she feels the same way towards me. In short, dear aunt, I am seeking your permission to marry Anne."

Lady Catherine de Bourgh stood quite still.

Then, raising herself as high as she was able, announced, "This is nonsense. It is out of the question. No such marriage can take place."

She waved her hand holding a kerchief as to dismiss his petition. Then span round to turn her back on him in order, apparently, to refocus her attentions on the prospect from the window.

Colonel Fitzwilliam held his ground. "My dearest aunt, Lady Catherine, my situation is very favourable and my connections are as good as any man in the country. Our union can only bring happiness to all parties concerned. You have been blind to one happy marriage. Anne and I are in love and want to marry to share the rest of our lives together. With or without your permission, sooner rather than later, with or without your blessing, we will be married. We have no wish to be disagreeable to you but we do have lives of our own. We would prefer to be married than to court your pleasure by not marrying."

Lady Catherine continued to apparently admire the view while announcing, "But she cannot marry without my permission." She turned to face her nephew to emphasise, "And I will not give it. No! Never! I cannot!"

She hoped to checkmate all his arguments.

The colonel attempted to explain that she would be standing alone in the family if she did not eventually give the consent. The effect of being isolated will become even more severe as the situation became common gossip.

He chose his words with special attention and continued. "Who will want to marry Anne thereafter knowing that she was forbidden to marry the man she really loved?"

Lady Catherine summoned a servant to request the presence of her daughter immediately. She followed her summons by ordering her carriage.

The colonel could not understand her thinking. "What," he thought, "was she intending to do?"

Anne, imagining that Lady Catherine by now had given her consent, leapt into the room ready to kiss her mother. At once Anne sensed, with much disappointment, the prevailing mood. Anne suspected that all had not gone well between her colonel and her mother.

"Go immediately to your room and pack your trunks. We are leaving for Rosings as soon as the carriage is ready." Lady Catherine ordered her daughter.

"But mother . . ."

"Now!"

Anne shouted at her mother with tears already in her eyes insisted, while stamping her foot, "No! No!"

It was now Anne's turn to stand her ground even though she was starting to cry. Never before had she said this word to her mother or addressed her in this way. Never had the thought of disobeying her mother's slightest whim occurred to her.

The servant returned from the stables.

"With your lady's pardon. The stablemen are unable to provide either horse or carriage tonight. There are problems with the horses and with the carriages. I am to convey to milady, apologies but that tomorrow morning would be the earliest."

With a respectful bow, he left.

Anticipating Lady Catherine's intentions, Mr. Darcy had given the strictest orders that no horse or carriage should leave

Pemberley until the following morning. It was fortunate he did. Mr. Darcy was well aware of Lady Catherine's deep-seated ambitions. She held them even now. His thoughts were to delay in order to give his Aunt time to reconsider more favourably. Darcy's mind dwelt on his own experiences. He had no parents to guide him or threaten him if he did not marry the partner of their choice.

"A union between Anne and the eligible Colonel Fitzwilliam is a matter of love between themselves and less on the ambitions of a parent." This thought resonated through his mind.

Lady Catherine fell silent. The prospect of dining with the family of nephews and daughter in such a confrontational mood imaged in her mind. This would be uncomfortable indeed.

The tactic employed by Lady Catherine was, "We will discuss this more, when we have had time to calm down."

Anne wanted to say something but Elizabeth whispered for her to remain silent. All three of the travellers noticed how Anne emerged from a cautious timid girl of a sickly disposition to a confident more outward going young lady. She developed during their journey. Somewhere between Rosings to Longbourn and then onward to Pemberley a girl was lost and a young woman was discovered. A headstrong young lady who wanted to marry the man she loved could prove to be a formidable force in any household.

Chapter Two

The Dilemma of the Lovers

Life at Pemberley did not stir very early the morning following the demonstrative refusal by Lady Catherine de Bourgh of Colonel Fitzwilliam's suit to her daughter, Anne. There had been much on which to contemplate. At the breakfast table there would be a consensual silence regarding to the important subject. Mr. Darcy was already breakfasting when Lady Catherine entered the dining room.

"The others have not come to breakfast yet?" The lady asked Mr. Darcy after exchanging morning greetings.

"I understand that Anne and the colonel are riding on the estate. They breakfasted early." Mr. Darcy replied.

"My daughter on a horse? But my daughter has never sat on a horse in her life." Lady Catherine informed Mr. Darcy. "I would never expose my daughter to the perils of the horse; I am attentive to all matters concerned with her safety."

"Perhaps the colonel is teaching her to ride. She certainly could not have a better instructor. Fitzwilliam has won military cups, you know. His horsemanship is quite outstanding."

Lady Catherine ventured, "I do hope that Anne was suitably attired. She has no riding clothes and the mornings have by no means warmed up yet; and that Bennet girl, should she not be with them?"

"*Elizabeth*," responded Mr. Darcy, "Is quite busy already planning her day. She desires so much to see and to learn. As for suitable habit, Georgiana has provided Anne with all essentials. They are much the same size and build. I am sure there is no need for any alarm at all."

A few more minutes passed in total silence. The Lady Catherine was not as comfortable as she might have been at Rosings. She was so far from Rosings Park and fresh from the informal atmosphere of The Two Black Cats Inn. These contrary situations combined to inhibit her behaviour to be less authoritative than she could exercise at home. Before the silence could be broken again, the lady of the house entered the breakfast room. She was smiling as she greeted her husband with a morning kiss. She then paid her respects to Lady Catherine.

Then added, "Please excuse my absence: matters of estate you know Lady Catherine."

In understanding the lady's ill humour, she was careful not to use words of attachment in her address to Lady Catherine which might cause discord to her temper.

Lady Catherine acknowledged Elizabeth's courtesies. In this environment she was witnessing the very opposite of what she was expecting and indeed hoping. Elizabeth conducted herself very well, confidently and just correctly as a lady should. Lady Catherine simmered still in the most earnest of her life-long wish. Mrs Darcy, Mr.

Darcy's mother and Catherine had made the solemn agreement that they would unite their two and only eligible off-springs in marriage. They further reaffirmed that promise on Mrs Darcy's deathbed. His mother's dying wish therefore, was for the union between their offspring. Such a marriage would be a triumph in every respect for the two families. Now she was witnessing Elizabeth as a confident and capable mistress of Pemberley. It was difficult to form any plan especially when her other nephew thinks that he has made an attachment to her daughter. In spite of all, she was determined to weave some design into the events in order to detach Elizabeth from Darcy. Her first task would have to be to remove Anne from Pemberley and from the company and the influence of Colonel Fitzwilliam.

As soon as Lady Catherine had completed her breakfast, she began preparations for her departure to Rosings. She would not call for the carriage until Anne had returned from her ride.

"It will be," She thought, "better to remain private and away from company until Anne returns."

Lady Catherine had arranged for their entire luggage to be packed and removed to her carriage. While the morning hours mounted towards midday, Lady Catherine was becoming increasingly angry and more anxious.

Whilst learning of the ways of Pemberley, of the staff and the farms and their families of the estate, Elizabeth had little time for leisure that morning. The young women of the Pemberley staff also had little opportunity for distractions as they went about their business of cleaning and tidying in all the rooms. The cleaning girl, on whom it fell to attend to Anne's room, noticed a sealed letter resting overtly on Anne's escritoire. The writing revealed the addressee's name to be Lady Catherine de Bourgh. She mentally noted the fact and continued to her duties until midday when she would be finished.

Noon came and went without the reappearance of Anne or the colonel.

Lady Catherine sought out Mr. Darcy who was consulting with Elizabeth over estate matters. Lady Catherine reminded her nephew that the colonel and her daughter had been riding since before anyone else had breakfasted and they are still not returned.

She added, "It was possible that some dreadful accident may have taken place."

This possibility did provide some grounds for concern. Elizabeth summoned a servant and instructed him to make all immediate inquiries as to the whereabouts of the Colonel Fitzwilliam and Miss Anne de Bourgh.

Within the hour, the servant returned with the cleaning girl to inform Mr. Darcy of the letter that the girl had noticed on the writing desk. The young girl explained to the company that while she was dusting the desk, she had noticed a letter resting on the top. She expounded further that it bore the addressee's name as Lady Catherine de Bourgh.

Darcy dispatched the girl with the authority to retrieve the envelope with all haste for Lady Catherine.

All domestic activity ceased. The attention of the staff of Pemberley was distracted while the servant girl retraced her steps to the room of Miss Anne de Bourgh. She entered the room. The envelope was laid still where it was some hours before.

Returning to the assemblage, she offered the envelope to Mr. Darcy who indicated that she should be offering the letter to Lady Catherine, "You have done well girl, take the letter now to Lady Catherine."

With a rather shy curtsy, she tended the letter to the lady and left with the servant. Lady Catherine de Bourgh took the letter from the envelope very timidly. This must be a very secret and a very important letter indeed. It would involve her daughter and perhaps someone else associated with her. Opening the letter tentatively, Lady Catherine began to read it silently to herself. Her faced reflected a state of total disbelief and horror. She closed the letter slowly and returned it to its envelope. As she turned to walk away from the company, the lady appeared to be a little unsteady on her feet. Mr. Darcy and an attentive servant together moved forward to support her. She fell onto their support. Mr. Darcy and the servant guided the lady to a nearby settle where she collapsed.

Lady Catherine gripped and held Mr. Darcy's sleeve and she pulled him down close to her, so that she could speak discreetly, "My dear nephew, you are good at this sort of thing. You could go after them and bring them back for me. Bring them back Darcy. They must not indulge themselves. Read the letter Darcy, read it now and then go after them with all haste."

Mr. Darcy read the letter. It related of the reason for the absence of the two young people. He read of elopement and going to Scotland to marry with or without consent.

"This is news indeed aunt, but I have not power to detain them. Besides I am suffering still from my wound which is healing well but still vulnerable."

"Darcy, my dear nephew, I will explain more later, send servants bearing letters with your seal and mine. It is only natural the two young people should have an affection for each other. Have you not noticed how alike they are? Send servants to search for them, scour the country but stop the elopement, Darcy. Colonel Fitzwilliam and my daughter . . . they are brother and sister."

Chapter Three

Matters of Estate

Alongside the personal situations and problems, the industry and life of the Pemberley Estate must continue and to prosper. One of the important principles Elizabeth wished to continue on the estate was for the management to involve itself in the welfare of all the levels of their people. This task Elizabeth wished to engage herself by visiting as many tenants she could manage on the first day of each week. The following Monday, the cycle of visits would continue from where she left off the previous week. Thereby, in time, she would make personal contact with all the tenants on a regular basis. Therefore, it was thus, this Monday morning, Elizabeth, accompanied by Georgiana and a girl from kitchen duties, set forth on her first round of visits. As this was Elizabeth's first encounter with Pemberley tenants, they took with them much bounty for the pleasure and benefit of the tenants. Apples and pears for those with no orchard, pork for those who kept no livestock and more material things for those who Elizabeth thought might benefit from such.

Their first call was to the Manning family. Elizabeth judged them the poorest of the tenants by virtue of the size of their holding and its potential. When Elizabeth and her two aides arrived, the family appeared embarrassed and a little nervous. The children, upon seeing the apples and pears were all glee and excitement.

Mr. and Mrs Manning were less enthusiastic. Upon Elizabeth inquiring of their circumstances they admitted to being behind with their rent and had little prospect of being able to meet the arrears or maintain the level of rent. The reason was that they were unable to profit sufficiently from the land to pay the rent or able to provide enough to survive. Georgiana made a note of all this for consideration later. Elizabeth did not want her first task at Pemberley to be the eviction of one of her tenants.

The remainder of the visits that day reflected a more fortunate side of the Pemberley Estate. The tenants' industry to improvements, of increasing yields and trying new methods, the continuing potential seemed boundless. Elizabeth gave lavish praise and much encouragement to the farmers' hard work. She promised to keep her weekly visits and to meet them as often as she could.

Every morning of the week after the Monday, Elizabeth set aside for writing letters and keeping her accounts. This Tuesday morning her first letter was to the father and as she understood, the only remaining parent of Colonel Fitzwilliam. Elizabeth was anxious to have Lady Catherine's story of the parentage of the colonel confirmed. She could never doubt that Lady Catherine was telling her "truth" but the timing of the release of the news lead Elizabeth to question the full reliability of the information.

Possibly, Lady Catherine may have overlooked some minor point. She may have been genuinely mistaken on something. Anne and Colonel Fitzwilliam, by now, firmly believe that they are brother and sister. They understood that they could not unite as man and wife. Notwithstanding this understanding, they still held each other in the highest regard.

Lacking an introduction, Elizabeth was reluctant to write to Colonel Fitzwilliam's father, though she begged that he should consider her as introduced by virtue of the contents and source of the letter and the intent to bring some peace of mind to his own family. She explained, in general terms, the events leading up to the statement by Lady Catherine de Bourgh of the parentage of his son, Colonel Fitzwilliam.

Elizabeth had written in tactful wording in order not to appear to be indecorously inquisitive. The response was not as she had hoped nor could have anticipated. Nonetheless, she was pleasantly surprised to learn from the contents of the letter of her good friends and cousins. General Fitzwilliam's secretary replied, not a little officiously. However, he did pay compliments regarding the recent union that made them close cousins. The secretary referred Elizabeth to a family by the name of Dubery residing on the Kent – Sussex Border in a place named Dagenbury. These people were privy to the family records. The Duberys, the secretary explained, originated from France near a town called Agen. The British Monarchy of the time awarded land to the Dubery family. The Duberys invested much money in the area. Consequently, a town, which they originally called D'Agen, grew and prospered and so did the family. The present Duberys are direct descendants of the original Duberys. They still own the town, in addition to another ham north of the River Thames, but prefer to engage at the occupation of inn keeping. That Elizabeth should better serve herself by soliciting their records.

In turn, Elizabeth wrote a full explanatory letter to her friends and relatives, Bob and Joy Dubery. She had by this time become somewhat inquisitive if not excited by the possibility of coming close to the resolution of her inquiries. Little time elapsed before the hoped-for response arrived from Mr. and Mrs Dubery.

In the meanwhile, Mr. Darcy learned of the line of inquiry that Elizabeth had pursued. He had no great enthusiasm for the venture or the release of the news regarding the desire of a brother and sister to consider matrimony. If his aunt, Lady Catherine, was correct in her announcement that would put his cousins, Colonel Fitzwilliam and Miss Anne de Bourgh, in a questionable integrity by their desire to marry.

Otherwise, if Lady Catherine is wrong, this puts her in a difficult situation because of her attempt to falsify the relationship between the two young people to deliberately attempt to prevent the couple's happiness for her own selfish reasons.

Both Elizabeth and Darcy understood the possible meaning of "those reasons". Elizabeth and Darcy dwelled much on those reasons. Whom would it be that Lady Catherine had it in her mind that her daughter should match? Could it be possible that she still fostered her hopeless plans for Anne and Darcy? In addition, what or whom did she intend for the colonel? Although they held each other in great mutual affection, Anne and the colonel would not, nor could they, legally contemplate marrying if they were brother and sister or if Lady Catherine maintained an objection.

Elizabeth was not too keen to explain to her husband that these situations exist and all these questions are yet unanswered. She added, "I was once most impressed when you insisted, "disguise of every sort is my abhorrence." I could only agree with you then and I do so, still now."

Mr. Darcy winced at hearing these words again but for the reason and occasion, when he spoke them for the first time.

"You are, of course, quite correct. I was thinking of others and not quite sure how far we should intervene." Darcy explained.

"We are the guardians of our own integrity so that we need make public knowledge only that which we consider appropriate." Elizabeth reasoned.

Darcy thought carefully for a moment and said, "Let us consider what news, if any, we have."

Elizabeth offered the letter to her husband but he held up his hand and shook his head in refusal, "No, no. It is your letter. You read it to me but very gently if there is much to shock."

She smiled at him and read,

— o —

Wednesday

Bob & Joy Dubery,
The Inn of the Two Black Cats,
Dagenbury

My Dear Elizabeth,

We were very pleased to receive your letter and your kind wishes. Please, in return, our best thoughts to you both. We hope that by now, Mr. Darcy is well recovered from his misfortune and that there will be no more discomfort for him and for you to have nothing more to worry about.

Regarding the lineage of your cousins the Fitzwilliams, I am able to inform you of the full facts. We do hope that you will be pleased with what I have to tell you but it is quite a story of misfortune. I have to add though, that the Colonel more than bears up his unfortunate history of lost parentage.

The first Lord Fitzwilliam had a very unfortunate first marriage. Lady Fitzwilliam fell during a riding accident. The accident caused her failure to have children thereafter.

Her sister, Lady Jane Smythame, did have a son but she died shortly after the birth. Lord and Lady Fitzwilliam adopted the boy. During the first year of bringing up their adopted son, Lady Fitzwilliam herself died. The cause was, they say, the riding accident. The Lord Fitzwilliam followed her shortly afterwards by dying, it is rumoured, of a broken heart.

Lord Fitzwilliam's brother inherited the title and took the child as his own before he married. During the time the lord was single he became engaged to Lady Catherine.

The young baby boy passed on again to the third brother, General Fitzwilliam.

He raised him to the fine young man we all know and love today as Colonel Fitzwilliam. The General already had a son. He is another Colonel Fitzwilliam being the stepbrother and cousin to our colonel. His pleasant disposition is everything equal to that of our cousin.

Anne de Bourgh did not arrive until Lady Catherine's marriage to Sir William de Bourgh.

We both look forward to seeing you later this year when we shall be in Derbyshire.

Until then, our thoughts and very best wishes,

Your affectionate cousins,
Bob and Joy Dubery

— o —

Historical Record of Colonel Fitzwilliam

Lord Fitzwilliam + Lady Fitzwilliam   Lady Fitzwilliam's sister
(died in cb)

No Children   **Boy**
↑----------------adopted---------------←

Lady Fitzwilliam deceased
Lord Fitzwilliam deceased
→---------**Boy** adopted-------↓

Lord Fitzwilliam's Brother (Becomes Lord Fitzwilliam II)

General Fitzwilliam   Lord Fitzwilliam II + Lady Catherine
Progeny - Son (Currently Lord Fitzwilliam III)
↑-----------**boy** adopted---------←

Lord Fitzwilliam II dies
Lady Catherine marries Sir Lewis de Bourgh
Sir Lewis de Bourgh + Lady Catherine
Progeny - Anne de Bourgh

Mr. and Mrs Darcy looked at each other both taking in the contents of the letter.

"It cannot be that they are brother and sister and not brother and sister!" Elizabeth exclaimed in astonishment.

Darcy, after examining the record, pointed out that it would indicate that there is no shared bloodline proven.

"The chart would suggest that Lady Fitzwilliam's sister, who died in childbirth, could not have had any previous children or they too would have been adopted. There does not show to be such a record. The boy, it appears, was for a short time, the stepson of Lady Catherine. Later Lady Catherine gave birth to Anne but there is no shared bloodline. Therefore Elizabeth, I would suggest you show Colonel Fitzwilliam the chart for his knowledge and satisfaction."

—o—

All the servants whom Mr. Darcy had sent abroad to seek out and bring back Miss Anne de Bourgh and the colonel, returned one by one from their fruitless search. That is, except the last servant. He had found the couple. The had arrived in Scotland.

The colonel then instructed the servant to write ahead immediately, to confirm, "Brother and sister returning, post haste, their situation unchanged."

Lady Catherine learned of the news with a show of great relief. So much so, that she condescended excessive praise to Mr. Darcy's servant for reason of his success.

However, she was dreading the task of giving her account of the young peoples' relationship. This was the motivation that led to Catherine wanting to quit Pemberley With great embarrassment and a measure of abasement, she must explain to her children how they became to be brother and sister and brought up as cousins.

Mr Darcy invited Lady Catherine to his office where they could talk privately. It was then that Elizabeth suggested she could lighten the burden by taking the task from her. Elizabeth explained that Lady Catherine was too much personally involved with the situation. Lady Catherine permitting Elizabeth the office to talk, as a confidential cousin, as cousins to cousins, would be easier for them also. Lady Catherine thought in great depth on this consideration. Distancing herself from the problems would be advantageous indeed.

From this moment onward, Mrs Elizabeth Darcy appeared as greatly elevated in the esteem of The Lady Catherine de Bourgh. Lady Catherine laid her hand on Elizabeth's hand to say, "Bless you Elizabeth. I must just add that I am beginning to see and understand a lot more of the exceptional qualities of my nephew's choice. Thank you Elizabeth."

Lady Catherine offered to relate the course of events to Elizabeth in as much detail as she could dare.

She explained, "I have harboured the family secret all these years with only Mrs Darcy, your predecessor, as a confidant. I find the event very humbling but I shall experience a deal of relief to share the past with a friend. We will talk of it again."

Elizabeth felt herself not wholly persuaded of good intent by Lady Catherine or of her words.

Chapter Four

Lady Catherine Leaves Pemberley

Alongside the personal lives of the staff and management, other matters were always in need of consideration at Pemberley. An occasion when the master and mistress were engaged in studying the varied duties of running a large estate helped to bring them together privately. They were pursuing this task primarily for the benefit of Elizabeth who was still finding more to learn and discover. No mistress of Pemberley had taken so much interest in details or had been so innovative. During a pause between tasks, Mr. Darcy drew Elizabeth's attention to something his Aunt, Lady Catherine de Bourgh, said to him earlier that morning at the breakfast table.

She insisted, "My dear nephew, please let me say how much I now admire your choice of partner."

Together they understood that this could only mean that Lady Catherine had now accepted their relationship; their good choice of partners and this was by way of giving her blessing to their union at last.

It was two days later that a carriage unfamiliar to Pemberley drove through the portal and stopped alongside the entrance. Colonel Fitzwilliam and Miss Anne de Bourgh descended the carriage without ceremony to enter Pemberley as brother and sister. The servant had delivered Mr. Darcy's and Lady Catherine's letter to the couple prior to the intended union.

As soon as Elizabeth learned of their arrival, she made haste to greet them. "My dear Anne and Colonel please consider yourselves very welcome and I am pleased that you have returned safely. I have the news from Lady Catherine and I must relate it to you, if you are prepared, as soon as you have recovered from your journey."

The colonel, a gentleman as always, thanked Elizabeth and confirmed that he and Anne would appreciate a little time before hearing of any new intelligence.

Lady Catherine de Bourgh witnessed the arrival of her nephew and daughter. Privately she hurried to the stables where men were now finishing the loading of her and Anne's luggage onto the carriage. She ordered them to harness the horses and to make in haste everything ready for immediate departure.

Lady Catherine then returned to the house for the purpose of gaining Anne's immediate presence, confidentially in the salon. Upon arriving, Lady Catherine spoke to her daughter in low tones to explain that the colonel would follow on horse while they quit Pemberley. His trunks are packed and on the carriage with ours. The reason she gave was that some shame might befall them if at this time they sought the company of outsiders.

"We must hold ourselves in privacy until we can rise above this low point in our personal circumstances." She said. "Otherwise it may be held against us. We can gain nothing here. By staying, we will have sneering of the servants amongst themselves at our expense. And who knows, much worse besides; perchance a good deal worse besides."

Anne had not expected this reaction from her mother. She felt confused, though readily agreed but she needed to change her coat and a bonnet. She also would like to see Colonel Fitzwilliam before they leave to have his assurance that he will follow immediately.

Lady Catherine continued in earnest, pressing her daughter to go straight away to the carriage, while persuading her that the colonel will follow very shortly. Her present bonnet is all that she needed while travelling and anyway the others were already packed. She offered her spare coat to Anne so that they could quit this place without ceremony and without notice.

To leave a house such as Pemberley without notice would be without precedence. To leave her friends without ceremony was such an undertaking as to be counter to the core of Anne's nature and sense of decorum.

Lady Catherine persuaded Anne to enter the carriage and her mother followed. Anne was thinking of the leaving of her close family without word. She wondered why their departure needed to be so hasty. How would Elizabeth think if she left without polite leave and Georgiana who had also become very dear and precious in her affections?

As the carriage jerked forwards and while she was looking up at this great house of Pemberley, she saw her Colonel Fitzwilliam looking through the window at the coach. He was not waving.

"What did that mean?" She thought.

Without any hesitation, without any other notion at that particular moment, Anne pushed the carriage door handle. The door flew open so that she fell out of the opened carriage. The carriage continued for several yards before pulling to a halt. Quickly Anne rose to her feet and ran towards the front entrance of the house. She was still fatigued from her journey from Scotland to Pemberley and her body was aching from the fall from the carriage but she ran. Anne ran with every ounce of energy she could summon.

All the time her mind was not on the running but on so many unanswered questions, "What is happening? Where is the colonel? Why is not Eliza here to say her farewells?"

She could hear her mother somewhere behind, calling to her. Her mother screamed her name now to order Anne to return to the carriage. Anne ran on. She came to the steps. She was half-running, and half-crawling, scrambling up the steps she reached the top with her mother following and gaining nearer and nearer. Anne reached the door. A servant opened it. He had been watching the drama. He closed the door again to the extreme anger of Lady

Catherine. She was obliged to push against the heavy door wide enough to step inside. Having lost those few precious moments, the distance between her and her daughter was now that much greater. Lady Catherine made for the stairs where Anne was now struggling with the labour of climbing step on step. Upon reaching the first landing Anne collapsed, exhausted of all strength, she fell into a faint.

Upon regaining consciousness, Anne found herself gazing up at the face she adored. She was tired, exhausted, and a little concerned though she felt wonderful as he cradled her in his arms. This was a contrast to the feelings she felt in the coach beside her Mother. Colonel Fitzwilliam stood erect with his lightweight but precious burden. He looked defiantly down the stairs at Lady Catherine. She was just a short distance away, a few steps further down the stairs and her face exuded a wrath that the colonel had never witnessed before. For some moments, they stood starring into each other's eyes. One set of eyes of challenge and anger and the other of defiance and love.

"My daughter, if you please?" Lady Catherine demanded in a contemptuous manner and with all the authority of her superior status.

The Colonel was at a loss for words for a few moments. During this time Elizabeth, Darcy and Georgiana together with servants had congregated on the stairs and the landing witnessing the scene. At last, he looked down at Anne. She smiled faintly back at him. Her face was pale but still beautiful.

He continued to admire her until finally he found the words. "Lady Catherine, with respect, Anne does not appear to be well enough to travel today."

"Nonsense! Bring her to the carriage immediately. We have no time to lose."

Elizabeth moved forward towards Colonel Fitzwilliam, "Carry her gently to her room. Follow me Colonel Fitzwilliam, I will show you the way."

They began climbing the stairs. Elizabeth, passing a nearby servant spoke to him to summon a physician, "Go quickly and request that he should come in all haste."

The servant obeyed. As he was passing Lady Catherine on the stairs, he felt uncomfortable and even threatened. This was a lady of some status and he could feel it. He looked back to Elizabeth to obtain some reassurance. Elizabeth nodded to him and he hastened on down the stairs ignoring the authority of the Lady Catherine de Bourgh. In a moment he was through the main door and off to fulfil his duty.

Lady Catherine could understand that this course of events had out-manoeuvred her. She stood for a moment in defiance, and then said, "Very well then, I will send for my daughter after you have considered the error of your ways. See that she receives all the medical attention to return her to good health."

Then added in continuing scorn, "If indeed, there is anything wrong."

Lady Catherine made straightaway to her carriage. By her order, the horses moved on. It was soon on the road to Rosings Park with its solitary charge seething with thoughts of revenge.

Darcy and Elizabeth exchanged glances. Both understood without words, of their meeting earlier and of Lady Catherine's confidence in his choice of partner. Yet, Lady Catherine's good opinion of Elizabeth did not apparently alter her vehement intentions.

Chapter Five

The Servants' Ball

There was much to attend to on such an estate as Pemberley. Fortunately, staffs were numerous. Elizabeth was trying to remember names and to fit the names to their tasks. In this and with this and much more Mr. Darcy was able to indulge his greatest passion, to be close to his new wife. It was very much to their liking that Mr. Darcy was not fit for sports or any arduous activity yet. This meant that they spent much time together at work and at leisure. From him, Elizabeth learned a deal more about the estate, so much of its history and of the people who were and are now presently working the farms around the estate. With the aid of the Pemberley Estate's steward, Elizabeth decided to make a list of her own of all the families and farms. This would be a new list in order of their size and productivity. She could then consult the steward on how to contrive to improve the farms, especially the poorer holdings. Then there were the domestic considerations to organise along lines to be more efficient. There were many innovations occurring now at these modern times in houses such as theirs.

During a moment of leisure, Mr. Darcy consulted his wife regarding a ball, "Something for the servants to celebrate our wedding."

Elizabeth embraced this suggestion with the greatest glee and enthusiasm.

"It was," As Mr. Darcy explained, "An opportunity to gain experience before attempting something more ambitious. I am thinking of a special occasion when we might expect very distinguished dignitaries attending."

"That would be an honour indeed." Said Elizabeth, "Could you quote me names and perhaps, titles?" She added.

"You will be informed in the course of time." He smiled and continued, "It is enough to say that we may be hosting some very great dignitaries but of the very highest secrecy."

"Please, sir, say no more. I shall be of the most silent, not a single word even when the time comes."

With the thought to increase the pleasure, Mr. Darcy suggested, "We could call upon our friends, Sir Rufus and Lady Penelope who reside as our nearest neighbours on the estate, Wynnstay Park. You have yet to meet them but they know of you. They are a family of long standing friendship of some generations. We could invite their household to join our ball. This will give twice the pleasure and the opportunity for our two households to make new acquaintances."

Thus, they declared the prospect of a ball for the servants and a date agreed. This announcement created great excitement among the staff. No sooner did Elizabeth tell the housekeeper of the intended staff ball but the news spread swiftly from the hierarchy to the lowest levels. The servants did most of the organising, though Elizabeth did involve herself as much as possible.

On behalf of his staff, Sir Rufus accepted the invitation to the celebrations as a pleasant surprise. Elizabeth herself sent out the invitations for her, "Pemberley Staff Ball" to those of Wynnstay Park. Darcy's neighbours, Sir Rufus and Lady Penelope, attended with their staff. Mr. and Mrs. Darcy were naturally pleased to be with their servants in an informal atmosphere and with so much enjoyment.

Elizabeth dutifully sent a formal invitation to Lady Catherine to join the family at Pemberley for the occasion of the servants' ball. Lady Catherine made much of the business of which the latest generations were going about. Spoiling servants and diverting their attentions from the duties to which they were born. In her day, the servants knew their place. However, the experience proved to be not an unpleasant one for her. Lady Catherine de Bourgh could easily exercise her status and dignity in the company of servants and convivially with Sir Rufus and Lady Penelope.

Lady Catherine de Bourgh agreed to join in to help make the evening a success.

"It is very much against my grain." She insisted.

The fare boasted chicken and pork and there were great bowls of punch, trifles, chocolate sweet pieces and cakes. A bounty of fruit displayed topped with pineapples to give overall, a grand effect of colour. There were red and green apples, pairs, oranges, grapes and apricots besides many others. The entertainment was of dancing with excellent music, singing and some short theatricals. Throughout there was much good humour and entertainment. Nothing was spared and nothing too good but everything pleasing for these good people at their ball.

For long afterwards, Elizabeth's "Staff Ball" was an occasion much talked about the country. Sir Rufus made the announcement to return Mr. and Mrs Darcy's compliments with the promise of a staff ball at their own house, Wynnstay Park, in the near future. Then Sir Rufus declared, "All of the good company here are invited!" This made it necessary for all the staff to cheer and clap to show their pleasure at the invitation.

The staff of both houses felt so much more appreciated on the days following the ball. No amount of words of praise was good enough for the masters of Pemberley and Wynnstay Park. There was special warmth felt by the staff of both houses for the new mistress of Pemberley. Her particular quality of character impressed all.

As the subject of the ball began to retire into a happy memory, other events were advancing . . .

Chapter Six

Before the Ball

Elizabeth noticed familiar writing on a letter in the morning post. It was of the hand of her father. She opened the letter with excited anticipation longing as she was for news from her family. The letter started with the assurance of everyone at Longbourn to be safe and well. Even her mother was in excellent disposition. Mr. Bennett had long desired to see his daughter again and expressed his wish to accept the open invitation for a visit to Pemberley. He asked if it was convenient and if it does not appear to be too forward, if he should pack his favourite gun in the hope of a little sport? Further, Mr. Gardiner wishes to test the renowned waterways of Pemberley for fishing sport. He added to give weight to his request, that Mr. Darcy had suggested to Mr. Gardiner that he could come whenever he wished. The letter continued and explained that they could travel by one single carriage between them.

There was some exciting news from the Parsonage at Hunsford, the letter explained "But it is so secret that it must wait until we meet."

"What can that mean?" Thought Elizabeth, "Has any exciting news ever come out of Hunsford?" She was echoing a biblical reference in good humour, which she thought appropriate considering the religious associations with that place. "It must be good news of the baby of course."

The addition of more news excited her sense of anticipation even to exasperate Elizabeth but with a deep regard and love for her father and the dear relatives, Mr. and Mrs Gardiner. Elizabeth wished to relay the information to her husband and set about the task immediately.

After she had explained to Mr. Darcy the contents of the letter, he seemed more pleased than she could have anticipated.

"My dear Elizabeth, why not invite any or all your family to Pemberley and Lady Catherine? This is a time for reaching out for opportunities. We may build bridges, may we not? Imagine, Elizabeth, reparations and preparations."

Elizabeth, much engaged by the questions, in return asked, "Whatever can you mean sir?"

Mr. Darcy added, "Our relatives could help with much of the preparations. This is a special time when we will need people around us on whom we can depend and trust. The time is approaching for the "Grand Ball" of which we have talked. The Grand Ball will be a special event. We must, therefore, expect many dignitaries: some out of the country."

Darcy Continued "Reparation? It may be possible to bridge our differences with Lady Catherine by inviting her again, this time to your Grand Ball when she can mingle with the dignitaries of her equal status. We will hold a very high regard for everyone and everything at the Ball. But, first" . . . Mr. Darcy held up his finger to his face, "We must organize a special fete for the folk of Pemberley, Wynnstay Park and all of Lambton."

"Mr. Bingley has now replied to my invitation and they have agreed to come. Mr. and Mrs Bingley have each expressed a deep wish to see you again. Further good news is that Mr. Bingley's sisters will be in the country shortly so we can renew our acquaintance with all at the same time."

Elizabeth did not feel overjoyed by the anticipation of seeing Bingley's sisters again or Lady Catherine. However, the idea of establishing a friendlier family unit made the attempt a sensible one. The thoughts of seeing her family complete once more were too much of a distraction to keep to herself. Elizabeth summoned for Anne and Georgiana who were practicing with the pianoforte in the music room. In their presence, she excitedly relayed the contents of the letter from her father and of Mr. Darcy's words. To envisage so many dear friends, a fete *and* a grand ball stimulated the imagination of the two young ladies. They clapped their hands and danced around the room as though with invisible partners while singing the music.

It was about two months later when the relatives began to arrive. First to arrive were Mr. and Mrs Bennet together with Mr. and Mrs Gardiner and their children. Sir William and Lady Lucas followed shortly afterwards. More relatives continued to appear at varying intervals. Great excitement accompanied everyone on arrival. As each settled in, they orientated to the personal pursuits of their choice. Mr. Bennet and Mr. Bingley were soon lost in the sport of the field. Sir William and Mr. Gardiner enjoyed the fishing. While the ladies indulged themselves of the leisure to pursue their own individual delights. Most popular was the music and singing. Whenever the weather obliged, the guests' activities ranged from riding and archery to croquet. The ladies and gentlemen spent evenings, usually communally, with music, singing, cards, or board games.

Somehow, between the sporting activities, the family managed the organization of the fete. Throughout the country, the anticipation of the fete became the main talking subject. Darcy's men roped off areas for the market stalls and standing for the horses and carts. The racing fraternity laid out a racetrack for point-to-point events for horses. Donkey rides and human athletes in various competitions. There was planned, bare fist fighting, wrestling, weightlifting, foot races and many more like events. When the great day arrived, Mr. Darcy in person officially opened the fete with a short speech of welcome. The people cheered. Then the musicians played and the multitudes of pedestrians set about to enjoy a perfect day, each in his own way. The following day of the fete was as hugely successful as the first. Many tenants of the

Darcy estate were pleased to sell their wares of vegetables, fruit, animals and paraphernalia of all kinds on their stalls. On the third day, the men took down the big tents with as much reluctance as a boy walking to school Men carefully restored the fields to their customary states. The great success of the event did not pass by forgotten. Mr. Darcy promised after many entreaties to hold the fete again the following year.

— o —

It had become the custom for most mornings for Mr. and Mrs Darcy to take to their horses for the benefit of exercise. It pleased Elizabeth to do so. The morning air, the often brief encounters with tenants and the relaxed, informal association gave the occasions very valuable opportunities to bond more deeply with all of this of which she was mistress.

By the following day, the staff had cleared away all signs of the fete. Mr. and Mrs Darcy were enjoying their early exercise. The fresh morning air set the horses apace with vigour. Riding together at a good stride, they directed their horses towards the open fields. The going was easy and the horses were keen.

Within a short riding distance, they could hear people creating an unpleasant disturbance. This was distressing to Elizabeth. She pulled back on her reins. Darcy rode on apace towards a spinney. He called back to Elizabeth to stay her ground until he gave a signal. As he approached the trees, he could distinguish women screaming and coarse men shouting obscenities.

Chapter Seven

The Handshake of Friendship

As soon as Darcy was close enough, he called out to the antagonists, "You men! Cease this unruly behaviour!"

More by the surprise of the interference than their desire to suspend their activities, the ruffians stopped chasing and beating the women. They turned to look at Darcy. They still held their sticks high in readiness to continue. The men hesitated. Darcy called out to enquire the reason for beating the women with such weapons.

"Thems just be gypsies zur." One of the men replied.

"I did not ask you who they were. I asked you, "Why you are beating those women?"

The self-appointed leader moved forward towards Darcy. He was still holding his stick. While he moved forwards, the gypsy women were edging away from the men while nursing their own wounds.

One of the men called out to the leader, "That be Mr. Darcy of the big 'ouse!"

The leader stopped, dropped his stick and spoke again to Darcy, "Thems be gypsy women Mr. Darcy, sir. Thems be stealing wood for their fires. Them cast spells and make our animals sick, them do."

"If they could cast spells they would cast spells to stop you hitting them."

The ruffians laughed coarsely and heartily.

"'E be roit there Eric!" One of the band called out.

"Whose firewood is it they are stealing?" Darcy called out to them.

The small band looked shamefully at each other and on to the ground. Before they were able to answer, Darcy's attention was distracted by three gypsy men approaching, hitherto unnoticed while he was speaking to the ruffians. The gypsies were running towards the gathering but making particularly for Mr. Darcy. Darcy recognised them each. He was at a loss to imagine why they were running in such haste except in response to the cries from their women folk.

As the gypsies closed in on Mr. Darcy, he held his ground but remained ready for anything, or so he thought. As the gypsies arrived, they were unable to speak for want of breath. Before the gypsies spoke a word, Darcy could tell that they were in earnest about something. He dismounted and gave his hand to one of them that might have been the senior. The gypsy took it. The ruffians were all agog. Mr. Darcy was the closest element to royalty in this part of the country yet appeared here, as a friend of the gypsies. The one gypsy spoke first to Mr. Darcy in between breaths so that Darcy could not make clear the man's meaning. However, the word, "Frenchie" came through sufficiently clearly for Darcy to feel concern and especially for the safety of Elizabeth. He glanced towards her to reassure himself that she was safe and well. Darcy beckoned that she might approach.

Meanwhile a member of the gypsy party had recovered his breath sufficiently to address Darcy, "We wos jumped on by some Frenchies. The Frenchies were trying to steal our 'horses Mr. Darcy, zur, but we overcomes thems and we got thems tied up with leather bindings."

Elizabeth now had approached near to the ever-increasing gathering so that she instantly recognized the gypsies. They were helpful indeed at a time when her party, particularly Anne, was in extreme distress. She also recalled that dear Anne may have died had they not helped and knew how to revive her.

The ruffians stood and stared at Elizabeth. Never had these men seen such beauty and such feminine dignity. One by one each man removed his hat from his head. They all felt the feelings of aggression drain from their bodies.

If anyone had cast a spell, it was not by any gypsy woman.

Darcy spoke quietly to her. "Elizabeth, please return with all haste to the house. Send for the doctor, Colonel Fitzwilliam and dispatch four stout men from the stables to come immediately on horse and bring with them a dog cart."

The ruffians and Darcy followed the gypsy men and women as they made their way back to their encampment. As they drew near to the field, they could hear cries of distress.

The gypsy-men ran forward ahead of Darcy so he called out, "Be on your guard!"

His words arrested the gypsies who now moved forward more cautiously. The ruffians joined the gypsies so that man by gypsy they approached the campsite. As the group closed on the encampment it revealed a sight of destruction and desolation.

Women folk were bent over bodies on the ground, bewailing and weeping. Two caravans had been overturned. Signs of wanton destruction lay all about. The men and the gypsies now all ran to give what aid was possible to the gypsy people and their encampment. Darcy felt great pity for these people for whom he had come to respect. He was not armed or else he may have given chase in blind anger. Being limited in his options Darcy waited for his party from Pemberley to arrive.

The four men, the colonel and the dogcart approached together. The scene was something of a puzzle to them.

The colonel approached Darcy,

"Are these not the gypsies we met at the ford? What has happened here? Who has wreaked all this destruction? Darcy, what is happening?"

Darcy reacted with some ire in his voice, "This, Colonel, is the work of your Marcel and his followers, the agents of the

French Republic. The enemy is running rampant in our own country, sir."

"These beasts must and will be stopped!"

"Exactly as I was thinking, Colonel. Is there no one you can influence to help us do something?"

"The best person to approach would be Wickham. He is only a captain but he has made good contacts with the higher echelons and not the least with close ties to certain generals."

The statement arrested Darcy in the way. In his puzzled thoughts, with total disbelief, posed the question, "Wickham, I understood was killed in action, surely Colonel?"

"He was wounded but like you, he recovered. Being the only man known to be able to identify Marcel, Wickham is a most important officer. As far as Marcel is aware, he killed Wickham. So he thought, but although the French had seriously wounded Wickham, he did survive. We did broadcast the demise of Wickham as true to all but his wife and special security people and the generals we need to influence. Not a word of this must be relayed to anyone not even your family, Darcy."

Darcy thought how much he would like to tell Elizabeth of this good news. He did not have much affection for Wickham in days gone by, but now an officer in the regulars he has found himself. To this, Darcy gave due respect to his boyhood friend. Wickham had advanced from a lieutenant to captain on his own merits. He has proved himself a brave and dedicated professional soldier.

His thoughts were that, "Even Elizabeth must wait for the good news for the sake of Wickham's safety and for military reasons."

Colonel Fitzwilliam continued, "I mean secret and security. We must endeavour to make contact with Wickham with all speed to organize a counter force for this foray."

At this conclusion, the doctor approached the two gentlemen. His first task was to pronounce the two slain gypsies as dead by wounds from knives or swords. He then examined the wounds suffered by the womenfolk by the French and by the ruffians. The latter were now more ashamed at their actions. To see the gypsies suffer so by the hands of the French then by their own hands gave them some cause for shame. It became greater by the reality of seeing the gypsies in their own camp. These were humans just like themselves with their own homes, own families, own animals and own hardships.

Without any persuasion, the ruffians were helping with the restitution of the encampment, collecting scattered gypsy tools and artifacts, up-righting overturned caravans and comforting the injured.

The colonel was asking questions of the gypsies. They told him of the two prisoners of whom they discovered, to their sorrow, had not been alone. Others were hiding in the woods waiting to seize the opportunity to rescue their comrades. In doing so they perpetrated the most vile abuse without due cause. The women should not have been harmed nor their caravans overturned nor their horses stolen.

Darcy called for Barnie, the gypsy who stayed behind to see his party safely across the ford while on their journey to Pemberley. Barnie came forward to Darcy, limping and half trying to smile. Barnie was plainly distressed. Once more, Darcy was extending his hand to his gypsy friend. Barnie took it and shook the hand again that he took so proudly some months previously.

"Barnie, stay as long as you wish on my land. Let no man harm you or your family during your stay. Moreover, I am deeply sorry for the tragedy here today. We will do anything we can to help. Just send a messenger if you need us. Will you do that Barnie?"

"Well, thankin e' zur. O'll do as ye says."

There was no appetite in his stomach for more talk.

Further words were superfluous. There seemed no further reason to stay. It was a very sad Darcy that urged his horse on to return to Pemberley and Elizabeth."

Chapter Eight

The Grand Ball

Elizabeth was in great determination that her ball should be an outstanding success.

All her family were to attend, including her dear "bereaved" sister, Lydia. It included also, Mr. Bingley and Jane. The Bingleys had not had the occasion to call upon Mr. and Mrs Darcy since their arrival in the country. The Bingleys had taken a house not too distant from Pemberley some 30 miles at most. Their choice was a much-admired address named. "Lilac Time." It stood proudly on a knoll with panoramic views extending for miles around. For the honour of the ball Mr. and Mrs Bingley arrived two days early. This gave two sisters and two husbands the opportunity to indulge most pleasantly each other's company. The men enjoyed a good shoot while Elizabeth introduced Jane to the joys of archery and croquet. The evening's entertainment consisted mostly of cards and music.

The evening of the ball began early with the arrival of the guests from the neighbouring country. They arrived with great style all in grand carriages. The ladies' gowns splashed colour and splendour while the lords and gentlemen appeared each one distinguished.

Soldiers and officers exhibited in gay regimentals rivalled but could not quite match the ladies in their satins and lace finery.

Every party was trying ardently to give the greatest respect to the occasion.

While the parties were arriving, the musicians played favourite pieces for the delight of everyone. Mr. and Mrs Darcy personally welcomed each guest, upon their arrival, individually in turn. As their guests entered the main ballroom, the master of ceremonies announced each by name and title. When it was thought the arrivals to be complete, the music sounded louder and then rested quiet.

The master of ceremonies announced next, "His Royal Highness, King George the Third."

For some moments, the gathering became silent as though in disbelief of the words of the announcement. As indeed, many were astonished to a high degree. A polite, subdued clapping began and continued for some minutes. It grew in intensity all the while until, as though by some collective agreement, the clapping ceased. Slowly, gradually the various sounds of a ball gathered apace to return to normal.

Mr. and Mrs Darcy having already received the sovereign privately now proceeded to acknowledge him to the rest of the guests about the rooms.

Every guest waited with stayed breath for the first dance to begin. As it was customary for the king to open the evening with a dance accompanied by the hostess, Elizabeth rose to the occasion with grace and confidence to the admiration of all.

As the king took her hand, He looked into her eyes and His face expressed a delight for the vision before Him of Mrs Elizabeth Darcy. The King of England and Mrs Darcy were to open the first dance. As they advanced across the floor, the king whispered to her, "My dear, this is indeed an honour."

As soon as they began to dance, the gathering clapped, politely at first. Soon it swelled into enthusiasm as the confidence grew.

During the course of the evening, the king received every lady and gentleman. Each bowed or curtsied accordingly to their king. Whispers behind fans and gentlemen in undertones made their amazement known to their friends and family. Eventually His

Majesty expressed a wish to dance again. He requested that his hostess should accompany Him. Surprised and enthralled though very conscious of the honour, Elizabeth consented to the privilege once more.

Occasionally the king danced during the evening with a few favoured ladies. Each time His Majesty stood up every one of the ladies hoped for the honour. Naturally, Mr. and Mrs Elizabeth Darcy regularly engaged themselves on the floor. Elizabeth tried to circulate among her guests especially her family. Lydia, never in want of a partner, was often the centre of attention, surrounded herself ostentatiously with officers of the regulars.

"It was her way." Elizabeth sighed.

She could feel no ill towards her youngest sister's behaviour. The evening, the occasion, the ball would not allow it. She thought how much they had worked and planned to achieve this. How wonderfully it had fashioned. Most of all she was puzzled why Mr. Darcy did not tell her until this evening that the king, of all people, would be in attendance. While dwelling on this question, Elizabeth espied her husband across the room talking earnestly with some officers. Together, the men retired into the library.

In the hope of engaging Mr. Darcy to ask of him if there was a reason for such secrecy even with her, she pursued them into the room. To her amazement, there were several more soldiers. They were in deep discussions or checking of their various armaments. As the men became aware of her presence, they fell silent looking at her with as much amazement as she felt, looking at them. One stood up, then another, then all the military gentlemen rose as one man to Elizabeth's presence.

"All this must be for the security for our king." Elizabeth ventured.

Mr. Darcy moved through the soldiers towards her smiling and confirmed her postulate, "Yes, you are quite right but he is in good hands as you can see. There is no danger at all. It is better if you say no more about this to avoid disturbing the guests now in their good humour, Elizabeth."

Elizabeth readily agreed and with apologies, left the room but not so fast that she could not help but hear, behind her, the key as it turned in the lock of the door.

Her thoughts were, "There is something afoot, which is not on the agenda. Something had happened or something is going to happen."

She felt locked out and not only out of the library. Mrs Elizabeth Darcy was none the less, as always, dutiful to her husband's wishes. She re-engaged herself with her many guests, each of whom wanted to congratulate her on such a ball as this and how surprised and delighted they had been to see the king. She responded as well as she was able but in the back of her mind, the scene of the library was a cause of apprehension.

"This is the King of England. Is he *really* in danger here at Pemberley?" Elizabeth looked around closely at her guests. She did not know all of them. Mr. Darcy alone would be familiar with many more of them.

She mused, "Some strangers have been invited in the hope of making a better acquaintance but nobody appeared dangerous. Dressed as they are in their eveningwear, they suffer too many encumbrances to engage in any dangerous activity. No, he must be right, there is no danger."

The music played on. The dancing continued. Elizabeth could hear somebody playing a piano somewhere. A person could be heard singing. Some voices talking and laughing made themselves heard above the cacophony. The occasional clatter of the plates or glasses sounded as the hands of the clock continued round the face.

The evening all too soon spent, the night heralded the end of the Grand Ball. Gaiety changed to thoughts of travelling home. Some guests would stay the night because of the distance they needed to travel to their homes. Laughter not yet all exhausted made itself heard here and there as the parting visitants made good their jovial good wishes to each other.

While bidding each parting guest a pleasant journey home, Elizabeth kept a watchful eye on anything that might be of interest or in the least threatening to her king. All was in accord with an estimable approval of the evening's entertainment.

The evening had dissolved into night and outside was darkness. A cloudy sky hid the moon intermittently but stars did their best to bring a supporting light. Men were lighting torches in order to prepare better for the leaving guests to take to their various conveyances. Lamps on the carriages, one by one, lit up to discharge their light on the scene. The lords, ladies and gentlemen were finding their coats, mufflers, hats and gloves. Their adieus spoken, one by one, they mounted their carriages. Soon they were moving off into the night one after the other but each to their various ways.

When the last of the guests had departed, Elizabeth's thoughts turned to her husband. Searching the rooms and following the sound of voices in conversation, Elizabeth had hunted down her quarry. Mr. Darcy and other men were in jovial conversation with the king. The servants were busy coming and going and cleaning, clearing and tidying up the mess they knew as Pemberley. She approached her husband who showed no sign of approval. Instead, Darcy insisted on her leaving immediately. He explained to Elizabeth, but not in undertones, of there being much matters of state they needed to discuss. With a heart heavy, full of disappointment at her husband's unusual brusque dismissal, Elizabeth turned to leave. As she did so, she was amazed to see a man whom she recognized. She could not believe her own eyes.

Shocked and puzzled by his appearance, Elizabeth called out his name spontaneously, "Wickham! Wickham!"

The king and Darcy looked at each other. Darcy vaulted across the table to attend to his wife. Simultaneously, four men dropped their pretence as household servants and drew swords hidden under their aprons and protective clothing. Four more that must have been waiting outside the room for the signal, joined them. Darcy was joined by six soldiers, officers and an NCO. Darcy and his allies then out numbered the first four intruders. This left Wickham alone to deal with the four who had entered from the door. The fencing continued for some minutes without any progress from either side. Elizabeth guided three of her menservants to stand around the king and waited for events to take their course. The king drew his sword and he too waited, but calmly watching as though surveying the scene with a detached interest. Wickham was giving a good account of himself and shortly wounded one of his four combatants. One of Wickham's adversaries left off, responding to a call for help from his allies. Darcy and four officers and two NCOs were gradually beating them back away from the king. Wickham began to tire. He had no respite, not for a single second and the effort was beginning to show on him. Realizing his danger Wickham rallied his strength and managed to wound another in the arm but the effort had taken its toll. The last of the four swordsmen thrust his weapon into Wickham's side. Wickham let out a scream of pain, which disarmed all the other fighters. While it was Wickham who tired first, the outnumbered enemy were in their turn beginning to wane. Good as they proved themselves to be, the Frenchmen were unable to match the superior fencing skills of Darcy. When only two assassins remained, a new turn of events developed. One of them pulled a pistol from his belt. As he did so, an officer lunged at him. The villain attempted to evade the officer but received an injury. The wound was serious, taking the villain to the floor. He rolled himself away from the soldier in order take another aim at the king. The mortally wounded Wickham spotted the danger. He strained himself to reach out for his sword that lay on the floor at a short distance from him. With his remaining strength, he grasped hold of his sword and threw it at the assailant. The attempt did little harm to the Frenchman but it did hit him sufficiently to spoil his aim. The gun discharged wild of any danger to anyone. The wounded man collapsed completely.

The last attacker remained standing with one arm held outward and the arm holding his sword extended in the opposite direction to challenge anyone to try to take him. His evil face grinned. He knew he had no chance of survival so was inviting the officers to try to kill him. By this means, he was taking away their attention from the wounded gunman lying on the floor. One of the officers went forward to face the challenge of the French assailant. For some minutes, they fought their duel furiously while the remaining soldiers now gathered around the two swordsmen who were each fighting for his life.

Slowly, surreptitiously the wounded assailant on the floor drew a second pistol from his belt. Carefully, while the attention centered on the fighting swordsmen, he lifted his pistol to aim his weapon at the king.

At a critical moment, the king's officer gained the advantage and was able to disarm his cheeky French opponent. He held the point of his sword at the villain's throat. The officer demanded, "What is your name sir?"

The reply came, "Je ne comprend pas monsieur!" as he grinned cheekily.

Two more officers ran forward to secure the man's arms and to tie him up. He offered little resistance but called out, "Vive La France! Vive La Republique!"

Darcy alone noticed this distraction. He realised that the focus of attention had been diverted away from the wounded gunman on the floor. Seeing that the gunman was once more taking his aim, Darcy understood the danger. He moved sharply towards the king to act as a shield. The report came just as Darcy reached the king. He took the bullet as it hit his shoulder throwing him into a spin. Elizabeth screamed. Frightened, she ran towards her husband who was now on the floor. Servants and soldiers rushed towards Darcy to attend to him and to lift him to his feet. Dazed and seriously shaken, Darcy was reassured that the king and everyone else were safe and the prisoner secured. Two officers had dealt with the gunman with the blades of their swords.

Mr. Darcy looked towards his wife to reassure her that he was not seriously injured. That it was only, "A minor flesh wound." He rejected all further offers of assistance. He held his right arm across his chest to hold the wound on his left shoulder. Mr. Darcy's sole concern was not for himself, it was with the safety of the king. He called the senior officer to him.

"Please make every effort to be sure that the area is safe and escort His Majesty to his chamber when he wishes."

The officer barked out orders to his men. Immediately they pursued their tasks.

King George called out, "Mr. Darcy!"

Mr. Darcy turned to see the king advancing towards him with his sword drawn.

Chapter Nine

The Close of the Ball

The sounds of human industry resounded. The clatter of dishes, the military activities and the sounds of people speaking and shouting echoed around the hall. It was at a moment that seemed to hold a hand up to time. Elizabeth looked on anxiously at the scene of her husband nursing his left arm. It showed signs of bleeding. The king had been exposed to real danger and might have been killed. What could His Majesty be feeling and thinking? He might be in shock. There were those who thought that King George was ill in his mind. One stroke from the powerful royal sword could finish her husband.

Elizabeth whispered her thoughts, "And this, after all he has done? Surely this is not so!" Elizabeth was transfixed knowing that she was powerless to intervene. She felt aware that she was bearing witness to the unfolding of history. A silence issued as the hustle and bustle of domestic staff and soldiers' activities gradually faded while all interest focused on the king's intentions.

With a very insistent royal demand, the king addressed Darcy, "On your knees Darcy. On your knees!"

The wounded man knelt while still holding his shoulder at the same time, trying to apologize to his sovereign for the evening's event.

The king uttered some ritual phrases; deliberately put his sword on to Mr. Darcy's bad shoulder and then the other, commanded loudly and firmly, "Arise Sir Richard!"

Then continued, "You saved the King of England from a Frenchman's bullet, Sir Richard. Such courage and loyalty do not pass without my grace and favour."

The officer in charge witnessed the event and could not stifle his enthusiasm.

"Three cheers for His Majesty King George."

Three loud huzzas rang out and echoed around the chamber.

Even in all the activity, the survivors had not forgotten Wickham. Two officers went to his aid. He had suffered a mortal wound. His last thoughts were with Lydia and asked, "My dear wife, Lydia, please send for her quickly."

An officer charged a soldier to summon her with the uttermost haste.

Sir Richard attempted to rise to his feet. Although his head was spinning with excitement, bewilderment, exhaustion and the pain of a wound, he tried, but stumbled then passed out. Elizabeth with tears flowing down her cheeks, first for the surprise and joy for the knighthood and now with fear and concern for her husband's well being, ran to his aid. She knelt on the floor to nurse his head. A soldier advanced with a wet kerchief for his face and forehead. Slowly Sir Richard rallied his senses enough to make his wish known that he needed to rest.

He assured Elizabeth that he was exhausted but otherwise he was well. The soldiers made up a stretcher and proceeded to carry him to a place of safety. Sir Richard could but accept his disposition and upon leaving spoke to his lady wife to say, "Good night my dearest Elizabeth."

Lady Elizabeth in turn replied, "Good night, good knight."

While Elizabeth leaned forward to kiss her husband on the forehead Sir Richard smiled at the good humour that was ever Elizabeth, it seemed.

Darcy's consciousness faded as he succumbed to complete exhaustion. It was with deep apprehension for her husband's condition that she watched him carried away on a stretcher by the soldiers to a place of safety.

Lydia arrived to the royal presence and went straight to her husband. Wickham was lying on the floor, his head supported by the officer. He smiled as he saw her.

"I'm glad you have come. I want to say good-bye also dear Lydia, to say, I love you. Tell Darcy how I did my duty."

She watched him as he closed his eyes but still semi-conscious so that Lydia lent over him and kissed him. The tears ran down her face and onto his. As his strength ebbed, he looked calm accepting his fate. She could feel his body relaxing while his life force drained away. Lydia let out a scream that expressed the pain she was feeling for her now dead husband. She collapsed onto Wickham as the soldier still supported his head.

His Majesty witnessed the scene and he felt justly moved by this poor woman's loss. The king knew that Captain Wickham had played a major roll in the arrangement of the security and understood that he was the only man who could identify the French agent they named Marcel. Once more, this French agent had evaded the best of the British plans to capture or kill him in this trap laid down at Darcy's ball. The King of England could not let these services to the crown go without due recognition. It was also essential that the French should not know of Wickham's demise. They should not know that British Intelligence had deceived them.

Somewhere a dog howled a long wail that spoke but without words, of grief, of a sorrow deep in the heart. The king and his subjects in the room each felt shivers run down their spine at the mournful utterance. No one moved. Within a few moments, the dog ran into the room. It ignored the other corpses and made straight to the body of Wickham. The dog was whining over the corpse still as Mary, Elizabeth's youngest sister, entered the room looking for her little pet.

As Mary entered the room, she felt extremely disturbed. She had heard the gunshots and heard a commotion but thought it to be the soldiers' revelry after the ball. Mary soon realised it was not that simple. She found herself in a room in great disarray and of soldiers and officers and many corpses, every imaginable dining utensil, weapons and overturned tables strewn randomly around. Some bloody corpses still lay on the floor while soldiers were removing other lifeless bodies. There was another gentleman; a gentleman apart. He was portly with a ruddy rotund face. Within seconds she realised she was in the presence of the King of England.

The encounter confounded Mary so that she was at a loss as to what to do or say. She wanted to apologize for the presence of her dog. Her nervousness must have been apparent.

Mary curtsied before the king whispering, "Mary Bennet, your Royal Majesty."

She wanted to continue but the king distracted by the dog interrupted her.

"Ach! Ein Dachshund, ein Dachshund! Come to King George my little fellow and brook sorrow no more."

The king picked up the whining dog from the body of Wickham and held it in his arms as though it was a baby.

"My little one, cry no more for our friend, cry no more. He is a great hero. Do you not know that brave soldiers who fall in combat go straight to Heaven?"

Upon hearing their king speak so, the assemblage of soldiers, men and ladies down to the servants all clapped reverently.

While the clapping continued more, the king put his arm around the shoulder of the distraught Lydia and spoke gently to her, "It is our duty to do our best to carry on. We must now be strong and think of your future."

Chapter Ten

A Second Surprise

The king was still nursing the dog. It had stopped whining. "We will start by giving your dog a medal."

"Thank you, your Royal Highness, but he is not my dog. The dog's name is William and he belongs to my sister, Mary."

"If we cannot give William a medal then we must honour your husband must we not?" The king smiled at her. His face was beaming as though with benevolent mischief.

Lydia was uncertain of the meaning of King George's words. She felt uneasy at what to expect. The king's intentions were not clear. Her education did include certain habits of royalty that wanted decorum but kings were kings.

Lydia's thoughts were racing to think, "How could he honour my husband now?"

The king's curt command interrupted Lydia's thoughts, "Bring the captain here!"

He barked out the order into the air as though not just to any one person in particular.

Soldiers, servants, and a number of guests who were staying over for the night were as nonplussed as Lydia. They stood waiting for something to happen. Silently two soldiers advanced towards the body of Captain Wickham. As they began to lift the corpse to carry it to the king, three more moved forward to aid the men in their grim task. The heavy body of the tall and well-built soldier told of its weight to the struggling men. They were also a little at a loss to know what to do with it. Slowly they advanced towards the royal figure. His Majesty stood with one hand on his hip, while the other held his sword to the ground with an outstretched arm.

"Over here! Over here!" The king indicated with emphasis by stabbing at the stone floor with his sword.

With a man at each limb and another to guide, they laboured with their inanimate burden towards their king. Wickham was a heavy man by any standards but now literally dead weight. It could have been a sack of turnips. The tired men pained the last few feet to drop the burden before their king. Each man a loyal soldier clicked his heels and bowed to his monarch, "Your Majesty."

"Ach! Nein, nein. Stand him up. Stand him up. I must have him standing."

The loyal subjects having discharged their duty had turned away from the king to return to their respective posts now stopped in their tracks. They looked at each other and spun round on their heels to face King George once more.

Lady Elizabeth watched with much apprehension and some curiosity at the gruesome scene acting out before her remaining guests and her family. Lydia cried but silently as tears streamed down her reddened cheeks not wanting to believe what her eyes were telling her. There was murmuring running around the guests and soldiers. Even the servants had laid aside their respective tasks to gape and guess at the intentions of their monarch. Elizabeth noticed one of them make a gesture with his finger to his temple to indicate his opinion regarding the sanity of the king.

Two of the men were uttering apologies while they undertook the task of lifting their captain to a vertical position so that the body stood limply and head bowed heavily forwards before the king.

"On your knees Captain Wickham." Ordered the king.

The soldiers did not understand what the king expected of them or how to do it. They continued to struggle with their weight. The two men dropped to their knees, while one of the men, holding the body at its arm, tried to kneel while taking the corpse with him but the soldier with the other arm remained upright but confused.

The king shouted impatiently, "Put him kneeling. Put him on one knee!"

All five men hurried to involve themselves in the almost impossible task of making a dead body kneel in a one-knee position. Five men held the body. They waited for the king's word.

King George lifted his sword to dub the Captain on each shoulder. He then added, "Arise Sir . . . . He looked round as though searching the ether for a name to come from somewhere, anywhere.

Mary had just recovered her dog, William, and offered, "With respect your majesty, his name is George."

"Arise, Sir George." The king ordered.

Then to the soldiers, "Well, pick him up, pick him up!"

Nobody cheered. Nobody clapped.

In the room were various guests, soldiers and Pemberley staff. They had stopped their various duties to witness, with amazement, the royal act of knighting a dead hero.

A guest whispered to his neighbours, "*This* will never find a page into the history books."

Nobody else spoke, the room was silent but for two soldiers entering with a stretcher for the Captain.

One of the guests had the presence of mind to call out, "Three hurrahs for King George!"

The response came but lacked enthusiasm. A half-hearted cheer came from a number of guests and soldiers.

Again, the guest called out but louder now, "Hurrah for King George."

This produced a little more enthusiasm from the assemblage though still unimpressive.

"This time, for King George *and Sir* George!"

The crowd cheered much louder for this, while some of the guests and soldiers cried out two hurrahs.

The effect seemed to please King George so that he stood in a proud stance, head held high with his sword in hand stabbing at the floor while his subjects clapped and cheered enthusiastically.

Elizabeth approached the king; "Your majesty has been very busy today. If you have no more tasks to undertake would you wish that we escort you safely to your royal chamber?"

The king smiled broadly at Elizabeth as He looked into her eyes.

Chapter Eleven

The King's Prerogative

Was it the food? Perhaps it was the music or too much wine. The King's thoughts were of the deep pools of sleeping passion looking back at him. King George felt strangely allured to primitive magic in those depths. They were more than beauty, more than compassion; these eyes appeared distant but welcoming.

"Your eyes are like gems of azure fallen from Heaven." He put his arm around her waist and said, "Dawn will soon be here. You and I must dance the night away."

Most of the musicians had by this time packed away their instruments and left or retired. There were three however, who had remained to fulfill duties. A flutist, a violinist and a harmonium player quickly reorganized themselves to play for their hostess and their monarch. In ¾ time, the two dancers fell naturally into a landler but just for two. Some say it was at this dance at Pemberley that the waltz was born. For some time they continued in this fashion with Elizabeth becoming quite dizzy. The king steered her to the door and into the passage. A retinue of Grenadiers hurriedly roused themselves to follow the dancers, finding their marching step as they went. In this manner, Elizabeth and the king danced while the soldiers marched in columns towards the king's chambers.

When the music from the ballroom became too distant for the king and his entourage to hear, the stride of the marchers took over and inspired a different pace, a marching beat which the king and Elizabeth stepped into. They marched along corridors and up stairs, royalty, subject and military escort marched and weaved their way towards the king's chambers.

Elizabeth sang aloud a military song in time to the soldiers' marching. Her voice struck a cord in the spirit of the fighting men. The men joined Elizabeth in singing but with a male force that made a shiver run down the spine of each soldier. Brothers at arms know this feeling well. Elizabeth felt something too. Lady Elizabeth was thinking that she did not wish to join the king and his retinue any further. Equally, she did not wish to court the royal displeasure. Elizabeth raised her voice to sing louder and louder while using her arms in time to the music but in an exaggerated way in order to obtain the best effect. Elizabeth now danced around in the 4/4 time while singing and raising her arms in an exaggerated marching manner. She dropped back from the head of the column to continue her extravagant style amongst her fellow marchers. All the while Elizabeth was gradually finding her way to the rear of the column of marching men. Upon reaching the end of the soldiers, Elizabeth dropped behind further still. At a convenient moment, she turned round and ran in the opposite direction, away from the king and his military escort. It seemed that nobody missed her. She continued to run so long and so far that she made good the way to her own bedchamber.

"With the danger behind me." She thought, "I need not run in haste further."

Lady Elizabeth adopted a more comfortable and dignified deportment. She panted and felt the effect of the effort she had made to return to her own quarters alone. Now walking at a normal pace, she soon reached her rooms.

Entering quickly Elizabeth closed the door immediately and turned the key in the lock. This was the second time Elizabeth heard that sound. It reminded her of the events of the evening, the slain Wickham and her wounded husband. In her room, she immediately gained a feeling of complete security. In the absolute darkness and peace of her chambers, Elizabeth was now alone, quite alone at last.

Elizabeth Darcy nee Bennet continued to reflect on the days events. She had risen from her bed in the early hours as Mrs Darcy but now, laying her head on her pillow at this late hour as Lady Elizabeth. She repeated the words several times trying to catch the sound of it. It sounded good to her. Again, she recalled poor Wickham. He died again but this time as the bravest man she had ever known. With these thoughts and of the ball, the guests and most of all, her dear Sir Richard, Lady Elizabeth laid her head onto the pillow, wanting to fall into a deep slumber. The room was in total darkness and complete silence. As Elizabeth was closing her eyes, she thought she heard a sound. She held her breath to listen intently for the smallest of interruptions to the quietness and peace of the night. There did not seem to be the slightest cause for any concern. It may have been the wind on the window or the creaking of her bed. She took a breath again. Again, she thought she heard something. Again, she held her breath until she could feel her heart pounding, demanding that she should take a breath. Breathing out, yet as she did so but gently and quietly, Elizabeth realized the sound came from close to her. There was no mistaking that a noise came from nearby. The darkness all about was such as to prevent her from distinguishing any form at all. Elizabeth summoned the courage to remain awake and alert to any danger. She lay struggling with her demand for sleep, while the concern for what monster that may be in her chamber waiting for the moment to pounce. Nothing disturbed the peace of the night. Her imagination fought against sleep but sleep laid heavily on her eyes and her senses. In desperation to escape a fate of unknown horrors, Elizabeth pulled the top covers over her head as she slid deeper into the bed. At the moment of disappearing beneath her covers, a canine whining sound complaining of the disturbance of his sleep quenched her fears.

She called out, "Barnie, is that you?"

The only sound in response to his mistress's voice was that of his tail thumping on the bed covers on which he lay.

A familiar voice sounded through the obscurity and darkness of Elizabeth's chamber, "Elizabeth?"

"Jane?"

The thumping continued.

"That sound is a dog."

"Yes, he followed me here. He would not let me lie on your bed so I found your chaise-longue."

"He has never stopped me from sleeping in my bed. You could try coming now while he is asleep. He may be more agreeable because I am here."

Within a few moments, two sisters and a dog were all slumbers. The silence of the night was unbroken, save for the occasional obligatory exercise of a dog's tail "Thump! Thump!"

Chapter Twelve

The Service for Wickham

$\mathbf{M}$any visitors came to the ball and stayed overnight. Some because of the distance they needed to travel back to their homes, while others remained simply as guests.

Elizabeth was eager to provide for these people, a breakfast table laid with an ample supply of all good things. The guests were coming and going from the table. It was not possible to accommodate all the guests at one sitting. Their appetites and enthusiasm for eating made it hard for the servants to keep up with the pace of the guests' demands.

Among those dining as Elizabeth arrived to breakfast were Mr. and Mrs. Dubery. It was the custom in their presence that company would entirely ignore common courtesies replacing them with informal greetings of much good humour. It was in the nature of Mr. Dubery to cause formality to melt into informality. His easy-going attitude to life had proved to be infectious on every occasion to any wholesome company. Then, so many of her guests around the table joined in when the conversation with Mr. and Mrs Dubery moved towards the matters of the previous evening. Elizabeth was surprised to discover that many of her guests knew nothing of the events of the previous night. She wanted to apologize to anyone who was disturbed. Some had heard the noises that they had put down to revelry of the soldiers.

On hearing the news of the troubles, everyone who was in ignorance of the events naturally became very inquisitive. Only a few who had witnessed the fighting knew that the Throne of England had been in jeopardy. Best of all, the company insisted that Elizabeth should tell the story how Mr. Darcy had saved the king's life and then honoured him with a knighthood for his bravery. The cry went up, "Hurrah! Hurrah for Lady Elizabeth! Story! Story!"

Lady Elizabeth became just as insistent that she did nothing but stand by the bye.

She supported this along the lines, "The infraction cost my sister the life of her dear husband, the very brave Captain Wickham. We must not forget the other soldiers who did not survive to enjoy a breakfast this morning: good men and good soldiers all. They too have loved ones. Let us not forget them also. I understand a Requiem Service is being organized even now to honour these brave Englishmen."

The more sober other truth of the previous night's victory over the French resulted in a vein of seriousness among the diners. The subdued company continued with their eating for some minutes. The sounds of knives and forks and general noises of dining mixed with the clatter of plates accompanied the modest entry of Sir Richard into the dining room. Just as one guest noticed him and so began clapping, another did in support. Then another and yet another so that soon, the whole room was clapping respectfully for the hero of the previous night.

Sir Richard wore a sling for his arm proving the valour of the man by his impairment. He looked at Elizabeth. She smiled back at him, that smile and demonstratively clapped along with the diners and standing up as she did so.

Sir Richard pushed two hands with palms forward then turned downwards towards his clapping guests, as best as he could, as the wound would allow.

"Please, please. Thank you my good friends. I hope you have all had a good breakfast?"

There were replies from the diners that substantially confirmed they had.

"I have come personally because I have a very important and, feel, a very personal, well . . . an important piece of news."

At this announcement, Sir Richard looked towards a servant who had accompanied him into the breakfast room. Sir Richard nodded towards him then took a seat.

The servant stepped forward and read from a sheet of paper,

"We wish to announce that there will be a memorial service in the chapel at 10.00 o'clock for the fallen soldiers. The men, who paid the ultimate price for us, saved the King of England and defended the English way of life. All who wish to come to give thanks will be very welcome. The service to be conducted, by Mr. Collins of Huntsford."

There were many among the diners and others who came into the room in order to hear what their host would say. A good number of the guests called out in subdued tones to confirm their assurance of attending the service. The guests continued their conversations in some restrained excitement due to the anticipated delivery of the service by the parson. Mr. Collins had now gained a reputation that stood on his previous service. The diners were now hastening to complete their meals in order to make good time to attend the occasion.

The family ancestors responsible had never intended that the Pemberley chapel would need to contain so many faithful. The chapel, commodious for its original purpose but would not accommodate entirely the people wanting to pay homage to the heroes of the previous evening. In addition, it was in their minds to offer thanks to the Almighty for the safe deliverance of their Sovereign. The congregation overflowed into the aisles, vestibules and even many people standing outside.

For several minutes, the congregation waited for the arrival of their parson while whispering their conversations. The time passed slowly while the congregation continued patiently to wait. Their talking grew to more than whispers, from reverent undertones to normal pitches. As the people started to be restless,

Mr. Collins and Miss Mary Bennet appeared. She was carrying a sheaf of papers, the notes for Mr. Collins. Mary accompanied Mr. Collins to the front of the congregation, handed his notes to him, and then turned to take her place with everyone else. She stood looking around, searching with her eyes for a vacant seat or even somewhere to stand. Elizabeth beckoned to her young sister to sit on the floor at her feet. Mary ignored Elizabeth's offer but swivelled around on her foot to find a small bench, close to the altar. She sat behind and to one side of Mr. Collins throughout the ceremony.

It was Mr. Collins who, being a relative of the main deceased, led the service. Mr. Collins delivered a memorial service that did not disappoint his congregation. Two locum tenens, who conducted services in the Pemberley Chapel on occasions, assisted Mr. Collins. His demeanour was again outstanding compared to previous services that Elizabeth had attended at Huntsford. Then, his duties were sufficient but ordinary. Now the lady of the house, Elizabeth was very conscious of the responsibility she had towards her guests.

At the conclusion of the service, the congregation remained silent, save for the sounds of weeping. No eye was dry, every soul felt moved, no thought was anything but feeling of loss but gratitude to the fallen and thanks for the safe deliverance of their sovereign. The outstanding performance by Mr. Collins pleased Elizabeth greatly.

Pleasing as it was, Lady Elizabeth could not help thinking it was something inspired, which elevated the presentation by Mr. Collins. Her thoughts dwelt on this for some time without forming a firm conclusion.

Mr. Collins, his ceremonial duties now completed, made his way to the entrance of the building to shake hands with the worshippers upon their leaving.

Elizabeth was due to follow close behind him. Elizabeth decided to wait for Mary to accompany her. While Elizabeth waited for Mary, she espied her recovering the parson's notes, tidying them up and then preparing to leave. It was now that

Elizabeth began to resolve in her mind that the improvement of Mr. Collins' performance at the pulpit coincided with Mary's volunteer to nurse Mr. Collins' baby daughter.

Elizabeth caught Mary's attention in order that they should leave together. Mary smiled at Elizabeth indicating that she understood her sister's wishes. They sat on the front pews as they waited for the last few members of the congregation to slowly make their leave. Mary placed her sheaf of notes on the seat beside her. While they sat together so, Elizabeth and Mary talked of superficial affairs.

As they rose to their feet to take their own leave, Elizabeth took hold of the sheaf of service notes and held them in her own hand. While they walked down the aisle, Elizabeth glanced downwards to see the notes. There was no mistaking her sister's handwriting. It was very much a woman's hand. It was well practiced and Mary's uniquely.

Elizabeth recalled her last visit to the parsonage at Huntsford. She remembered the wastepaper basket so infested with failed attempts of a sermon in a gentleman's hand.

The congregation's rate of departure was so slow that Mary and Elizabeth found that they had reached the tail of the leavers. The sisters took to the pews again to allow the congregation more time to withdraw.

Chapter Thirteen

Questions for Mary

Elizabeth and Mary remained in the chapel until the last guest had departed. They talked of their experiences since their last contact. Initially, they spoke of general matters. Eventually, Elizabeth questioned Mary of her decision to usurp her sister's prerogative go to the parsonage to care for Charlotte's baby.

"To own the truth, Elizabeth, Kitty did not relish the prospect of Mr. Collins' company even for the baby's sake. Lydia and Jane both had other commitments. Therefore I was alone and felt it prudent to seize the moment."

"This was very good of you . . . and *for* you . . . and for the baby's sake. Yes, I think it may have been a good decision for all, Mary. Though, I cannot but wonder who is attending to the baby at this moment?"

"You need not concern yourself on that matter. Mrs Bushel from Meryton, a friend of the wet nurse, is well experienced with babies. She has accompanied us for this visit to your ball. Mr. Collins enjoys the music and dancing so. We came with Lady Catherine, in her carriage."

"With Lady Catherine . . . in *her* carriage?"

"Why, yes. Indeed, she insisted that we should accompany her."

"Accompany Lady Catherine? You meant to say, you accompanied her? Is that not so?"

"Yes. We were entering her carriage. She, Lady Catherine I mean to say, well, when she saw the party climbing into her personal carriage, she seemed to change her mind. Then we had to wait for her ladyship to arrange everything. We then joined her in another carriage before we could leave. She had a most disdainful journey. However, she, or perhaps we, all suffered it quite well considering."

"So, if this Mrs Bushel is tending to the baby, what duties are you performing for Mr. Collins or are you now considering your situation again and returning home?"

There was a long silence. Mary broke the peace not by a reply to Elizabeth's question but by standing to ask, "Is it not time for us to follow the congregation? The parson will miss us. He will be wondering why we have not yet come."

Following this last pronouncement, Mr. Collins re-entered the chapel. He was apparently searching for Mary and Elizabeth.

"I thought I had missed you both. I knew really that I could not. No, not in any way."

He smiled at the two sisters who were now advancing towards him. Elizabeth responding to his smile, offered the sheaf of papers to Mr. Collins. He took them showing some degree of surprise.

"Oh, thank you Elizabeth. Our notes, yes, of course." He responded and took Mary's arm on one side and Elizabeth on the other. They exited the chapel all blinking as they encountered the noonday outside. The change from the dark to the light imaged the turn of events in Elizabeth's mind. Mr. Collins' words of thanks in which he referred to the sheaf of papers as, "Our notes." did not pass without Elizabeth's recognition of the significance of the collective pronoun, "Our." Knowing the previous attempts of Mr. Collins' work, though adequate, did not match his most recent standard. She knew also of Mary's studious nature and especially her leanings towards the sacred works. Combined with her natural female disposition towards creativity and expression and with the attraction of a possible romantic encounter would be enough inspiration for Mary. Elizabeth thought that in her own way and long before anyone else, perchance, her younger sister recognized her life's destiny.

Elizabeth looked around and said, "Such a fine day. The kitchen is preparing an outdoor lunch for all. We thought the breakfast room too small to accommodate everyone and the dining room too large. The outside is neither too large nor too small. It just is. Do you not think so Mr. Collins?"

Mr. Collins felt taken aback by Elizabeth's musings and again by her question. For some moments, he was at a loss as to a reply.

"The good Lord must have dined in the open on many occasions. Therefore, I see no evil in it. No, indeed! What is your opinion Mary?"

That Mr. Collins should apply to Mary for her opinion was further support of Elizabeth's suspicions. The family never solicited Mary's opinion in all her life. On the contrary, whenever she offered it, however correct and moral it may have been, she was generally dismissed and sometimes ridiculed, sometimes contemptuously but often in good humour. It had become a habit to do so. Mary was now discovering her sister's strategy.

Elizabeth had already suspected that Mary's duties were less in caring for the baby but more towards Mr. Collins' needs. Elizabeth feared that harsh judgement might befall her sister. This, in turn, could jeopardize Mary's situation with Mr. Collins and the baby. It was now that Mary must make the proper response to Elizabeth's inquisitions.

Mary re-countered, "Oh, I have no opinion in it at all. I believe that if Mr. Collins and our good Lord both agree on it, then I am sure the repast will be more than pleasant, a feast in fact. What do you think Elizabeth?"

Elizabeth had underestimated her younger sister. She was outmanoeuvred and cleverly so. It was not by accident that Mary followed this strategy. Though, by such methods she told her own story. It was now time to change the temper and leave Mary and Mr. Collins to contemplate their affairs in private.

Elizabeth responded, "If it proves to be a feast, then the good Lord and Mr. Collins will be both tested correct."

The good humour gave relief to the mounting tension. They laughed and parted company, Elizabeth to find Sir Richard; the "Collins' household" attending to the baby daughter.

With the preparations for the afternoon tea well advanced, Elizabeth felt her presence superfluous in that direction. Her interests lay in her husband's welfare. She could not trust him to care for his wound, as he should. After some enquiring, an attentive servant suggested to her that she could find the master in his chambers preparing for an afternoon in the saddle.

Elizabeth made haste to find Sir Richard. Her suggestion that she accompany him on his afternoon ride he received with alacrity. Within a short time she had changed into attire more suitable for riding. A little later still she was in the saddle. They set off on at a gentle pace so as not to impair the healing of the wounded shoulder.

The ride went well. Elizabeth was enjoying the easy going. In this way, they were able to appreciate better the views and talk of them as they rode.

Elizabeth opened the subject that was most upon her mind.

"The congregation at the memorial service was very impressed with the affair. Mr. Collins has performed his duties so well of late. Have you not noticed, Sir Richard? I believe that my sister Mary and Mr. Collins are forming an attachment and that Mary is writing his sermons. It is possible. Yet Charlotte has not so long parted from us. Do not think that it would be a critical error for them to publicly demonstrate so?"

"While Mr. Collins and your sister, Mary are sojourning at Pemberley you could take the opportunity to discuss the matter with Mary. I will speak informally with Mr. Collins. However, I would never come between to people who hold each other in mutual admiration. You must know me better than that by now!"

Sir Richard would speak no more on the subject.

Later, on the return to the stables, Sir Richard opened another topic. It concerned news of Colonel Fitzwilliam.

"We may have been mistaken all along upon the matter. When I have had time to speak with the colonel, I will be able to relay the news to you. It would seem to me that these human affairs can become complicated more by our own devices rather than by natural means."

Elizabeth pressed her husband to speak further on the subject but Sir Richard would not give ground.

From the stables they proceeded together to enjoy the remainder of the afternoon with their guests and many culinary delights from their own kitchens.

* * *

Chapter Fourteen

Dinner the Day After the Ball

There were still a few guests remaining and were dressed or still dressing for dinner. Elizabeth sought some private time with her husband. They too had been dressing. By now, Elizabeth had dismissed the girl who helped her to dress. Sir Richard, almost finished with his man, talked of the day's activities while Elizabeth listened attentively until he had quite completed his dressing.

Only then, Lady Elizabeth ventured to ask. "Had you noticed this morning how well Mr. Collins conducted the memorial service, Sir Richard?"

The sound of the title by which people were now pleased to address him, Sir Richard found agreeable indeed. He had never expected such a title in his life. Nothing he did or said was for the purpose of securing such an honour.

"If only my father was here to see the king at Pemberley and my status raised to that of a Knight of the Realm." He thought.

Attending to Elizabeth's question responded, "No, indeed I did not so at the time, Lady Elizabeth, but later reflecting on the service, I am obliged, and pleased you understand, to admit that Mr. Collins has improved considerably." Sir Richard informed his ladyship.

Elizabeth laughed. She liked the sound of the titles when addressed abroad. In the privacy of their chambers, they seemed fun but far too serious for all the time. Elizabeth said so but as she was always, politely. Sir Richard admitted that he too enjoyed the drollery adding that he imagined that his lady did too and all the time.

"Yes, yes, perhaps but what of Mr. Collins? We were discussing Mr. Collins sir."

"Ah! Yes, Mr. Collins, the expert on the art of delivering the message of the gospels to his flock. What? Have we more to say on the subject?"

"You are very well aware that we judge people on their past, do we not? Have we misjudged Mr. Collins or have we been blind to his arts that we become prejudiced?" Elizabeth inquired of her husband.

"Mr. Collins is keeping us from dining. Can we meet Mr. Collins at the dinner table, do you suppose, your ladyship?" He asked teasingly while smiling at his wife.

Elizabeth knew her husband had his priorities and she knew when to stop.

On this prompt therefore, in good humour, the party descended to join their guests for the evening meal.

The Pemberley hosts led their guests two by two into the dining room. It was an occasion that gave Elizabeth the opportunity to study her friends and acquaintances. Among the last to arrive were Mr. and Mrs Bennet. They seated themselves as near as they could to their daughter. Mrs Bennet was eager to speak to Elizabeth to congratulate her. She was ardently speaking to an adjacent guest on her left.

"Ten thousand a year . . . and a knighthood! We all knew she would do well."

The guests next to Mrs. Bennet but on her right were Mr. and Mrs Bingley and their sisters. They found the Mrs. Bennet's words extremely indecorous. They found themselves much indisposed by Mrs Bennet's conversations. The two Bingley sisters looked at each other and with a look of distain rose from the table and withdrew early to the drawing room.

At length, Elizabeth withdrew with rest of the ladies and encountered the Bingley sisters and her sister Jane in the drawing room. The sisters immediately sought out Elizabeth with the intention of engaging her interest.

Mrs. Hurst spoke first, "We have been trying to speak to you but you are always so busy or surrounded by others who seem ardent to speak also to you. Elizabeth, we want to personally thank you for inviting us to your ball, for having such a wonderful time. We are also genuinely sorry for the loss of the Captain Wickham. We both admit to misjudging him harshly in the past and we are sorry for having done so. May I be so forward as to add that my brother and sister in law and my sister, all of us, would like to offer our friendship? If there is anything we can do or say to make amends for our past differences, please let us be friends from now on. We were wrong in the past and we own to it with some shame. Can we put it all in the past, our false pride and our foolish prejudices?"

Elizabeth greeted this submission with some suspicion at first. The Bingley sisters had proved to be unseemly especially to Jane. As she tempered the initial surprise of Mrs. Hurst's words, she turned her own thoughts to take the opportunity to mend their fences. She recalled her husband's wishes of reparation of the family.

"Yes, indeed, let us be on the best of terms now that we are all cousins. There is nothing but ill thoughts to be gained in malice and everything good to be wished for in friendship"

"If I can be of any help with the differences you have with Lady Catherine I should be pleased to be at your service, Elizabeth. Personally speaking, I think that Catherine is treating both you and her own daughter very ill indeed."

This was more surprise and Elizabeth said so. She could not imagine how these two sisters could help to turn the obsessions of Lady Catherine or mend the disallowed affections of Anne and the colonel.

"How can anyone mend the illicit romance of a brother or sister?"

"We have learned that there might be an indiscretion in the affair."

"Well yes, even Lady Catherine owns to it."

They laughed at this indignity of the Lady.

"No, no, this is something outside the field of influence of her mother. We have some cause to doubt the veracity of their sibling relationship."

This was very much of interest to Elizabeth. If the rift can be bridged it would bring the whole family together again. If they could open the way for the Colonel and Anne to wed then this would permanently thwart the historic ambition of Lady Catherine. Elizabeth, quite intrigued by the concept of Lady Catherine rejoicing in the union of Anne to the colonel, was at the same time excited with the pleasure it would bring to her husband if Lady Catherine accepted the status quo of their own marriage.

This was then, an opportunity for Elizabeth to cement their new found friendship.

"Sir Richard is pursuing a line of enquiry also. My dear cousin, why not talk to him about your doubts and together you may establish something substantial?"

"My dear Eliza, thank you for the information. I will most certainly solicit his opinion and share mine with him. Was it the Hydra who said that two heads are better than one?"

Elizabeth had the most difficult task to refrain from laughing as she responded,

"Ach! Nein, Nein."

As she mimicked the royal personage of the previous evening while making reference to the nine Hydra heads.

On realizing their error, the sisters and Elizabeth together, laughed so loudly amongst the ladies present that they drew much attention to themselves. This attracted the interest of Miss Anne de Bourgh. She approached the gathering of her friends. She was pleased to see them in such pleasant mood and enquired as to the reason for their joviality.

The sisters attempted to explain but the humour of the moment was lost also for want of laughing, they were incapable. They did become serious to inquire of Colonel Fitzwilliam and to explore her reactions to his reference.

"My brother is leaving early tomorrow morning. He has important military duties to perform."

Elizabeth reflected aloud, "You will miss him, no doubt. We all will, of course."

A tear droplet trickled down Anne's cheek as she nodded her head.

"He informs me that he is not convinced of Lady Catherine's assessment of his relationship. I did not know that he is Lord Fitzwilliam, heir to the Earl. He uses his military title only until he inherits but I will always think of him as my colonel. His father, the earl, told Colonel Fitzwilliam that he has never had any relationship with Lady Catherine. The Colonel wants to believe him so much and so do I. Tomorrow morning I shall leave with my mother after I have said my farewell to the colonel. We are to return to Rosings."

Mrs. Hurst put her hand on Anne's hand and said, "We were just discussing your situation. Believe us when we say, that you have our deepest and most sincere sympathies. We will do all we can to help you."

Elizabeth joined in to add that she would attend to her leaving tomorrow morning.

"Remember, my dear Anne, we are still sisters under the skin? We will do all that we are able."

⁜

Chapter Fifteen

The Last of the Guests Depart

In the early hours, the stables of Pemberley were alive with activity. Horses and carriages were being organized for departing guests. Stable boys carefully loaded luggage on luggage and all on the correct carriages.

As dawn began to break, on the steps in the courtyard of Pemberley a small group gathered. Colonel Fitzwilliam shook hands with his friends and cousins. A small number wished him well and urged him to return soon. One particular young lady with tears in her eyes made her parting farewells in as much privacy as the occasion would allow. The Colonel then took to his saddle. He turned his horse to the portal gates of Pemberley. Two attendants opened the gates as he rode towards it. The men smiled and saluted him as he passed through. He did not turn round or look back but passed through the gates, took to the road and was off apace.

For several minutes, his friends looked to the opened gates and the road beyond as the colonel rode into the morning mists and out of sight. No one could tell if it was the morning cold air or the event of the colonel leaving, for each onlooker felt a shiver of a kind that was unfamiliar to each of them.

Anne was ready to leave with her mother. Their carriage, arranged for a comfortable return to Rosings, now waited patiently while the two ladies completed their farewells to the hosts and a few friends. Mounting the carriage, the doors shut; Anne lowered the window and began flourishing her kerchief. She continued to wave as they approached the gates, waving the same as they continued along the road, until they too dissolved like phantoms into the mist. Inside the coach, Lady Catherine then relaxed with an air of self-satisfaction. This time, she enjoyed a feeling of triumph as her daughter now accompanied her.

Many more parties took their leave after Lady Catherine's carriage. By the time the last one had left, Elizabeth was quite exhausted even before her day had started. Jane and Elizabeth were alone to talk in depth for the first time since the day of their joint wedding. They had the time to relax and enjoy each other's company. Jane wanted to tell her sister of her news since the wedding and at the same time, Elizabeth wanted to share with Jane of her adventures when travelling to Pemberley.

With so much to say and so much to do, the parties remaining at Pemberley had little time for their normal routine. Georgiana, however, felt the loss of her new friend, Anne, exceedingly. Now that Elizabeth was much engaged with Jane and her other sisters; she felt the loneliness more deeply.

—o—

Elsewhere, at Rosings, a young lady recently exposed to lively company and an admiring suitor, was now at a loss for entertainment. Her natural industrious disposition found her often at the pianoforte to practice her newfound skills. Even this distraction was growing tedious as a solitary entertainment.

Anne recalled the journey to Longbourn and then on to Pemberley. She pictured the strange but good gypsies, the inns they visited and the informal meeting of the Bennet family at their manor house. As the recollections flooded back in more detail, she realized how happy she had been. Most of all, to recall her newfound friend but dares she think love, the love that gave her most pleasure, yet more heartache? She had actually eloped. She had eloped with the colonel because her mother would not agree to their union. Pemberley seemed so distant and another life. It was a life that she no longer had and that she longed for again. Anne tried to formulate a plan in her head but everything seemed to have problems and risks attached to them. How could she approach her mother? Her mother was responsible for the fiasco before the ball. Her mother insisted they left Pemberley together without Colonel Fitzwilliam, her own brother. She left him behind, left her brother at the time when they were becoming acquainted as brother and sister. Somehow, she could not believe she had felt what she did, yet they were now brother and sister. The thoughts tortured her mind and she was at a loss as to what to do. Wrestle as she did with her recollections, no solution presented itself. The more she dwelt on her problems, the greater they appeared with no answers to bring any comfort at all.

Final deliberations led her to put pen to paper and write a letter to Elizabeth. Such a letter she thought it politic to guard from her mother. She wrote how unhappy she had become with her life at Rosings that she missed the companionship of Elizabeth and she yearned for her experience of the relaxed informality at Pemberley again. Anne continued that now she hated the strict formality at all times at Rosings. It seemed so unnatural after her short visit to Pemberley. She has no companionship, no conversation worth the name and no more distractions except the pianoforte that she now finds tiresome as a lonely and solitary pastime. More than all of this, her longing for the company of her colonel was a torture that she found impossible to bear on her own.

Writing a letter in the privacy of her room was without risk. She must solve the problem of delivering it into the care of the post rider. Anne devised her plan, to pay a visit to see Mary at the parsonage on the excuse to see the baby. She bore the challenge of the cold with a heavy coat with large pockets. The large concealed patch pockets of the coat easily accommodated the letter. It was by this means that Anne transported her missive to the parsonage.

Upon arrival, a girl met Anne who ushered her into the parson's study. Both Mr. Collins and Mary received Anne cordially. Mr.

Collins was at his most self-abasing. Mary gave a hint of an air of some intrusion and disturbance of their work of the day. They did indeed appear to be deep in some study. Anne could see open books of reference on every flat surface in the room.

Anne made some small apology and gave the reason for her visit. It was to see the baby again. Was she well? Had she a name now? This did not draw Mr. Collins or Mary into conversation. Anne enquired if they had a comfortable journey back from Pemberley. To this, they responded positively. They spoke of the solemn journey to Pemberley they had made as a party, themselves, Lady Catherine and Anne. The return journey was in separate carriages. Sir Richard loaned them a carriage because his aunt was so uncomfortable travelling with the young baby and the inconvenience of all its needs. Mary summoned a girl to the kitchen with the message for her to return with the baby for Miss Anne de Bourgh to see.

While waiting for the girl to return, Anne showed great interest and asked questions. Anne learnt much from her host and Mary. Anne noticed how intimate their behaviour was one to the other. "This." she thought, "Must be included in my next letter to Eliza or sooner perhaps." At length the baby arrived from the kitchen. One of the domestic staff was holding her.

"Has she a name yet?" Anne asked in the direction of Mr. Collins and Mary. Neither replied but simply looked at Anne with blank expressions.

"Please ma'am we call her Boo-Boo, because that is what she does of most."

"That is hardly a Christian name. Do you like the name Elizabeth; she was Charlotte's best friend and cousin? Did not Charlotte make a decision on a name before she left us?" Anne asked.

From her questioning earlier and considering that the domestics gave the only name the baby has, there seems little interest in the mite and by implication of the account of the name, cries much but for her mother, no doubt. She will boo-boo in vain for all the interest the father and Mary appear to have for her.

"How different." Anne thought. "To my previous visit to see Charlotte's baby."

At that time, with much cuddling and cooing from everyone, the baby appeared happy. There did not seem to be any boo-booing then. This was self-evident.

What was not so self-evident was that Anne had a different agenda. Her thoughts were with the letter for Elizabeth. Anne had unbuttoned her coat while remarking how warm she was. Pulling her hand out of one of her coat pockets, she purposefully produced the letter and then allowed it, as though by accident, to drop onto the floor.

Immediately Mr. Collins stooped to pick it up. Mr. Collins was about to say something to the effect that she had dropped her letter.

Before he could speak, Anne said, "Oh! My letter to Elizabeth. Or should I say Lady Elizabeth now? I shall be too late to catch the post by the time I return to Rosings. Has your rider arrived yet Mr. Collins?"

Mr. Collins readily agreed to see her letter for Elizabeth put safely into the hands of the post rider.

With her purpose complete, Anne made her farewells. She then walked home through the glen that she and Elizabeth had shared together so agreeably during those brief times together.

Chapter Sixteen

On the Road to London

The post rider delivered the morning mail while Sir Richard and Lady Elizabeth were enjoying their breakfast. The knight and his lady would normally be in conversation while enjoying their leisurely morning repast. As it was that morning, they were both discussing general matters of the estate.

The letters would then not be open until later in the morning. Elizabeth casting a casual eye on the several letters espied one that was evidently from Rosings and addressed to her.

"This could be from Anne to confirm her safe arrival at Rosings." She thought. This, she mentioned to Sir Richard.

He responded with the suggestion that they should save it for later. It will prove a distraction for the afternoon.

With the meal well addressed, the daily round of duties started to take their course. Sir Richard and Lady Elizabeth had adopted the routine of taking their exercise in the saddle for an hour or two. Now that the renowned wound had nearly healed, the morning ride was more enjoyable and lively.

Most mornings they would decide on a route that would take them to a tenant or near to a tenant, just for the pleasure of bidding a good morning. On occasions, tenants drew him into a more serious level of conversation. Now that the knowledge of the knighthood had circulated, the tenants were most desirous in their wish to be correct in their address to their landlord. Elizabeth noted that the elevation had not dimmed Sir Richard's concern for his people. He returned morning compliments with as much enthusiasm as the farmers gave their greetings. Elizabeth had not allowed the social events of Pemberley to interfere with her weekly visits to her tenants. Under the good guidance of the steward, Sir Richard's respect for the tenants and Elizabeth's concern for her people, the Estate of Pemberley continued to prosper. This was so much so that Sir Richard was obliged to seek further investments outside of the estate.

At this time, a stock market in London was gaining a reputation for the exchange of shares in enterprises of diverse varieties. News of this means of investment had received much attention in the national daily newspapers. Sir Richard was of the mind to test the system in order to diversify the Pemberley wealth. While they rode back towards the stables, Sir Richard introduced the subject to Elizabeth. He explained that it would take him away to London for a few days. This then, would be the first time that her husband would be away from their home and her company. The thought of his absence and the attractions of London society formed the idea in Elizabeth's mind to join Sir Richard for the "few days". Elizabeth made her thoughts known to Sir Richard so that their conversation continued around this possibility.

The imaginations of her introduction into London society was of some excitement to Elizabeth. In London, she would not be too distant from her aunt and uncle, dear Mr. and Mrs Gardiner, which would enable Elizabth to visit them. Now that Bingleys' sisters, Caroline and Louisana had made their peace with her, there would be further social advantages to exploit.

Sir Richard warmed to the idea of Elizabeth's company in London. "I had intended to leave for London within a day or two. I wish to make myself acquainted with a jobbing broker as soon as possible. If you feel for the attractions of London still, is it possible for you to be ready to leave almost immediately, by tomorrow or the latest, the day after Elizabeth?"

"Sir Richard, I can be ready and at your disposal by tomorrow with little inconvenience." Elizabeth was eager to reassure her husband.

Each withdrew to his or her own office, Lady Elizabeth to inform the housekeeper, while the master to his study.

In his office, Sir Richard examined the mail and set about attending to anything that required immediate attention. The letter bearing his aunt's coat of arms he observed to discover it was a letter from Anne to Elizabeth. He placed it in a pigeonhole to save for Elizabeth to read on their journey, as they had agreed for "it to be read later". He continued with his paperwork for the rest of the morning.

With such short notice, the household of Pemberley was in a state of industry, choosing what to fold and pack while the stables prepared Sir Richard's own equipage. Cases packed, loaded and all preparations complete, the party left Pemberley for London the following morning. The way through the gates and onto the road was smooth. Elizabeth felt that leaving Pemberley she was leaving something of herself behind.

"Perhaps I will re-unite with it when we return." She thought. In the strengthening morning sunlight Lady Elizabeth turned back to gaze upon her Pemberley. "Most pleasantly situated." She thought thus once again.

Sir Richard and Lady Darcy were on the road to London for two days. They stopped only for essential refreshments either for themselves or the horses or both. Otherwise, the journey was uneventful. As the evening of the second day began, they were into London and driving ever closer to Park Lane. On arrival, servants reversed the whole procedures of packing and folding while grooms attended the carriage and horses. The evening meal was at least the equal they would have expected at Pemberley. Glad as they were to be in London, the journey had stamped the mark of exhaustion on the two travellers. Their retirement was as early as possible. Elizabeth however, could not contain her excitement and sleep was thus, a reluctant visitor. Her thoughts were of shopping for clothes for balls, of the balls and all the new people with whom she would make acquaintances and so much, so much, so much. Sleep came but lately.

Sir Richard was awake early and about, preparing for his day. He sought out his business case. It contained not only his important business papers but also Anne's personal letter to Elizabeth. Making good time by starting early, Sir Richard arranged his papers. He made a schedule for himself and made a copy for Elizabeth. This was so, in order that she would know where he was at any time and when to expect him home again. With his case loaded onto a carriage Sir Richard made good with an early start to his day.

Chapter Seventeen

Anne Rides Northwards

The lack of correspondence from Pemberley led Miss Anne de Bourgh to write again. She could not believe that her "sister" would not reply and would not reply immediately. Her belief therefore was that her last letter had gone astray. As indeed, one could consider that while her letter to Elizabeth was languishing in London in Sir Richard's chest of business papers, her letter was suffering exactly the fate as Anne imagined. It was therefore prudent in Anne's mind that she should immediately write again to Elizabeth at Pemberley. This time, Anne wrote most carefully and clearly the recipient's address and name in bold lettering. This caution was a further insurance that proved the safe delivery of her letter to "Lady Elizabeth Darcy" at Pemberley House in Derbyshire.

After a lapse of some two days without a reply to her second letter, Anne became very agitated and somewhat dismayed that Elizabeth had ignored her letters and the urgency that she expressed in them. Her agitation gave way to concern as it occurred to her that some evil might have befallen upon Elizabeth. Indeed, her imagination extended to the whole of the Pemberley including the staff and the horses. Meanwhile, her own situation at Rosings did not improve in any way. Her feelings of loneliness increased. Her natural desire for the informality of other men and women of her own age grew. There was no compassion for her predicament from her mother. Anne knew that her mother did not understand her daughter's feelings. It was necessary therefore for Anne to act as the adult that she was and make her own life decisions. She formulated a plan to go from Rosings to Pemberley without her mother suspecting anything to be amiss. That is, until it was too late, then Anne would be well on the road to Derbyshire.

To implement her plans she needed to complete two tasks. Firstly, she wrote two letters. The first addressed to Elizabeth at Pemberley for the post rider. The second letter addressed to her mother, which she would leave in her room for the domestic staff to find as she had done previously so successfully but at Pemberley. The second task was to visit the kitchen to ask the cook to prepare a picnic lunch with a bottle of white wine for her for the following day. She further explained that she would take her sketching kit and that she would not be home until much later. Anne added that, "An early breakfast and her lunch packed and ready would enable me to have an interesting and rewarding day sketching in the country."

Then she walked to the stables to request that a horse to be ready as early as possible the following morning. This, the grooms were pleased to arrange for her.

Anne and Lady Catherine ate their evening meal in silence as usual with Mrs Jenkinson. There was little conversation between them because they had little to say. Mrs Jenkinson and Anne both felt subordinate below the great lady because her conversations usually took the form of dictums. With the meal complete, Anne announced her intention of retiring early because with so much to do and she wanted to make an early start in the morning. After a round of "Good nights" Anne made her way to her bedroom. Anne's thoughts were all excitement of her adventure the following morning. She did not feel at all tired and was not ready yet to sleep. She packed a pillowcase with a few clothes and things she imagined she might need for her ride to Pemberley. Not until she had completed every small task of preparation and thought of as much detail as she could, then did she take to her bed. The excitement deprived her of any natural tendency to sleep. Her thoughts were active until the early hours of the morning. However, after a short sleep, she did wake early and took her breakfast. She ate well with the intention to stay in the saddle until lunchtime to make better progress.

Anne took her packed picnic, pillowcase and sketching kit with her to the stables. As promised, they had saddled her horse and he was ready for a day's ride. A groom helped her into the saddle, wished her an enjoyable day in the countryside and she was off. As soon as Anne was out of sight of anyone who might see her from Rosings, she urged her horse to a livelier step.

The weather was fine and ideal for a ride in the country. Her horse kept up a good steady pace for about three hours but finally showed signs of wanting distractions. It wanted to drink and eat the lush vegetation along the way. As the horse tried to stop to eat by the wayside, Anne urged the horse onwards. As the horse became more insistent Anne's control of the horse became less. As much as Anne wanted to continue her journey unbroken, she realized that the horse had his needs. She arrived at a village and dismounted near a pond. The horse drank from a trough provided for travellers and local drovers. While the horse drank, Anne looked around. She wondered what it was like to live in a small hamlet such as this. A few houses were visible and only one person, an old man sitting outside his front door, smoking a pipe, seemed the sole occupant of the place. The horse now satisfied of his thirst was more compliant to Anne's needs. Instead of mounting into the saddle, Anne felt she wanted the exercise of walking awhile. She walked, leading her horse by his bridle along the road in the direction of the old man.

As she was passing him, he called out, "A good day to e missy."

This had a lifting effect on the young lady's spirits and Anne, with a smile, returned the compliment. She now felt ready for the saddle again. She mounted her horse and was soon trotting off northwards towards Pemberley. Anne was not at all perturbed that she did not recognize the road; she was going northwards, the way to Pemberley as she thought.

Anne realized that she was beginning to feel tired. Her journey was now four hours and beside the tiredness, she felt the first pangs of hunger. The distance between villages seemed further on horseback than when she was enjoying the comfort of Elizabeth's carriage and jovial company.

At a convenient place somewhere along the road going north, Anne stopped her horse. It was an isolated spot. Here was a meadow with plenty of grass and something that looked like a stream further over the field. She took her provisions and a bottle of wine from a saddlebag and sat down to a picnic. The horse made good the opportunity to take his own picnic from the bounty of the countryside. It might have been the country air, the wine, or the fact that she had not slept well the night before but Anne completed her repast, lay down on the grass, and fell into a deep sleep.

Anne woke before the evening had set in. She suddenly felt very cold. She sat up and looked around for her horse. He was grazing some yards off. He appeared contented but she had it in her mind to make as much progress as possible to reach Pemberley before nightfall. In fact, Miss Anne de Bourgh was into the first quarter only of the way into her journey to Pemberley. Though she had no understanding of the distances, Miss Anne de Bourgh had travelled nearly thirty miles into her journey of about 150 miles.

Chapter Eighteen

The Fate of Anne's Letter

At Pemberley, a servant took the mail from the rider and placed it in the usual tray in his master's study. As he did so he noted that there was, on top, a letter addressed to Lady Elizabeth. The steward would normally open any relevant mail in the absence of Sir Richard. The steward made the letter available for Lady Elizabeth the next day by forwarding it on to London.

Elizabeth's engagements for that day took her away from her London house from early morning before the mail had arrived. The following morning, from her bed she inquired of her maid if there were any letters for her.

"The one letter only, milady. It has come from Pemberley."

Elizabeth's interest was immediately aroused. She thought, "What has happened at Pemberley that somebody should write to me?" She then remembered her letter not yet read.

It was on opening the second letter did she understand that it was from Anne. Elizabeth read with much consternation of the distress that Anne was expressing in her letter. She read on to discover that Anne wanted to go to Pemberley to be with her and Georgiana.

It was necessary to answer the letter as soon as possible. Firstly, for the comfort of words that she could give Anne. Secondly, to inform her that Sir Richard and family were in London for two weeks. Elizabeth wrote that it might be possible for Anne to join the party in London and return to Pemberley with them in due course. She was confident that such a proposal would not meet with any objections.

Elizabeth made her reply and secured its collection for the following morning.

The fourth day after Anne left for Pemberley Elizabeth's reply arrived at Rosings. The household at Rosings was already in turmoil because Anne was missing.

In the absence of Anne, Lady Catherine opened the letter from Elizabeth and its content surprised her.

Anne had left days before the letter arrived. Lady Catherine was in a state of high anxiety. She had several servants searching the immediate countryside for Anne. Lady Catherine knew by now, through Anne's note, that she planned to ride to Pemberley. Therefore, Lady Catherine knew of Anne's intentions. She knew also that the distance of about 150 miles was too much for Anne to ride. Anne was still a novice rider. 50 miles would be too much for just one day's ride. Lady Catherine was at a loss to know where Anne would sleep at night. Anne never had money. She never had need of it nor consequently, known the value of it. Elizabeth's letter gave no solace for the lady but simply confirmed Anne's note to Elizabeth.

Lady Catherine immediately replied to Elizabeth in London to explain the drama that was unfolding. She asked if she might solicit help from the servants at Pemberley to search for Anne in the immediate countryside of Pemberley. Not wishing to suffer delay by waiting for Elizabeth's agreement, she wrote a similar letter to the steward at Pemberley to instigate immediate searches.

Already, Lady Catherine was receiving communications back from her staff of sightings of a lone horsewoman on a grey speckled stallion. However, the concern was for her safety during the hours of darkness. To expose herself to the country at night when the temperature drops so much could be very detrimental, even lethal.

Therefore, it was a consideration to judge how far Anne may have travelled in one day and towards Pemberley and concentrate the search accordingly. Lady Catherine's first concern was for her daughter's safe survival of the inclement night. Anyone acquainted with the countryside will be aware of how complete the darkness can be. Anyone acquainted with the night temperatures will be aware of how much the thermometer level will fall. Lady Catherine was acquainted with all this and more, of the wild creatures abroad, the dampness, and villains, besides there are all sorts of evils unknown.

Upon receipt of Lady Catherine's letter, Elizabeth wrote to her father at Longbourn.

She explained to him that Miss Anne de Bourgh had taken it upon herself to ride her horse from Rosings to Pemberley alone. She would have no money with her or any knowledge of the world that will sustain her through five or six days journeying. She wrote further, that it occurred to her that Anne might take the same road as we did on our first journey to Pemberley. We stopped at Longbourn and rested overnight to start fresh and well fed early the following morning. It is possible that she intends to do the same again.

"Please," She wrote, "Spare no expense. Rally a few riders to search the country. A bonus to the man who can locate her first! Also tell the post riders to keep alert for a young lady on a grey speckled stallion."

Elizabeth's next letter was to the Pemberley steward. The letter was with much the same general content as her letter to her father.

After seven days since Anne first left Rosings to ride to Pemberley, no enquiries or searches found any further trace of her. Lady Catherine did not surrender any hope at all. She decided to engage permanent riders to search systematically across the country between Rosings and Pemberley. It occurred to her that Anne might have given up and decided to return to her home comforts. This would mean that Anne might very well be in the immediate vicinity. It was of some encouragement to learn that in a small hamlet, walking past an old man sitting outside his house while smoking, a young woman leading a grey speckled horse passed by to bid him politely

"A good morning to you."

Beyond that hamlet, there was no further information.

As the days passed into weeks and without any more news, Lady Catherine paid off the searchers. The mystery became a talking point in every inn across the country for weeks after. Many people hoping for a reward kept a close watch on anyone who might fit the description of a young lady with a grey horse. There are even tales of a ghostly figure of a lady walking abroad at night leading a grey horse. Even to this day.

Chapter Nineteen

A New Development

To keep warm, Anne wrapped herself up as best she could. On the horse, she felt better. She urged the horse back onto the road. They continued at a trot in what she thought was a northerly direction. Anne felt hungry but she decided not to stop again but wait until she arrived at Pemberley. Gradually the tiredness returned. Again, she had difficulty keeping awake but the darkness now increased her resolve to continue her journey. The moon was almost full but the occasional cloud obscured it so that visibility was lost from time to time. When the clouds blocked out the moonlight, Anne let the horse go as he would. She found herself falling asleep in the saddle and then waking up with a start. Several times this happened until she fell forwards over the neck of the horse, quite fast asleep. The movement of the horse's body caused Anne to fall further forwards until she fell down, out of the saddle on to the road. The surface was not hard and Anne was so relaxed in her state of sleep that she did not sustain any injury but some pain only. The fall caused Anne to awaken into a half sleep and half awake manner. She rose to her feet. Her horse stood still. In the moonlight, she could see a tree or bush with overhanging branches under which she could shelter and gain some rest before she completed her journey. Half walking, half-stumbling, she made her way to the bush and gained the shelter. She wrapped her riding coat around her and before she put her head on the ground, she was already asleep.

There is a time between early morning and late morning and it was at that time that Anne woke. She did not feel the cold so, but very hungry. Without any ceremony, she rose to a kneeling position to crawl out of her shelter. She could see no horse. She stood up and looked around but still there was no horse. It was unlike her horse to leave her. She realized that she was alone. In addition, Anne did not know where she was. She had no knowledge of which direction to take. For some moments, she stood still taking stock of her new situation. She had no food or drink. She was lost and had no horse. Alone and helpless she began to feel some sense of panic. Anne covered her eyes with her hands and fell to the ground onto her knees. She wanted to block out the reality of everything. For sometime, she remained this way. She began to feel herself crying. It was tears of despair.

She felt as though the world had deserted her or had she deserted the world? She began to feel cold. For some time Anne stayed like this, not knowing what else to do. She would have stayed longer if it had not been for a voice calling her name. It was a man's voice but she could not recognize it. Because of this, she did not respond immediately. It might have been a voice in her head. Who in the great wilderness of this country with a voice she did not recognize could possible know her name?

Slowly she allowed her hands to drop.

Again, the voice called her. "Is that you missy Anne? Is that you we 'elped cross t'ford?"

Anne was overjoyed but that did not stop tears falling freely and abundantly down both cheeks. She turned her head and looked at her gypsy friend from the meadow by the ford. His rough, weatherworn cheeks seemed manly but gentle. He stood holding a brace of rabbits and looking at her he spoke again, "Yu's alright are you missy? Oi thought oi recognized yer 'air. Oi 'elped t'save yus loif, oi did. Lovely 'air yus 'as missy."

Anne could not find the words. They seemed to refuse to come. She continued to kneel and look at him with her body twisted round in his direction.

The gypsy spoke again, "Oi' be goin cross t'next field. If 'e follows me you cn 'ave som'ing to eat. Som'ing 'ot oid wager."

The gypsy walked away from her to go towards the next field expecting Anne to follow. After a few paces, he stopped and looked round at her. Anne was still kneeling. She was now so cold and stiff she found it difficult to move. She did feel hungry but she still could not move. The gypsy stood for a moment or two just looking. He was waiting, expecting her to rise to her feet. As she did not move, remaining kneeling, looking at him as though pleading, he walked back to her. He cupped a hand under each elbow to lift Anne up to her feet. Her knees remained bent so that the gypsy had lifted her completely off the ground with her bent legs dangling. With his strong arms that were used to picking up and carrying heavy weights, he let her down gently towards the ground and as he did so, her legs straightened out more and more as they reached down to meet the ground.

The gypsy squatted down and spoke to Anne. "Put yer arms round m'neck an' oil take e piggy-back."

She obeyed him. He stood up and secured his long eared dinner to his belt; put his arms round Anne's legs to support her. Soon he was striding across the field, and then the next. The encampment came into view. Already she could smell the gypsy smells that she remembered from her last experience with them. It was while they were walking the final few yards that the other gypsies came to look to see what was coming into their camp. Dogs were barking and children's laughter echoed her memories. She felt now she would be safe.

Another gypsy was entering the camp at about the same time as Anne. He was leading a horse, a grey horse, a grey speckled stallion. She tried to call out to him but what came was a croak. Her throat was dry and her muscles were too stiff to obey her wishes. Still on the piggyback, Anne wheezed into the gypsy's ear, "That is my horse, sir."

He answered in one word, "Aye?"

Then he set her down by the campfire. Within a few minutes Anne could feel the fire's warmth unlocking her body. A wooden bowl and spoon were proffered. She accepted the food and instantly smelt the same aroma of herbs and meat as she had had before. Gratefully, she looked up at the young woman who brought her the broth and smiled at her. The gypsy woman smiled back. They spoke no words. While she took of the broth, she became aware that a crowd had gathered round her, inspecting her. They were talking and laughing amongst themselves but keeping their distance. After finishing the bowl of broth and with the fire or the broth or both she felt an inner glow. She had felt the same as she did the previous time and had since wanted to feel that glow again. Anne laid her riding coat on the ground and fell onto it. By the warmth of the fire and the sounds of laughter in her ears, Anne fell once more, into a deep slumber.

·⁜· ·

End of Volume Two

Volume Three

Chapter One

The Dead Speak

Elizabeth made short her visit to London in order to focus her attentions on the search for her missing cousin, Anne. Sir Richard continued in London to study his affairs. With all the attentions of so many people already engaged, he might not be an asset to the search for his kinswoman.

Lady Catherine de Bourgh was now in a great deal of fear for the total loss of her only daughter. She had engaged agents of all descriptions to make enquiries. They were authorized to offer generous rewards for any intelligence of proven value. All the counties between Rosings and Pemberley failed to offer more than the last sighting by an elderly pipe smoker in a small hamlet in the County of Hampshire. Tales abounded but hard evidence was virtually nonexistent.

Due to the fruitless searches and amount of time that had passed since the last sighting of Anne, interest of the people in the affair was beginning to wane. Elizabeth, however, was determined to continue. It occurred to Elizabeth that there were just four possibilities.

Firstly, Elizabeth thought that the first credible explanation for Anne's disappearance was that she wants to disappear for her own reason.

The second explanation might be that she has died in some isolated spot and no one has yet discovered her body.

The third reason is that villains might have abducted Anne, perhaps to obtain a ransom or some other vile purpose.

Fourthly, Anne may be well and happy living somewhere, perhaps oblivious to the anxieties she is causing.

With a retinue of three men and her carriage, Elizabeth set upon the task to tracking Anne and her horse. The Pemberley search party set forth passing from village to village to make the fullest possible enquiries. It was of some help to discover that the complete lack of anything positive from each enquiry of the different villages was that it was most likely that Anne had not reached so far north. They were yet to find the furthest extent of her travels. They stayed at inns along the way and leaving with full instructions to each landlord that if he or anyone else should see a young girl of Anne's description, to take her in under his protection and to contact directly Lady Catherine de Bourgh for an immediate reward.

The party continued towards the south making their enquiries along the way and occasionally making diversions in order to cover the area to best advantage. The journey so far proving fruitless, the retinue felt discouraged by all the negative responses. They had started out with a spirit of so much determination and optimism but had now turned to cynicism. Elizabeth was always encouraging her men on and urging them to ignore the lack of response so far.

"In its own way, the negative is positive from our point of view because it gives us essential information that helps us to come closer to Anne's last sighting."

The weather turned colder and the men were complaining of so much discomfort. With a final attempt before turning away from the search to obtain a fresh retinue, the party arrived at a small village that she recognized. It was the village where they had encountered the young boy who sustained an injury by her horses. Here too, the men made their enquiries but with the same complete lack of results.

"The search was proving fruitless and it was" The men said, "Time to return to Pemberley."

Elizabeth knew that it was not wise to press men on who were in such poor spirits. Such men would be detrimental in every possible way.

It occurred to Elizabeth that while she was at this particular village she might call upon the woman and the little boy to discover his condition now. With the three men, she approached the area where the boy was injured. She had no difficulty locating the mill again and the cottage that leaned against it. Elizabeth walked along the path to the little cottage.

She thought, "How much better the woman was attending to her garden."

It was full of produce destined for the table. The woman however did not appear, nor was there any sign of the urchin. One of the men knocked firmly on the door. Within a short while, the door opened to reveal a woman of much younger years than Elizabeth had been expecting. She stood half concealed by the open door. Elizabeth introduced herself to the young woman. The woman did not seem to know how to conduct herself with such obvious high company as the lady before her.

Elizabeth enquired of the woman who once lived here, ". . . In this cottage with a little boy by the name of David?"

She continued to explain that the boy had sustained an injury from one of her horses and she was hoping to see him now well and fully recovered.

The woman showed some embarrassment and appeared reluctant to speak.

Eventually, by gentle persuasion from Elizabeth, the woman explained that the little boy had died and the woman had left. "The child was her life and joy. When he died, she seemed to lose all interest in life. She went off with . . . until the . . ."

She stopped and looked at Elizabeth and her retinue of men.

"This is nothing to do with me. I just help the miller for the house and mind my own things." The woman defended herself. "Have I." She thought, "Said too much or the wrong thing."

She began to close the door. Elizabeth was too quick for her. She held out her hand to grip the handle of the door to stop it from closing.

"Until what, woman? Until what?" She raised her voice with some impatience as she asked the question.

The woman's knees nearly gave way as she heard the question from this lady demanding her answer.

"Until the gypsies come." She replied with tears running down her face. She took the opportunity to slam the door.

A cold shiver ran down Elizabeth's back. She went cold all over her body as the realization of the fate that Anne may have met. She turned to her men and said, "I want that door opened. I must speak more to that woman."

Evans, the tallest of the three, strode forward and banged his huge fist on the door. He shouted to the woman to open the door, making the reason that milady wishes to talk more. Slowly, silently the door opened and half of the face of the woman looked round it. There were still tears of fear running down her face.

Elizabeth calmly explained that a young lady had gone missing and perhaps she was with those gypsies. She asked if she saw anyone like a young lady of some quality amongst them. The woman shook her head. Elizabeth pressed her further to think and tell her what she had seen. The replies provided nothing more useful for Elizabeth. She thanked the woman for helping her. This was information of some interest but by itself, of little value. Elizabeth thought of Anne living with the gypsies. What miseries she must be experiencing, what deprivations she must be undergoing. Elizabeth half turned round to make her departure, but turned back as a thought came to her mind. She asked the woman if the gypsies had any horses with them.

"Why, yes. Some." The woman replied.

The expression on her face showed that she wondered at such a question. "Gypsies always had their 'orses. Their 'orses goes with them and their dogs."

"What were they like?" Elizabeth enquired now tentatively.

"'Orses? Just gypsy 'orses. Them 'orses goes with them gypsies." She replied.

"What were they like? What colour were they?"

"What colour? Thems gypsy 'orses, piebalds they be."

"Think woman, think. Were there any other horses not like gypsy horses? What colours did you see?"

"Thems were all piebalds, I think." The woman searched the air for the pictures in her mind. "There was one dark brown un and a large grey 'orse."

"Was it a large grey speckled stallion?"

"T'would be hard to say but aye, t'were speckled, a big un too."

Elizabeth turned round to her retinue. The looks on their faces showed their amazement. With all the miles they had covered, all the people they had met and all the questions they had asked with no avail, here were all the answers. Their ladyship's persistence wrenched it out of the one and only person in all of England who could have given them their information. She held out her hand. "A sovereign, I think." Her man tipped a shiny coin from a purse into her outstretched hand. She turned to the woman who was still standing half exposed behind the door.

"Good woman, I want you to take this. You have earned it. With this sovereign goes my thanks to you for your help."

The woman took the money, opened mouthed she tried unsuccessfully to pronounce words of thanks. She had not held so much money at one time in all her life. She fell back into her cottage without a word.

Elizabeth turned to her men and smiled. She thanked them for their support and persistence, "For now we must return to the carriage."

"We have all been asking the wrong questions in the wrong places. Who could have guessed this? We can return now to Pemberley. Let us go home."

Chapter Two

The Search Continues

Elizabeth was thinking as she made her way back to the carriage. Now that the nights were drawing in and the road to Pemberley was more than one day's ride. Longbourn, in the other direction was just a few hours away. A visit to Longbourn would mean a delay in returning home. The matters in hand were more urgent and she could manage the correspondence from her family's Manor House as easily as at Pemberley.

"The retinue would not welcome this change in plan but it must rate as a minor inconvenience for the greater good." Elizabeth thought.

The carriage had already moved off, northwards, towards Pemberley. Elizabeth called to the driver, from the carriage window, her new instructions to go south to Longbourn.

Before dusk, the carriage approached Longbourn. The driver gave the signal for the horn to sound their imminent arrival, turned off the road and into the driveway of The Manor House.

Lady Elizabeth's arrival at Longbourn caused great excitement with her parents and Kitty and their entire staff. Kitty was now the last of her sisters not attached or intended. Elizabeth had arrived in time for the evening meal. She explained fully of her reason to be abroad and arriving at Longbourn without notice.

During dinner, much conversation took place regarding the disappearance of Anne. Many speculations caused ideas of the most unlikely possibilities but Elizabeth was keen to consider anything that might help in her search for Anne. The family also reflected on the similarities between Anne's disappearance and their dear Lydia's event. When Lydia eloped with Wickham, Lady Catherine was most indignant and scathing towards Elizabeth. Since then, Anne had eloped with no one less than her own brother. She has now run away without support from home or family, that is, as far as they knew.

Following the completion of the evening meal, Elizabeth set about writing letters to Lady Catherine and to Sir Richard.

The two letters were, in essentials, similar. Upon hearing the conversations at the table that same evening, Elizabeth was careful to word her letter to Lady Catherine to avoid any hint of her daughter deliberately running away for the second time. She wrote in terms of the hope that kindly people were caring for Anne along the way. Each letter expressed some information but at the same while, specific information she constructed to minimize distress to either party. It was therefore, that Lady Catherine did not learn that her daughter may have been in the hands of unknown gypsies.

— o —

Lady Catherine read her letter with a great falling down of her spirits. For her to read again of her daughter's disappearance was bad enough but to learn of the discovery that she may be consorting with ""People" along the way." was, in her mind, "People of little or even worse, no consequence." as a worse fate that could possibly befall Anne.

Elizabeth's letter to her husband detailed the events at the village where the young boy was injured. She described how the gypsies normally own piebald horses but a band passing through the village were leading a grey speckled larger horse matching the description of Anne's own horse. The village could very well have been in the proximity of the furthest extent of Anne's journey northwards.

Elizabeth also explained her plan, which was, she was setting out from longbourn to return to Pemberley.

— o —

The following morning, an early breakfast made good the time for starting the journey to reach Pemberley by nightfall. Before the party had travelled one mile, the thought came to Elizabeth a visit could be a great comfort for Lady Catherine. She opened the carriage window and called to the driver to turn round and make for Rosings Park in Kent.

By early afternoon, Lady Elizabeth's carriage turned into the drive at Rosings Park. Lady Catherine and Mrs Jenkinson with two servants in attendance were waiting on the steps in response to the driver's signal. They were surprised to see Elizabeth's carriage speeding towards them. In the driveway was a carriage of which Elizabeth was very familiar. She saw the owner turn round to see this new arrival to Rosings. At the realization of the identity of the carriage, a broad smile spread across his face and he turned to retrace his climb, to descend to meet Elizabeth at the bottom of the steps. They embraced briefly and laughed together because Elizabeth had written that she was returning to Pemberley. She explained why she had changed her mind at the last moment.

Lady Catherine's welcome was very much warmer than usual. She was ostensibly indulgent to her two family connections. With her arms encompassing one of each guest, the three of them proceeded up the steps. Lady Catherine was eager to learn of any intelligence of her daughter, of her whereabouts or welfare.

"Let us go inside. We can talk in comfort there." Lady Catherine said as they continued up the steps.

Inside they did talk indeed and in depth. Lady Catherine began to realize how she had failed her own daughter. Further, how she had caused the problems with Anne's relationship with

Colonel Fitzwilliam. Many years ago while she was in low spirits, she explained how the marriage of Anne to Darcy would have guaranteed that she would not be marrying anyone in her family bloodline. The great problem with charts is that they never show the results of illicit encounters. From her early days, she believed there were many such relationships of which she knew definitely only a few.

To make certain of the safest marriage and a good connection was by the arrangement to which Catherine and Mrs Darcy's swore that she would keep on her deathbed. That is, that their own offspring should be united only to each other.

"I am sorry now. I realize that the reason for making the promise for both Darcy and Anne to marry outside the bloodline was achievable without them having to marry each other. It was, unfortunately, the promise I made on his mother's deathbed and that is a difficult promise to break."

"A consolation Lady Catherine, that is, that you have kept your promise in the spirit of the intention. Mrs Darcy's son has married outside the bloodline and you have been brave enough to prevent your daughter marrying into it. I see no occasion so far for you to feel any guilt. You have had a difficult task with difficult decisions to make. I respect all you have done or tried to do." Elizabeth assured her aunt.

Sir Richard followed Elizabeth's assurances, "Elizabeth expresses my mind even better than I can. Pleased be assured aunt that Elizabeth and I hold you always in the highest esteem."

Lady Catherine felt very uplifted by Elizabeth's speech. Here was honesty; here was the true dignity of a real lady.

The family enjoyed an excellent lunch. Afterwards they discussed the possible actions they could take in order to discover if Anne might still be alive and if so, where she is living.

Lady Catherine wondered if they could engage the militia. Sir Richard expressed his approval of the idea and that he would make enquiries.

Lady Elizabeth said, "If we could enlist the help of Colonel Fitzwilliam we might have a whole army to help us find Anne."

For a moment, they were silent waiting for these considerations to settle in their minds.

"You may be aware that Bonaparte has escaped and that he is in France?" Lady Catherine asked.

Elizabeth and Darcy agreed that they did know, "But, aunt how can Bonaparte's being in France affect our search for Anne?" Elizabeth asked, speaking also the thoughts of Sir Richard.

She continued, "Colonel Fitzwilliam is surveying the entire South Coast of England to prepare defences against a possible French invasion. We could ask him if he is able to employ any means to search the areas in which he works, to discover Anne. Of course, we understand that no such undertaking should interfere with his work or the national security. I will write to the general today."

With these resolutions and after all other ideas were exhausted, their meeting broke up. Lady Catherine wrote a letter to the General. Sir Richard sent a message to the local militia. Lady Elizabeth decided to take the opportunity to visit the parsonage to see the baby and her sister Mary.

Protected by warm clothing, Elizabeth made her way through the grove that she knew so well and was so familiar to Anne and Charlotte. She thought she could feel the presence of Charlotte again. The thoughts made her feel even colder and she pulled her coat and scarf tighter around her body. Elizabeth was trying to picture in her own mind, the scenes that she might encounter at the Parsonage. The different ideas that came to her she considered carefully and was well prepared mentally to remain composed for whatever she might encounter.

As Elizabeth entered the forecourt of the parsonage, she noticed how deserted and lost it appeared. Before she reached the front door it opened by a servant who curtsied.

The young maid greeted her with a generous smile. "Good Morning, your ladyship."

The lady returned the compliment and asked of her health and how baby Boo-Boo was faring.

She received a very enthusiastic and positive response to both enquiries. This was a good start to her visit indeed. The servant girl ushered her guest towards the study, knocked and upon opening the door announced, "Lady Elizabeth Darcy."

The opened door revealed the parson and Mary busily working but in such close physical contact while so engaged as to be most indecorous for any normal moral acceptance.

The maid left the room, closing the door without showing any outward reaction to Miss Bennet's and Mr. Collins' behaviour.

"Perhaps," Elizabeth thought. "This is because such a sight was all too familiar to her. It cannot be that her sensibilities are so dulled that the young girl cannot understand its significance."

Mary greeted her older sister with some guarded pleasure. Mr. Collins advanced to Elizabeth to put his arm round her to guide her into the study to make her feel the more welcome. Elizabeth noted how different his behaviour had become. This was a different Mr. Collins. She mused briefly on the probability that Mary must be the person responsible.

Elizabeth addressed her hosts, "I have come to see you and the baby. I do hope all is well?"

Both Mr. Collins and Mary were jointly eager to reassure Elizabeth that everything with the baby was well and besides, they wished to impart some news to Elizabeth. That she should be the first to learn of it was appropriate, as she was the one responsible for their coming together. Elizabeth felt that same, cold as ice feeling she experienced upon learning that the fate of Anne might be that gypsies may have captured her. She felt it wiser to hold her silence and wait for the declaration of their news.

Mary was about to speak but Mr. Collins had been waiting with some eagerness to tell someone of his new and happy intended alliance. "Mary and I have become very close during the time we have met. I have helped Mary with her studies and in return she has given me quite some help with her observations as a young person on the scriptures and in particular the Epistles."

Mary was equally keen to add. "It is by some greater providence that we have come together in this way. We feel a Heavenly power at work when we study the fashion by which our separate lives have drawn together and been so affected that we have come to know each other, and of being such equal dispositions."

For some time, there was silence.

The one thought that Elizabeth had was, "Is this close relationship seemly? In view of the relatively short time since Charlotte's demise. Some people would judge such behaviour as disrespectful."

Elizabeth added, "I wish you both well and all happiness but be advised. You should keep this friendship, outwardly at least, on a formal basis for another few months yet. Sir William and Lady Lucas may be very offended. And there are dear Maria's feelings to consider. We must not hurt our cousins."

As she finished the sentence there was a knock at the door and it opened slowly. The young servant girl that Elizabeth had seen earlier curtsied and walked into the room with Charlotte's baby in her arms. The girl curtsied again to address Elizabeth, "We knows you want to see her, your ladyship. We still call her Boo-Boo."

Elizabeth could see she had grown and was looking very healthy. "Why, does she still cry so?" Elizabeth asked.

"Er . . . No, she hardly cries now, hardly ever." The servant girl replied.

The girl was looking down adoringly at the baby. She was obviously enjoying the experience of looking after the mite.

"You may hold her yourself milady if you have a mind to." She suggested to Elizabeth and continued, "We have asked Mr. Collins to name her Elizabeth after you, your ladyship.

Chapter Three

Familiar Family

With the demands of their business, Anne's disappearance and Mary's secret intended alliance to Mr. Collins, Elizabeth and Sir Richard concluded their visit to Rosings earlier than they had wished or expected. They had agreed in private that they must make known their knowledge of the affair of Mr. Collins and Mary discretely to Mr. Bennet. As a consequence, Sir Richard agreed with Elizabeth that they should call at The Manor House while making their journey northward to Pemberley.

Their arrival at The Manor House was greeted with as much surprise as pleasure. Great humour was made of the possible reasons for Sir Richard's and Elizabeth's calling at such frequent intervals.

It was not easy to find sufficient privacy to explain to Mr. Bennet that they wished to speak to him secretly. Many hints were surreptitiously made. However, shortly after the evening meal completed, the ladies withdrew to leave the gentlemen to themselves. This allowed the gentlemen the privacy that Sir Richard was waiting patiently to obtain with Mr. Bennet.

Sir Richard explained in general terms that he wished to discuss a topic of some delicacy and have Mr. Bennet's opinion on the matter. The subject is a family affair so should be guarded with great care.

Intrigued, Mr. Bennet assured Sir Richard of his earnest attention and that he had his word as a gentleman that he would remain discrete regarding the subject.

The dialogue took half an hour to reach the salient point. While Mr. Bennet did, as promised, give his entire attention to Sir Richard as he detailed the events at The Parsonage as related to him by Elizabeth.

"So you are saying that Mary has formed an attachment with Mr. Collins?

"Quite, quite so. The fear that Elizabeth holds is that such an untimely affair could invoke the displeasures of Sir William and generally, disapprobation of everyone."

Mr. Bennet looked thoughtfully at Sir Richard. He was trying to speak, to put his thoughts into words with which Sir Richard would not feel uncomfortable.

"Sir Richard, I feel I owe it to you to inform you of something that everyone else seems to have neglected to explain. Please do not be offended in any way . . ."

"Mr. Bennet, father in law, what could you ever say at which I would take offence?"

"Well, Sir Richard, I will be blunt. We are aware of the circumstances that you describe at The Parsonage. Sir William and his family also are informed and their approval obtained. We all feel that if Charlotte was able to speak to us, she too would give her approval. The coming together of Mr. Collins and Mary was unexpected, though with a little insight one would imagine a greater power had a hand in bringing about the union. When it happens, that is. So there cannot be any ill will at all."

"Mr. Bennet, I am of the same opinion as you have described and now I feel ashamed at raising the subject."

"Please, Sir Richard, do not feel disquiet about anything we have discussed. You have done your duty. Our business this evening will be held in confidence. I am sure that Elizabeth will be in accord with the rest of the family when she thinks of about it and what is best for the child. And I have to add that Mrs Bennet approves most enthusiastically, you can depend on that."

Sir Richard held out his hand to Mr. Bennet, "Thank you, sir, I am glad to have had the opportunity to talk. We should do so more often."

Sir Richard made good his leave to seek out Elizabeth to inform her of this piece of good news and make preparations to return to Pemberley immediately.

Chapter Four

Return to Pemberley

Once more, Elizabeth was waving to her family as she left, this time for Pemberley. Sir Richard seemed to enjoy the visit and her father's company. The driver had instructions to make all haste for the hills of Derbyshire for which he had a great affection. The two carriages sped along the same route that they had followed on Elizabeth's first journey to Pemberley as mistress of that great house.

With their private company in the seclusion of the carriage, Elizabeth enquired of Sir Richard of his opinion of the fate of her cousin, Anne.

For several minutes, he was obviously cogitating on the subject. Holding her husband in the highest esteem, Elizabeth hoped to have some definite judgement. He began shaking his head slowly indicating that he was unable to come to any other conclusion other than the considerations already discussed in detail.

"Surely, Sir Richard, if she had died or was killed, someone would have discovered her body and reported the news?"

"That is the most probable theory, yes. This is not definite because her body could be lying undiscovered or eaten by wild animals."

"Consider, sir, the area in which she was last seen and the immediate surroundings. Is this not the most difficult country? Would it be most feasible to lose a body, dead or alive?"

"Difficult, yes, but not impossible, my dear."

"Consider also sir, that Anne was actually running away from home to join us at Pemberley. She leaves home without money, little sustenance, no knowledge of the road and Anne, a novice horsewoman. Against this background, if she met with some convivial company she may have the inclination to join them, would she not?"

"That would be a possibility, but one among many. We have to approach her disappearance with an open mind. I am as concerned for Anne as much as you are. I cannot imagine an easy solution for which you are trying to reason. We shall have to depend on good providence."

Elizabeth continued, trying to think it through to some resolution. As the miles passed by, she began to tire and eventually fell asleep. She woke to the voice of Sir Richard repeating a whispered call to her.

Sleepily she stepped down from the carriage to find herself before the inn that her party visited on their last journey to Pemberley. In the doorway was the same jovial innkeeper. He smiled broadly at his guests as they advanced to the inn.

The innkeeper greeted, Sir Richard though not aware now of his elevated rank, and led them into the dining room. The room appeared the same in all essentials as they had left it those months before. A serving girl arrived to take their order and invited Elizabeth to refresh herself in their new facilities. While Elizabeth left the room, the innkeeper stayed with Sir Richard to discuss the weather and other general topics. He eventually arrived at the recollection of their previous visit.

Sir Richard enquired if he had again seen the man they missed on their last visit at the inn.

"He has returned twice since you were here last. Your friend, a military man, I think seemed to want gain his attention for some reason?"

"Yes you are right my friend is a colonel. The other man, the Frenchman, we are wanting to meet him. Can you help us find him again?" Sir Richard asked.

"Oh, French is he? I suspected him to be foreign but I did not know of his country. He spoke perfect English but with an accent. He hasn't given any trouble."

"Does he always come alone?"

"Yes, always alone. That is so until now."

"Do you expect him to call again soon?" Sir Richard asked.

"It is impossible to say sir, he may never come again. This often happens with my guests. They come a few times and then they go and sometimes I never seem them again and sometimes I do."

Sir Richard thought for a moment and then asked the innkeeper, "Could you possibly check your records to find the three dates on which he visited you, Landlord?"

"I will do that now for you, while you and your lady dine, sir."

"That will be very much appreciated landlord."

Elizabeth returned and the food arrived. Husband and wife ate their meal and enjoyed their wine. The landlord entered the room. He tended a piece of paper on which he had written three dates.

"This is what you asked for sir." The landlord spoke as he handed the paper to Sir Richard.

"By which route did the fellow leave? Was it always the same or did it change?"

"The first time, as you know sir, he went nor'wards towards Derby, I think. The second time he went southward and last time he went nor'wards again. I didn't see him myself but I asked the ostlers and they was in no doubt about it, sir."

"Thank you landlord for your good service."

Elizabeth listened to this conversation and as soon as the landlord left their presence, she was keen to have her curiosity satisfied.

"Of whom are you talking? Is it anything to do with Anne's disappearance?"

"No not at all." Then after a pause for thought added, "Oh, at least, I hope not. We were talking about the French agent we call Marcel."

"It is not possible that your French agent would want to secure Anne for some advantage?"

"Possible but unlikely, Elizabeth."

"Did you not say to me earlier that we should consider every possibility?"

"I sincerely hope that she has not fallen into a trap of that scoundrel."

With little ceremony, they left the inn to mount their carriage to continue the final passage to Derbyshire.

Less conversation passed between Elizabeth and Sir Richard, while both were in deep thought considering the alarming concept of Miss Anne de Bourgh to be a prisoner of the French.

"Look here, Elizabeth, do you know where we are? We have come to the site of the gypsy camp. I have a strong desire to see it again."

"Oh, yes, please do and I shall accompany you."

Sir Richard called to the driver to stop the carriage. The bemused staff, watched as the lady and gentleman indulged their nostalgia.

Together they climbed the embankment and on to the campsite. There were no gypsies, no caravans, no fires and no horses or dogs barking or children laughing. The grass had grown long and the cold wind blowing across it bit deeply into Elizabeth's body. She wanted to return to the carriage but the memories of their previous visit pulled her further to where Anne lay at death's door in Colonel Fitzwilliam's arms. She discovered some charcoal remains, now almost over grown with wild vegetations.

"This is where the fire blazed and where we spent such a pleasant time."

In her mind, she could see the gypsies dancing and recalled the smells and the music. These poor people who squeezed so much pleasure from so little resources found life's fulfillment in their own special way. The cold biting wind reminded her of the comfort of the carriage. Sir Richard was obviously reminiscing also and she had to bring him back from his reverie.

"It will be much warmer in the carriage, Sir Richard."

He responded immediately and they returned to the carriage. Their journey home was without incident. Even the ford favoured their crossing without disadvantage.

Husband and wife sat silently both engrossed in their own thoughts. They felt deeply moved by the recollections of the magic of that evening. The memories were so strong yet the event seemed so distant.

Their journey completed as they passed through the portals of Pemberley while some light still left. It was the opportunity for Sir Richard to write a letter and to have it dispatched hastily before nightfall.

Chapter Five

An Event at the Manning's Holding

At breakfast the morning after their return from Longbourn, Sir Richard and Lady Darcy were discussing their engagements for the day. They agreed that they should take their exercise while visiting their tenants because there was otherwise much business to occupy their time.

While on their way to their nearest farm, they met with Mr. Mannings of their estate. He was making his way, in a much-distressed discomposure, towards the big house. The man was wringing his cap while tears ran down his face. His condition gave him such distress that he had difficulty to speak.

Sir Richard demanded, "Mannings, what ever is that matter with you? Why are you so put out?"

"Sir, my child is sick and I can't make the place work. I must find employment somewhere with a house to earn my keep."

"It is as you wish Mannings, but before you leave let us call the physician to make your child better. What is the child's state of health now?"

"Oh, oh, she is in a bad way and I fear for her life. I must try to do something, sir."

"Elizabeth, you can arrange that can you not? I will talk to the man to discover his problems."

Elizabeth turned her horse round to make for the big house. Upon arrival, she summoned a servant to hasten a physician to the Mannings's holding to attend a sick child on Sir Richard's order. She then engaged two stable lads to accompany her return to her tenants' dilemma.

She arrived again at the Manning's' cottage to discover that they had packed their belongings onto their cart hitched to a horse ready to make their leave. The sick child lay on a mattress thrown onto the very back of the cart. Elizabeth demanded that they wait until the physician arrived. Mrs Mannings was for staying but her husband demonstrated an eagerness to leave early because of the long journey ahead of them. Already he was seated on the cart with the reins in hand. Elizabeth remonstrated that the child was too sickly to travel. There was much argument with pleadings and counter arguments until the physician arrived accompanied with two servants.

Whereupon Mr. Mannings insisted that, he could not pay the doctor. Sir Richard intervened to say that if Mr. Mannings wished to leave the estate then there was nothing to stop him but cautioned him to stay until his daughter was in better health to travel. While he remained as a tenant Sir Richard pledged to meet any physician's fee until the child was fit and well again. Mr. Mannings still insisted that he was not in any way capable of repaying Sir Richard and he certainly could not stomach charity. Sir Richard continued to urge Mr. Mannings to stay and wait until his daughter's health improved.

"Have you any idea, sir, of the problems a child gives? The responsibilities that are so out of proportion to their size?"

Sir Richard thought the question irrelevant but replied, "No, Mannings I have no child of my own, not a daughter, not a son either."

"Well, sir, with the greatest respect, you have no idea of the problems and responsibilities that go with being a father."

Elizabeth could hear the conversation and thought, "We have never discussed the subject."

She had felt something was missing in their lives. They enjoyed every luxury that the world could offer but there was this big empty space, a chasm wider than her mind could comprehend and she felt it.

All this time the doctor took the opportunity to examine the child. Having done so, he made for the front of the cart and joined Sir Richard in his protestations. The physician and Sir Richard called the two women to help persuade Mr. Mannings to stay until at least the young girl's health improved.

Anticipating that Mr. Mannings would concede Elizabeth dispatched the boys to return to the house and come back in a dogcart.

"Bring some vitals for the Mannings and bring anyone we can spare from their duties to help put the cottage back into order for Mrs Mannings and her daughter."

Mr. Mannings did give way to heavy persuasion and began the lengthy task of unloading the cart and moving back into the cottage. While he was undertaking this work, Sir Richard was noting that his tenant was thin and wiry looking but he was certainly strong. As he lifted furniture and paraphernalia off the cart, he demonstrated his physical abilities.

"The thinness, perhaps it was a poor diet." Sir Richard thought.

Sir Richard also noted the cart was old but in an excellent state of repair. The woodwork was a mixture of old and new but all very well preserved. The axles displayed a good greasing for heavy work and the whole was a very useful tool.

Sir Richard thought, "The estate needed a carrier and there must be plenty of work otherwise, outside the estate. This must be even more so at special times like harvest and other farm events. With the small holding that Mannings had it would be better to regard some enterprise of business and anything he could earn from his small farm as a bonus."

Mr. and Mrs Mannings were coming out of their cottage and approaching Sir Richard to express their gratitude for his help. Mr. Mannings was crying, "The Lord thank you sir, I do not know how I am ever going to repay you. Your physician said that my little girl was very ill but she will pull through with good management. She will get very hot and we must help her sweat the disease out."

Mrs Mannings gave her thanks and added that she always knew you were a good man and that they would both make good their debts to him.

Sir Richard said, "Perhaps we can help you do that."

Both Mr. and Mrs Mannings looked astonished at Sir Richard for his remark.

"With the problems of your making a living we have failed to see what is before us all the time."

Sir Richard realized how much he had now engaged the attention of his tenant. He judged this a good sign, at least to start with.

"We would be glad to do anything for you, Sir Richard" Mrs Mannings blurted.

Mr. Mannings enthusiastically followed her with, "Yes, yes, anything I can do, Sir Richard."

"Well, Mannings, I see you have an excellent cart and horse. Very useful on a small farm but even more useful put to work to move goods for other people. I have, for instance to move some items to Sir Rufus. He has requested the loan of certain items that he would like to have for his servant's ball. If you could do that for me, my patronage should give you a mark of good service. What do you think, Mannings?

"Your recommendation would be the best I could ever hope for, sir. Please consider me engaged."

While Sir Richard and Mannings were talking, other tenants had arrived to help the Mannings. They had heard of his misfortunes and these people, his neighbours and fellow farmers, were in sympathy for him. Some came bearing their various gifts of food items mainly. It was with great glee that Mr. Mannings accepted the further orders from two of his neighbours. One was to move potatoes to Lambton and the other to move furniture to the auction rooms.

Sir Richard was about to take his leave when Mr. Mannings sought him out. Overwhelmed with the Christian kindness from Sir Richard and his neighbours he was with tears again, Mannings discovered his biggest problem of the day was to find the way to express his thanks to his master and his neighbours.

Lady Elizabeth approached and saw the state of Mannings. She knew exactly what to ask before she and her husband made good their leave. "Will you be staying now, Mannings?"

He fell to his knees, his hands clasped over his face and tears releasing the pent up emotions of two years of failure and worry, of starvation and illness, and hopelessness. In less than an hour, Sir Richard had shifted his world from one of despair to one of hope and opportunity.

Manning's homestead was now all industry of his neighbours. Some engaged in activity while others in discussion on various matters. One neighbour had brought a barrel of cider, which was proving very popular.

Sir Richard astride his horse turned to Elizabeth, "We must be returning now. This matter is resolved but it has put out our timetable, do you not think?"

Elizabeth would have agreed with him but all she could think of was, "Sir Richard, I would like a dog of my own."

Sir Richard felt much dumbfounded by her remark. It seemed out of context of the immediate endeavours as he saw them.

They rode together in silence, taking their exercise and returning to Pemberley where Elizabeth was now beginning to feel it to be more than just her house, but more their home and something of a nest to keep everyone in it warm and comfortable.

Chapter Six

News from Rosings

Sir Richard and Lady Darcy normally breakfasted without any interruption but this morning a special delivery arrived before the usual post mail. A manservant tended the special letter to Sir Richard who took it eagerly from the tray. His hopes were for news from Colonel Fitzwilliam who was still on a task of surveying the South Coast of England for defences against the French. The letter did bear the coat of arms of Colonel Fitzwilliam in his capacity of lord to the earldom.

With a careful hand, Sir Richard unfolded the letter. As he was reading it, Elizabeth was becoming increasingly frustrated.

"Read it to me, sir, please, I beg you."

Sir Richard stopped reading and looked, smiled at Elizabeth and said, "I was hoping to hear some good news from the colonel.

He writes, "Several detachments have been deployed to search the Southern Counties for any trace of Anne or the gypsies. We agreed in committee that such a comprehensive exercise of the country could return much valuable information on the details of various strategic components. This is of bridges, roads, and elements valuable to the military. The exercise has proved very worthwhile indeed. The men did encounter ten separate gypsy family encampments but no grey speckled horse among the gypsies nor sightings of any people matching the descriptions to which you alluded to me in your letter."

"With regard to the inn where we stayed on route to Pemberley, we have stationed four men and an officer. They are acting undercover, working in the stables and on nearby farms in order not to create suspicion or alarm. In the event of any traveller remotely matching the description of Marcel, he will be carefully investigated and appropriate action taken. Until now, there has been no communication from them. I will keep you informed at all times. The colonel ends with his best wishes to me and to somebody called . . . er, Elizabeth."

She smiled as she heard this last sentence and continued her thoughts on the subject.

"Surely, no-one can just disappear and gypsies also, in our country?"

Elizabeth expressed her thoughts to Sir Richard, "With both Anne and the gypsies missing at the same time, could there be a connection? It is very strange that my cousin and the gypsies should both disappear together, is it not?"

His response was to point out that to make a connection does not take us any closer to finding them or Anne.

They finished their meal in silence and deep in thought.

Their morning exercise ride they took together. They rode across their land to the site of the gypsy encampment at the time of the Pemberley fair. The couple scanned the deserted site. This is where the French miscreants had slaughtered the two gypsies then escaped with their lives. They recalled the women wailing for their dead husbands.

"And all for the want of a few horses." He thought.

Sir Richard and Elizabeth were both preoccupied with the idea, "Could there really be a connection? Is it possible that Anne's sudden disappearance has anything to do with the French or the gypsies or both?"

After a few minutes, they turned away from the empty site. The wind now seemed colder and Elizabeth felt it biting into her.

She thought, "Would the gypsies ever return?"

Then, back in the saddle, she pressed her horse on to a gallop. She rode fast and recklessly while Sir Richard had difficulty in keeping up with her. Eventually she began to tire and Sir Richard leaned over to reach out for her reins to pull her horse to a halt. They both understood that her impetuous riding had been very dangerous but he said nothing.

For some time they walked their horses in silence. Sir Richard did not refer to her outburst but did suggest that they return home and talk about the dog she wanted. To this, Elizabeth readily agreed.

In the warmth and comfort of the salon, Sir Richard and Elizabeth took a glass of wine and talked of dogs. The reason Elizabeth gave for wanting a dog was for companionship when she was alone in the country. She further explained how she feared for her safety because the disappearance of Anne was always on her mind.

This provided the reason enough to persuade Sir Richard to make immediate enquiries to the local kennels. He dispatched five letters to kennels with whom he had previously made purchases.

The rest of the day, they engaged with affairs of the estate. The Mannings family were often in there minds and hoping that their sorry saga was over and happier times will come for them. Soon, they hoped, the Mannings would be self-supporting and paying their rent. It did impress them both how so many neighbours turned out to help the family.

"This may have been." Sir Richard thought, "Only natural but possibly due, in part, to the camaraderie found at the servant's ball and the Pemberley Fair."

He resolved to repeat the fair again in the summer. This year, it was Sir Rufus and Lady Penelope who would be catering for the staff ball. It would be a new experience for them. Sir Richard and Elizabeth agreed to call upon Sir Rufus before the event to help with ideas for the ball.

While engaged in these thoughts and affairs of the estate, a manservant brought the day's mail to Sir Richard. He extracted one letter that bore Elizabeth's name. She recognized the hand of her sister, Jane. Elizabeth was eager to read news of her closest sister. She opened up the letter and read quietly. For some time she sat quietly with the letter still in her hand.

Sir Richard looked up from his writing to observe his wife in deep contemplation.

"You have received good news, Elizabeth?" He asked.

Elizabeth folded her letter and with a serious countenance informed him, "I must go as soon as possible to see Jane; she will be having her baby very shortly."

Sir Richard had no knowledge of this happiest of events but did recognize an opportunity to visit his very good friend, Bingley.

"We will go as soon as you wish, Elizabeth."

"If we tidy things up here we could be on the road within 2 days. I would like that we should go in my carriage. The horses will be pleased to have the exercise and with my carriage you will not be mistaken for an Admiral."

At that, they both laughed. Sir Richard always enjoyed the humour of Elizabeth. She wrote a letter immediately informing Jane of their intentions.

The following day, the mail contained two replies from the dog kennels. Sir Richard held one of the letters and said to her, "These kennels are in the vicinity of Bingley's house. We can visit them during our stay."

Elizabeth's thoughts now, were more for her sister. Would she be an aunt to a boy or a girl? She recalled Charlotte's baby, newly born. She remembered Anne's adoration of the baby, her baby talk and then her joys and then her agonies of unrequited love.

Now Charlotte has gone and Anne has gone. Elizabeth felt very sad for these events. She decided that she would pray for Jane, for her confinement and for the new baby. She would also pray for Anne's safety. That is all she could do. It was all in God's hands.

The carriage waited for Sir Richard and Elizabeth while they attended to some last minutes instructions to the steward. Prepared for the journey, as they approached the carriage, they could not but admire the carriage and the horses. Elizabeth spoke to each horse, as was her custom before mounting the carriage. The journey will be less than four hours barring any delays along the way.

Within four hours, the horn sounded of their approach, uphill to Bingley's house. Elizabeth was eager to see it. She leaned out of the window to capture the expanse of the frontage. There were two ancient walls with wisteria cascading down to the ground each side of the approach to the house. The house was not as large and imposing as Netherfield Park but more as an over sized homely cottage. The chimneys told of its Elizabethan origins.

Bingley, surrounded by servants was displaying his winning smile to greet his favourite cousins as he waited at the front of his house. As the carriage pulled up Bingley stepped forward to greet his good friend, Sir Richard, with a warm handshake and a broad smile then helped the lady to descend. The threesome walked together towards the house. Bingley was excusing Jane's absence because she was presently in confinement and that he expected to be a father of something very soon. Elizabeth wanted to say that she desired to be with Jane at this time but the heavy week of the Mannings, arranging the affairs of Pemberley and the journey, left her exhausted. She asked the gentlemen to excuse her and possibly a maid could show her to her room. Elizabeth explained that she would rest for half an hour before seeing Jane.

Elizabeth did not wake until the following morning. She stirred only when her maid opened the curtains to let in the sunlight. At first, she had not realized that she had slept through the afternoon and throughout the night.

The maid bid Elizabeth a good morning then said smiling, "Your ladyship, I have instructions to inform you that you are an auntie again."

Elizabeth was surprised and taken aback. Her first thoughts were that she must hear from Jane first if the baby was a boy or a girl.

"Oh please, do not say if I am an aunt to a boy or a girl. I wish to learn this from my sister."

"I have had strict instructions on this very matter, milady." The maid assured Elizabeth while smiling more broadly this time.

With all haste, Elizabeth dressed to prepare herself to meet Jane and the baby.

The maid guided Elizabeth along seemingly endless corridors and staircases to a corner of the sunny side of the house. She knocked gently on the door, opened it and announced, "Lady Elizabeth Darcy, curtsied and left closing the door on the three sole occupants.

Elizabeth advanced across the expanse of the room to Jane's bedside. Jane was nursing a newborn baby. Elizabeth caught her breath as she saw the beautiful child, sleeping peacefully.

"I do not think that I can ever get used to seeing a new born baby. Each time, each baby seems the more handsome. Was there ever such a baby?"

Then she turned to Jane, but now with tears in her eyes. Elizabeth leaned over the bed to cuddle Jane and kiss her.

"How I have missed you Jane, my dear sister, so many times I have wanted to talk to you; to ask you a question or to tell you of piece of news. Tell me now, how are you?"

"I am well and have no discomfort at all. I know what you mean about wanting to talk with me; I have felt exactly that way."

Elizabeth responded, "Even now, I want to ask you a question."

"Ask."

"What am I an Auntie to?"

To this they both laughed.

At length, Jane replied, "Since late last night, she has been longing to meet you."

"That explains why she is as beautiful as her mother." Elizabeth replied between giggles.

For about an hour, they talked like this until a breakfast tray arrived laden with enough for two young ladies who had not yet dined. Enough food indeed for two young ladies as though they had not eaten for several days. That was in order that no one should go hungry. By nearly mid-day Sir Richard arrived to see the baby. He expressed his pleasure to learn that Jane had delivered a daughter.

"But good looking enough to be a boy." Sir Richard confirmed to the two ladies.

Much merriment in this vein continued until lunchtime and the father arrived to join the family gathering. They followed lunch by the promised outing to some local kennels.

The party travelled in Elizabeth's coach and consisted of Sir Richard, Elizabeth and Bingley. Within about fifteen minutes, the party arrived at the kennels. This was evident from the canine expletives emanating from the premises. They were quickly ushered to the nurseries where the bitches with their puppies lived in special quarters. At each enclosure, they studied the bitch and the puppies. When they reached the third enclosure, Elizabeth stated firmly, "I want that one!"

It was a light brown dog of the Great Dane variety.

The proprietor picked up the puppy for Elizabeth to examine more closely and said, "He will be ready in about three weeks, your ladyship."

Elizabeth looked at Sir Richard who seemed much amused by the situation. "Do you also like him?"

"I do Elizabeth; I think you have chosen well."

This pleased her. Elizabeth cuddled the baby dog to her. She felt something that she could not explain but that she did want the puppy more than anything else in the world.

The formalities were completed and they returned to Lilac Time. Here was news to impart indeed.

Upon their return to Lilac Time, Elizabeth made her way to Jane's rooms. The sisters engaged themselves in conversations of their families and general affairs. Jane held little enthusiasm for Elizabeth's puppy while so engrossed with her own new charge. The subject of Anne they examined but they were unable to throw any further light on the affair.

During the evening, after dinner, Jane received everyone in her room. She missed having company and so much wanted to re-engage with the family and worldly affairs. In addition, she wanted to announce the name of her baby. Sir Richard and Elizabeth entered Jane's room together after the hour for dinner. Jane was nursing her baby to show her to everyone. Some of Bingley's neighbours had arrived with presents for the baby. All were keen to learn of Jane's decision regarding the baby's name. Glasses were filled while they all waited in anticipation for the announcement.

At the time, Jane, nursing her baby had her back on the company. Turning round and with a big smile and much obvious pleasure Jane declared her choice.

"We have pondered on many names. We have thought at some length on this commission. After much consideration, her name I have chosen is my favourite name of all. She is to be Christened "Elizabeth" after my dear sister and her aunt".

Jane and Elizabeth looked at each other, both smiling to express much happiness.

The party cheered and wished the baby Elizabeth a long and happy life. A hearty toast followed with more congratulations and all avowed the baby to be the prettiest thing they had ever seen.

The following three weeks, the men pursued their hunting and fishing while the sisters engaged with the baby and domestic affairs. When the time came for departure, Elizabeth and Sir Richard were made to promise to return and often.

"As soon as the baby is old enough to travel we shall bring her for you to see." Bingley avowed.

In good humour, Sir Richard replied, "If you do not, we will be returning here to know the reason."

Sir Richard and Lady Darcy stopped at the kennels to collect their new charge. With much persuasion and a little force, they got the puppy to enter the carriage but spent the whole journey whimpering on the floor. He appeared decidedly unhappy all the way to Pemberley. Upon arrival home, Elizabeth let the poor animal descend with much trepidation from the carriage by himself. Once on solid ground he ran round about, sometimes in circles and sometimes investigating his new surroundings. Whilst behaving in this puppy canine fashion he would return for short seconds to Elizabeth for, apparently, reassurance. Sir Richard declared that the dog would be all right and they proceeded into the house.

Chapter Seven

From Lilac Time to Pemberley

The morning that followed their return from Lilac Time, Sir Richard and Elizabeth breakfasted with conversation that centered around the beastly pest that insisted on playing with the ends of Elizabeth's skirts and Sir Richard bootstraps. With the morning dining complete, they took to the stables to begin their morning exercise. The puppy not yet named, remained at the stables to familiarize him with his equine friends while the master and his lady rode on the estate. To give some purpose to their outing they decided to call at the Mannings to enquire of their young daughter.

While on the road to their tenant's house, they met with the steward riding away from that very place. His countenance was one of great pleasure. The morning greetings completed, their attentions focused on the Mannings.

"Mannings called on me early this morning. He needed access to the furniture you promised to lend to Sir Rufus so I let him into the store. It is even now being delivered, Sir Richard."

"That's very good Jenkins. This is excellent, to find him reliable."

"And, that's not all, sir. He must be prospering. He has given me this very morning the quarters rent in full. Good luck to him, I say, sir."

"Just so, just so, Jenkins. Is this due to his new business do you know?"

"I am given to understand it is sir. He is now planning to buy another horse and a larger wagon."

"Is that wise so soon, do you suppose?"

"He seems to know his business. Let him prosper I say."

They made their good byes and parted in good humour.

"Your trust in our tenants appears to be justified, Elizabeth."

"Yes, so it would seem. Let us go to enquire of the daughter's health now and we may learn more."

The two riders took their horses apace to reach the Mannings in good time. After their neighbours had worked hard to help the family and with good management by the Mannings, the cottage and the surroundings looked impressive with a promise of much production.

As Sir Richard and Elizabeth reached the front door, it opened and Mrs Mannings presented herself and invited her guests to enter. Sir Richard had to stoop to enter through the door and inside he seemed almost to fill the living room. Mrs Mannings began to apologize for the absence of her husband.

"He has a delivery to make with his horse and cart." She explained. "If he had any idea that you were coming he would be certain to be here."

"Please do not concern yourself, Mrs Mannings. We wanted to see how well your daughter was recovering." Elizabeth assured her.

"Oh, your ladyship, she *is* improved. Mr. Mannings has taken his little Jennifer with him on his delivery this morning. The doctor said she would be well in a week and she was. She is the light of his life. Er . . . my husband's I mean. That she is."

Elizabeth asked, "His business is going well?"

"Why, yes your ladyship. He is busy from morning until night. I rarely see him now. He is always out this way and that and he comes back with such tales."

"And you, Mrs Mannings, how have you managed through these troubled times?"

"Your ladyship, I beg your pardon but I do not give much attention to myself. My concerns are for my family. If they are well, I am well. Just now, I have never felt better in my life."

Much warmed by this good news, Sir Richard and Elizabeth took their leave.

Elizabeth was in some haste to return to the stables. Her concern was for her puppy. She found him yelping inside the stables apparently completely lost. As soon as he saw Elizabeth, he ran towards her as excited as anything she had ever seen. The animal was so excited that she feared that he may cause himself some harm. To prevent him being over excited a stable lad came forward and picked him up. The boy stroked him until he was still. He calmed the puppy and then put him on the ground before Elizabeth.

The boy bowed slightly to Elizabeth, "Your ladyship."

"What is your name, young man?"

"Edward Harwood, your ladyship."

"Well, thank you Harwood. That was good of you."

Elizabeth picked up the puppy to take him to the house. She was following Sir Richard. As Sir Richard realized that Elizabeth was following him, he stopped and waited for her. As she approached, Sir Richard suggested that it would be more comfortable for her and the puppy to let him walk along with them. She put the puppy on the ground and to her amusement discovered how loyal he was even at this very young age. The puppy ran alongside, and then he would veer off to examine a blade of grass or a flower then return to her side.

As they walked along with the dog, she thought how everything seemed, at last, to be going well. Jane had her baby without mishap, they had solved the Mannings problem without eviction and her puppy gave her so much pleasure. Sir Richard, who had a good eye for a dog, had approved of him even from the beginning. The sun was shinning and she could feel the warmth of it.

The only blot on the horizon was that of the fate of Anne. Nobody could find her nor had any idea what fate could have befallen her. "Could she still be alive?" Elizabeth thought.

Then her mind recalled the tragedy of Charlotte. Charlotte was not alive and never would be. "Is it better that Anne should be missing for ever, not knowing if she is alive or dead and if dead, by what deed? Or is it better to know exactly what has happened as with Charlotte?"

Sir Richard brought her back from her introspections by, "We may have mail this morning. Let us hasten to the house."

Elizabeth increased her pace to keep abreast with her husband though she was in a thoughtful mood still. "We must give him a name so that we may summon him to us."

Sir Richard responded, "We? Madam, he is your dog so you must name him."

At the house, he examined the mail and pulled out a letter bearing a familiar coat of arms. "A word from the colonel, at last!" Sir Richard announced.

"What news sir, will you read it aloud this time?"

He unfolded the letter and while reading, "I will leave out the personal pleasantries. He says that they nearly captured Marcel at the inn but he escaped . . . They are on his trail . . . more men sent to engage him . . . we are confident of an arrest soon."

"That is good news indeed sir, is there more?

"Yes. He writes that he wishes to pay a visit to Pemberley. Would next Wednesday be convenient for about seven days, perhaps a little more?"

"But yes! The dear colonel does not have to wait for an invitation. By all means, come next Wednesday or sooner if he prefers and longer if he wants."

He adds, "There have been no sightings of our family of gypsies. He fears the worst. The French who killed two of the gypsy men may have found the gypsies again and finished the rest off. Over the entire South of England the regulars and the local militia have searched every bye way and village of the country. Many gypsies have been encountered but none of that would fit the description of Barnie's family"

They both fell into a very pensive mood for a while. Sir Richard picked up another letter. Upon reading the recipient's name, he looked at Elizabeth to say, "This is for you, my dear."

Elizabeth sprang back from the depths of her thoughts to discover her letter was from Mary. "My sister Mary is caring for Charlotte's baby. They call her Boo-Boo because she used to cry so much after her mother died poor thing."

Unfolding the letter, Elizabeth read and recounted to Sir Richard but omitting the details, "My dear Eliza, I have important news for you. Please do not be alarmed, the baby and I are in perfect health and so is Mr. Collins. We have discussed the situation in detail and we now consider the time is right to make an announcement. I am so apprehensive because I am afraid of your disapproval. However, beyond our love for each other, if you think about the arrangement it is the most sensible, even a God given opportunity for us. I do hope that you will rejoice with the entire household and Mr. Collins and I, here at The Parsonage, as we announce our engagement this week. Our father agrees. He even considers the event providential to help to calm our mother's nerves."

Elizabeth looked up from reading the letter to learn of her husband's opinion of this announcement.

"Yes, yes, I am surprised how often I agree with your father. Very providential when you think the events through. We must send them our best wishes and hope for an invitation to the wedding."

"Elizabeth read on, please."

She continued, "Lady Catherine has been taken uncommonly ill with anxiety just recently due wholly, we think, to the disappearance of Anne. Lady Catherine approves also of our engagement and goes as far as to offer the facilities of Rosings for the wedding celebrations. Mr. Collins and I wish to send you both our love and all best wishes. Your loving sister, Mary.""

Elizabeth put the letter down and looked for a reaction from Sir Richard.

He responded, "If my aunt approves there can be no impropriety, you can depend on it."

"So Mary and Mr. Collins are to be married after all. I will reply immediately and assure them of our blessings and good wishes. I shall ask for dates and details. Of course, I will press for an early response."

"Be sure, when you write to your father, to send him my best regards."

"Thank you sir, I shall be pleased to send your best regards to my father."

"Also, inform your father that the autumn fair will be held shortly and he is welcome to come."

"That will please him greatly. I . . . shall call him . . . Ganymede."

"Does your father not already have a name?"

"But of course he does. I mean my *puppy*,"

Chapter Eight

The Colonel Calls

The following morning, after breakfast, Sir Richard waited at the stables for his lady to arrive. He was impatient to start as early as possible because Colonel Fitzwilliam had confirmed his arrival this day. Sir Richard summoned a stable lad to send a message to the house to inform her ladyship that he was eager to make an early start.

The boy returned and delivered the message that her ladyship would be along shortly.

Sir Richard decided to remain in the saddle and to take Elizabeth's horse towards the house so that she had not so far to walk. At a distance, that would be about halfway to the house, he met Elizabeth making haste towards him. He was surprised to find that she was not in her riding habit.

"Elizabeth, are you not riding today?"

"I regret not sir, nor for a little while yet."

"What is the matter, are you so indisposed? Are you not well?"

"I am very well, thank you sir. The doctor suggested that I refrain from riding in case I have a fall."

Sir Richard dismounted and looked at Elizabeth more closely.

"The doctor? You look well enough, why should you have a fall? You sit well in the saddle."

"Thank you sir. It is not I for whom I fear to hurt from a fall."

"Elizabeth, I do not understand you. Who else could you hurt? You would not hurt me if you fell, or your horse, or my horse either. Why should the doctor tell you not to ride because you might hurt someone else?"

In some corner of Sir Richard Darcy's mind, a primitive yet timeless arousal seemed to expand to the most distant outer reaches of the cosmos and even beyond. At the same time, he knew that he was standing on his Pemberley ground. In the fresh morning air, and the smell of newly cut grass, Sir Richard could hear the birds singing. He could feel the sun on his shoulders beginning to warm on him and on the earth and everything. With that warmth, a new light was dawning.

"Elizabeth, are you trying to tell me something special?"

"Sir Richard Darcy, I think you may soon become a father."

"My dearest Elizabeth, my dearest Elizabeth, are you sure you feel well? Is there anything I can do?"

"Shall we walk to the stables Sir Richard? I shall not be wanting my horse for a little while."

"Yes, we will walk him back, and mine also I have other things on my mind today."

"We both have sir."

On their return to the house, Sir Richard was particularly attentive to his lady. They took their morning wine earlier than usual. They talked of Colonel Fitzwilliam and of Anne. "Now that she was no longer among us, it is of no consequence if she was alive or dead, for all practical purposes. We shall never know if they are brother and sister." Elizabeth mused.

Sir Richard agreed and added, "If her mother does not know, who else could know but the Good Lord?"

"They could never take the chance. Their marriage would have been unthinkable."

The door opened and a servant stepped into the room to make the announcement,

"Colonel Fitzwilliam." He bowed and left.

Sir Richard greeted his friend and cousin with the warmest of handshakes. With no delay, the colonel then engaged Elizabeth with a warm greeting. He remarked on her healthy appearance.

This he followed by, "Elizabeth, I have a surprise for you. I have brought someone with me I know you will be pleased, no . . . *very* pleased to see again."

Elizabeth looked at Sir Richard. Sir Richard looked at Elizabeth. Both were of one thought, "Anne"

Elizabeth pleaded, "Wait but a moment, for I know Georgiana would most earnestly wish to see her."

Without waiting, the door began to open but just a little. With the door ajar, a head peeked around the gap, a smiling giggling face appeared.

"Hello, everyone." She called out and the sylph like body of Lydia slipped into the room.

The tension of the suspense broke and everyone laughed. All the attention was on Lydia and she was enjoying it.

Elizabeth was delighted to see her. She could see that Lydia was holding something under her arm. "May I enquire what you have under your arm Lydia? It is not a soldier's hat, I hope."

"Lord no, sister, it is William, Mary's dog. They are so busy at The Parsonage that Mary asked me to care for him until afterwards."

"Afterwards, Lydia? Afterwards what may I enquire?"

"It is a secret, I promised not to tell anyone, it is such a secret"

Elizabeth knew the secret but was determined to have her fun with her young sister.

"If it is such a secret why should they tell you and ask you to care for William? Surely you are exhibiting that Mr. Collins and Mary are about something?"

"Surely they cannot be about anything special." Lydia declared.

"What could possibly cause such a disturbance in their household that would be such a secret? What could be so *engaging* that Mr. Collins and Mary must be planning that would be such a secret? Elizabeth emphasized, "Engaging."

Lydia put her hand over her mouth and looked astounded, "You know!" She laughed followed by the party who had been studying the event.

Lydia held William up to show him and said to Elizabeth, "William has met the King of England. Dogs are so adorable. You should have yourself a dog, Elizabeth, they are such good fun."

"Perhaps, one day I may." Elizabeth answered, preparing good humour with her sister until she discovers Ganymede.

"We have come from home and I have a letter for you from your father, Elizabeth."

"You mean that you have come from Longbourn?"

"We have come from home because . . . can I."

She looked towards the colonel for approval.

With a resigned smile and a nod from the colonel but all in good humour, Lydia concluded, "We want you to be the first to know why we called at Longbourn to speak to father. Colonel Fitzwilliam has asked me to be his wife and father has *agreed*!" Lydia emphasized the "Agreed."

There was an extended silence, broken by Sir Richard almost shouting with high approval. He took the colonel's hand and shook it so violently that the colonel was in fear of it falling off. Elizabeth summoned a servant to advise Georgiana that they required her presence in the drawing room, to hear some good news. She had another servant to bring a bottle of Champagne.

Sir Richard overheard her words and called to the servant, "Make it two bottles, Benson."

Benson acknowledged Sir Richard's request with a slight bow.

Within a few minutes, the Champagne and Georgiana arrived together. The celebrations continued for the rest of the morning, broken only by Lydia's protestations of hunger.

Georgiana and Lydia were not well acquainted but began their friendship immediately upon meeting. Over lunch, Lydia spoke incessantly about The Earl, the colonel's father. Lydia told of their meeting and how well disposed he was to give his approval. "Lord, the Earl was so, that I wondered who I was to marry, the father or the son. Anyway, after that we visited Longbourn to see my mother and father. She, Heaven bless her, was almost ill with the pleasure of it all. My father, well, being so far distracted, he could not speak, I must tell you, for a five whole minutes.

Eventually, he removed his glasses then he said, "I always thought you were destined for greater things. My dear Lydia, my blessings on you both and your union."

During an informal lunch, Lydia and the colonel learned of the course of events at The Parsonage at Hunsford. The conversation steered itself towards the fate of Anne de Bourgh. All declared a deep sorrow for the loss of one of the family and promised never to forget her. From there, the conversations lead on to the gypsies. It fell upon the colonel to detail the events of the gypsies and the investigations made all over the South of England.

The colonel continued with first, the near arrest of Marcel. "He slipped through our fingers again but I am confident that it will not be long before we have him behind bars. His first escape at the inn was too good to have been just luck. We are now of the persuasion that the innkeeper is in league with him. We think that he gave assistance to Marcel. One reason for our thinking is that the rider who took flight was not Marcel, so that when our men caught up with him it proved to be a diversion. The rider, who ever he was, left a trail that was easy to follow. However, a trail that would slow down his pursuers. When my men returned to the inn, the innkeeper was very chirpy, displaying an outward appearance of uncustomary light spirits."

Lydia and Georgiana were not interested in the news of something they had no prior knowledge. They talked together for a few minutes and then asked the company to excuse them. They continued their conversations still as they left the company but bent on pleasure.

Elizabeth was disgusted that an Englishman could even think of betraying his own. Sir Richard was the more shocked because he had engaged the innkeeper in conversation.

He searched his mind for the words that passed between them trying to recall if he had said anything deleterious.

The afternoon absorbed the interests of everyone who could point a gun. Elizabeth introduced Ganymede to his, "Aunty" Lydia and William, which proved great entertainment. They concluded the day with cards and music after the dinner.

It was another week until the Servants' Ball would take place.

Chapter Nine

The Ball at Wynnstay

Nearly a week had passed since Colonel Fitzwilliam arrived at Pemberley, when the housekeeper of Wynnstay House called with the invitation for the servants' ball. Sir Richard received the invitation on behalf of the servants with great alacrity. With further delight, he discovered from the invitation that it was to be a masked ball.

Sir Richard passed on the invitation for the pleasure of the staff. That day, at Pemberley House and for the following week, the hearts, minds and steps of the staff were lighter than they had been for a full twelve months.

Finally, the day and time arrived for the Ball. Several carriages and wagons were engaged to transport the servants from one house to the other. As the servants left in their divers means of conveyances, Sir and Lady Darcy, the colonel, Lydia and Georgiana were present on the forecourt to wish the revellers an enjoyable evening. They waved to the merry passengers as they left and continued waving until they were out of sight.

Sir Rufus was keen to equal the previous year's ball at Pemberley. The staff had laid out a lavish buffet banquet. Sir Rufus and Lady Penelope opened the dancing. The staffs applauded them enthusiastically. Sir Rufus then wished them a merry ball and left the staff to their own pleasures. The ball continued in excellent good humour all evening. As the time had come to close the event, Sir Rufus reappeared. He held his arms outstretched, forwards, hands waving downwards faced, in a manner to subdue the merrymaking. The gay staffs stopped their talking and laughter and all activities ceased. When all was quiet, he raised his hand, holding high a sheet of paper. He very solemnly announced some news from Pemberley House of which he thought they should learn. He looked down at the paper and began reading.

"I and my Lady Elizabeth would take pleasure in inviting all our staff to join that of Wynnstay House to our staff ball at Pemberley this very day next year. Signed Sir Richard Darcy."

The people exploded in many variations of noises expressing their delight. These noises gradually reduced into a collective hand clapping to demonstrate their approval. The festivities then ceased and the staffs went their way. The staff of Pemberley sought out their conveyances to return home.

Sir Richard and Lady Elizabeth met the returning staff of Pemberley to greet them with their best wishes and hoped that they had an enjoyable evening. There was much jocularity as the staff still in a gay celebrating mood arrived at the house. One staff member remarked in good humour as he was passing by Sir Richard, "At least next year we will not have so far to go."

The following morning, Sir Richard engaged the colonel to accompany him riding on the estate. Sir Richard was eager to show off the improvements he and Lady Elizabeth had brought about. One call they made was to the Mannings family. Mr. Mannings was abroad with his deliveries but Mrs Mannings made them both welcome and expounded profusely on her improved situation.

They left Mrs Mannings. The colonel much impressed with the exercise that had been so successful, he was trying to congratulate Sir Richard for his aptitude. Sir Richard would have none of it. He explained how it was that Elizabeth did not want her arrival to Pemberley to coincide with an eviction. Sir Richard explained she even suspended their rent until we could find them a better situation.

"Darcy, you certainly found yourself a worthy lady there. I have no loss of pride to say to you, if you had not seen her first, I should have thought seriously of her."

"Colonel, I am pleased you did not notice her earlier. Have I told you that she refused my first proposal, just as she did with Mr. Collins?"

"How could she compare you with Mr. Collins that she should refuse your proposal? No Darcy that cannot be."

"She said in refusing me, "You are the last man in the world I would ever marry!""

"Yet she did, with a great deal of persuasion on your part, I'll be bound."

"You are mistaken again, colonel, I did not ask her again and she did not say yes at any time, except at the ceremony. It just happened in conversation. The persuasion, as you put it, was due to the learning, she said, of my true character. Her ideas of me had been so ill that nothing could tempt her at first. She informed me so."

So deep in conversation were Sir Richard and the colonel that they had not realized their horses had wandered towards the site of the forthcoming fair on the Pemberley Estate. Upon realizing their location, Sir Richard stopped and looked round. Even now, there were people camping, some in tents and others in makeshift shelters.

"Let us take a closer look at these people."

They edged their horses slowly up to the nearest shelter to engage the occupants and discover what they could. The shelter was half a tent-like covering and half of a small cart, pulled by their nearby tethered pony, they presumed. The occupant was on a cushion sitting half in and half out of his shelter. Deeply engaged as he was with the activities of his trade, he did not at first notice the gentlemen on horseback looking at him.

The colonel leaned forward in his saddle, introduced himself to the man and asked of his business.

"My business? My business, zur, is pots and pans for cooking. All me life zur, 'Oive bought and sold and mended pots and pans all over.

"Good life then sir?"

"Wouldn't wont no other zur."

"Why," Colonel posed the question, "Have you come here to Derbyshire?"

"T'is t'e fair zur. We all cum for t'e fair."

The man look around at his fellow itinerates camped about and passed his hand about with a wave of his arm to indicate the others.

"Do you know them all? Are they all your friends?"

"I knows 'em not zur, but many oi 'av seen afore."

"Were you here at last year's fair?"

"Nay zur, but t'folks says it be t'best un in t'country. So's I cum 'ere zur."

"Well, I do hope you have a very good fair and your friends also."

"Why, thank 'e zur. You're a gent that you are."

"Tell me, are there any foreigners amongst the others here. Perhaps French people?"

"Oi knows of none zur."

"Well, thank you. A good day to you."

"A good day t'e too zur."

The two gentlemen continued on their way. They talked of the preparations they needed yet to be making for the fair. Their progress halted as they realized that they had arrived at the field where the gypsies made their camp the previous year. Their memories of the terrible dealings of the Frenchmen brought their senses some disgust.

The colonel looked around at the deserted field, "I imagine that this will be unoccupied this year. It is all very sad. It is the not knowing. Human souls lost in time and country. If I can do anything to avenge those deeds I will use my powers to the utmost."

"Perhaps we should let it be unoccupied until they are avenged? I shall call this field, "Gypsy Field" and allow it remain fallow and for the grass only. When we return to the house, I shall have the grass cut and the farmers can have it for their animals' winter aliment."

"That Darcy is an excellent idea."

They walked their horses around the field while both concerned in deep introspections. Darcy stopped by the hedge and looked down at the ground. I shall have a sign erected here immediately to make it known that this is Gypsy Field. The colonel said nothing; he was still deep in thought. They then made their way back to the house.

The return to the house by the two men lifted their spirits and gained a better humour. A messenger was waiting for the colonel with special military dispatches for his immediate attention. In haste, the colonel took charge of his communications. One paper in particular he pulled from the sheaf and declared, "By gad we have him sir!"

Sir Richard who was just leaving the room turned quickly to hear the details, for those few words were all-informative to him.

"You have the Frenchman, Colonel?"

It is a secret, Lord; we are all secrets here, that we captured him on the road to London . . . Marcel, we now have him detained in Reading under strong guard. The colonel continued reading then announced, "We have him securely behind bars and under examination. We have much to question on his activities and on the possibility of the disappearance of Miss Anne de Bourgh."

Pulling out more sheets from the sheave, the colonel engaged himself enthusiastically to their study. "I read here that he has been questioned and that his men hold Miss Anne de Bourgh captive. His release and safe passage back to Calais will secure Miss Anne de Bourgh's safety and freedom in return. Darcy, they have my sister. They are holding Anne prisoner."

"Colonel, we must keep calm heads and take our time. If you have the man, the lady is safe."

"Now this has become personal. I must think this through."

In need of distraction, the gentlemen sought out the ladies. They were practicing their archery. Elizabeth proved to be the most competent but Georgiana and Lydia were improving under her tutelage.

With the arrival of the gentlemen, they all agreed on a competition. They would know who was the best archer.

In jovial spirit, each suggested prizes. The only solution was. a hat for a gentleman if he won, or a bonnet for a lady, if a lady won. Because they all felt the need for refreshments, they abandoned the exercise for another time. That evening, after dinner, the colonel excused himself from their company in order to write military dispatches. Sir Richard and the ladies made a play at cards. By this means and with some music by Georgiana and Elizabeth in turn, they engaged the evening pleasantly.

The colonel gave orders for the dispatch of his letters at an early hour at the following morning.

Several days passed in this fashion. The colonel eventually won the bonnet a hat not being available.

The colonel was always in haste to write some letter, either of something of his thoughts, or in reply to one of the many dispatches that arrived for him.

The fair grounds and its surrounding areas were filling with newcomers. Even now, many traders had erected their stalls and trade between the stallholders appeared brisk.

As the time became closer to the opening day, the environs of the fair site began to fill up with traders and buyers. Musicians played their instruments, tumblers exercised their skills and stallholders crying out their wares gave a festive atmosphere as though it was already open properly. However, on the morning before the fair was to begin officially, a party of gypsies arrived and camped in the field with the sign, "Gypsy Field" displayed on a board.

As quickly as they made the discovery of gypsies in their field, the whisper of the gypsy presence passed all around the camp. The gypsies often brought novelties from distant places. They always lent colour, an excitement, and a certain curiosity to the events. The word of the arrival of the gypsies soon travelled to the stables of the big house and then to the big house. A servant had reason to attend Sir Richard and while carrying out his duties he took it upon himself to pass the information to his master. Without exception, the staff was aware of the interest that lay with Sir Richard and Lady Elizabeth in the gypsies.

The moment that Sir Richard received the information, his thoughts threw him into a mental maelstrom. His own anxieties were in confusion for not being certain. He tried to compose his mind, "If there really were gypsies in the field, were they the gypsies we have been looking for all over the South of England? Could this be possible?"

He thought also to tell Elizabeth but realized that if they were not our family of gypsies she might raise her hopes only to dash them down to utter disappointment. Breaking from his accounting, he sought out the colonel. He was examining military papers but appeared to be pleased to attend his friend.

Sir Richard explained of his problems with the gypsies. "Should I go with or without Elizabeth to see them, or check first to only to discover who they are? If they are our own gypsies I could return for Elizabeth."

"Sir Richard, let us go together. We must first discover them. I have to tell you that we have sought the family all over the South of England and could not find them or anyone who knew of them. I cannot imagine this party to be our own gypsy friends."

It was thus agreed and the two gentlemen walked briskly to the stables. Both were in deep thought each not wanting to raise the expectations of the other, they walked in silence.

Both in the saddle, they approached the field, Sir Richard was certain that he could identify a figure walking towards the field. He pressed his horse faster and as he approached nearer to the figure, the old man turned round. Upon seeing Sir Richard, he took off his hat. Sir Richard dismounted even before his horse had stopped. He held out his hand and with the most agreeable smile said, "Barnie, where have you been?"

Barnie standing looking at Sir Richard, did not at first, know him for certain. As they came closer together, Barnie could see who he was. He took Sir Richard's hand and said, "Mr. Darcy zur, t'is very good t'see 'e again."

Chapter Ten

The Pemberley Fair

With the greatest of enthusiasm, Colonel Fitzwilliam descended his mount and took the hand of Barnie. They talked for some minutes while Sir Richard studied the gypsy encampment at a distance. Everything appeared to be normal. He recognized some faces but not all. He could not see the women whose child had the accident with Elizabeth's horse. He had not seen her within close proximity but should be able to recognize her general appearance. He returned to the colonel and Barnie.

"I am so very pleased to see you here again, Barnie, and in robust health. I know my wife would also like to see you all again. We have been looking for you all over the country and here you are again, safe, sound and altogether. Perhaps we could spend another evening as we did before?"

"Oi would be onered t'ave e as my guest Mr. Darcy."

"Thank you Barnie. In much better circumstances this time. My wife would be delighted to see you all again. May I go and bring her back?"

Barnie smiled and nodded.

Sir Richard turned to the colonel and said, "Will you go too? Elizabeth will insist on seeing Barnie again but she must not ride. We must find a dog cart."

The colonel had not learned yet of Elizabeth's condition and he puzzled over Sir Richard's words. Thinking that there was something more in his words than he could decipher, agreed readily.

They assured Barnie that they would return with all haste. They then spun their horses round to take them at a pace, back to the house.

Finding Elizabeth was an easy employment. When the colonel told her about Barnie, she was all excitement. Georgiana and Lydia could not understand their cousin showing such extreme delights because a gypsy had camped in a field close by.

Sir Richard sought out a stable lad to secure a dogcart and take it to the house for Lady Elizabeth and Colonel Fitzwilliam. The cart arrived with a groom in full livery for her ladyship.

With Elizabeth in the dogcart, Sir Richard and the colonel rode back towards Gypsy Field. Elizabeth was all excitement but at the approach to the site, the ground became so bumpy that she could not cope. She insisted that she should walk. As she descended carefully from the cart, Elizabeth espied a figure that she thought she recognized. The face was a little dirty and the clothes looked less than the best but the countenance was unmistakable. The woman was carrying eggs in an apron that she had, tied around her waist. Elizabeth stood and stared all the time trying to make sense of what her eyes were telling her. The woman turned her head to look in Elizabeth's direction. Immediately it showed that she recognized Elizabeth. The woman gathered the top of her apron to hold the eggs in a big sling, slipped off the apron from her waist and gently laid the eggs on the ground, then ran towards Elizabeth. Elizabeth tried to call the woman's name but her throat would not. Her throat was dry because of the shock. Elizabeth opened her arms in welcome and showed a smile to match. Anne threw herself into Elizabeth's waiting arms, "My dearest, dearest Elizabeth."

Bewildered to distraction, the two men could not understand why Elizabeth was showing such affection to a gypsy girl. As the ladies parted their embrace, they chattered garrulously to each other both asking questions, though neither gave nor waited for any answers.

For sometime the gentlemen continued talking with Barnie while occasionally, throwing concerned glances towards the ladies. The colonel was the first cry out, "Anne!" In spite of the gypsy clothing, the smudgy face, and dishevelled hair, the colonel recognized his sister. Sir Richard became startled and again, he could not understand what had overtaken his friend. Upon hearing the cry of "Anne" from Fitzwilliam, he turned from Barnie with a polite bow to say, "Please excuse me one moment, Barnie."

Slowly and in utter disbelief, he made his way to the threesome of whom the ladies were weeping tears and the gentleman with moistened eyes yet.

Sir Richard reached the party and stared at his cousin. She looked just like another gypsy but this was undoubtedly his cousin and at one time, intended partner. Looking into her eyes, he noticed no difference. This was indeed Anne, for whom the military had searched the South of England all over.

"My dearest Anne, where have you been?" He took her in his arms and held her close in spite of her state.

"Mr. Darcy, I have been with my new family. I am married now. Happily and gloriously married to the man I love. I once thought it would have been the dear colonel but our family affairs decreed otherwise. Would . . . could I introduce my husband, Sacha to you? I think you might be too proud?"

"If he is truly your husband, he is part of the family now. Pride has nothing to do with anything. Is your husband a gypsy then?"

"Yes he is and I want to follow him wherever he goes. I truly love him more that any other man I have ever known. It is of no consequence to me whether he is a king or a pauper, I love him and he is my husband and my life."

"But you are the heiress of Rosings Park; do you not wish to live there in comfort and luxury?"

"These things are as nothing to me when I feel my love for Sacha. I have little, perhaps less discomfort, amongst my new family, I believe. Come let me introduce you and the others to my husband."

Anne took his hand and turned to Elizabeth and the Colonel, "Come with me to my caravan and I will introduce you to the man in my life."

Barnie watched them go towards the camp then turned to continue his work.

Anne ran forward up to the embankment surrounding the field and the camp, clambered to the top and stood looking. She leaned slightly forward and with her hands cupped around her mouth called out her husband's name, "Sacha" and waved enthusiastically. Sacha stopped with his work and looked up. He waved back to his wife but curious to why she should be calling him. Anne turned to urge her relations to climb the embankment to see Sacha. As they reached the top, they too waved. The gypsy also was waving but upon seeing the party waving apparently to him, he waved back more vigorously without knowing to whom he was waving or why. He stopped his work to make good his way to the party who were descending the inner side of the rampart. Sacha made his progress towards Anne to discover what was afoot. They met as the rest of the party was still making their way.

"These are my relatives and your relatives now, Sacha."

He looked up at the approaching company.

"I will introduce you to our family. This is Lady Elizabeth, Sir Richard Darcy and this is my brother, Colonel Fitzwilliam."

She then turned to Sacha and introduced her husband to her relatives.

Barnie arrived on the scene.

Sacha jocularly introduced his family, "And this is my family, ladies and gentlemen, my father, Barnie."

To which Sacha added, "I remember you all, at the time of the river crossing."

The assembly laughed heartily, putting them in a more jovial and relaxed mood.

As they continued to talk, the subject of an evening with the gypsies arose. Sir Richard promised venison and would have offered more but Barnie insisted that they had all they needed to feed a whole regiment of infantry. However, he would not refuse the venison.

The party from the house stayed at Barnie's request in order to introduce them to the family. They visited every caravan in turn with Barnie presenting each caravan owner. Elizabeth was amazed at the orderliness and cleanliness of each caravan's interior. The caravans were small and barely adequate but so appeared that gypsies proudly maintained their homes inside and out. The wheels looked like new to the visitors, as shiny and freshly painted as any wheel they had ever seen. The campsite all over, they kept clean and tidy. Having completed the round of every gypsy and their caravans, it was evident to the visitors that the woman who lived in the village and was the mother of the little boy who was injured, was not with them.

The colonel explained to Barnie of their concern for the woman.

"Oh yes, she joined us for some weeks but she wasted away, they say of a broken 'art. She had lost 'er 'usband and then er boy. Then we lost 'er, Lord bless 'er."

"That is very sad, Barnie." The colonel reflected on the harmless stripling and his proud but poor loving mother. "It must have been a preferred relief for her, Barnie?"

"T'is as we think also, zur."

"Barnie, did you know that we have been looking for you all over the country? We searched with many companies of soldiers but could not find you anywhere."

"Well, zur, that as may be but we try t'ide ourselves like cos of them Frenchies."

"You made an excellent job of it, Barnie. You outwitted even our best soldiers."

They both laughed.

It was time for the Pemberley party to return to the house. They said their goodbyes and promised to return the following afternoon with the venison.

With the dogcart turned round and the riders mounted, they made their way back to the stables in a very thoughtful mood.

At least they had learned that the gypsies were in good stead. That Anne was with them was something strange but that she was well and apparently happy was good news to learn also.

"However," Sir Richard thought, "How do I explain this to her mother and that she is now married? Not to have told her own mother was indecorous of her and beneath her family duties."

Sir Richard confided with the colonel of his thoughts.

The colonel has also been deep in thought, "I was thinking otherwise. I cannot understand how the family of gypsies could have evaded our searches. I cannot understand how we missed them, if we did. We traced them to the village where the widow woman lost her son. She joined the gypsies there and from there we tracked them southwards a short distance further. Then they disappear. There was no further trace of them. They go south, they say for the winter but there they disappeared. It is as though they walked into a mist and melted away. There must be some lessons from this which we can learn."

"We can question Anne of their travels."

"The colonel shook his head, "I doubt if she could relate any worthwhile information. She has little navigational skills, if at all. From her own account, she was lost while travelling on horse from Rosings to Pemberley without any plan or provisions. It was a desperate and a foolhardy attempt. We can try, perhaps, learn at least something from her."

There was much to consider with regard to Anne's new situation. "I wonder how legal a gypsy wedding would be." Sir Richard mused.

They arrived at the stables and Darcy dismounted to help Elizabeth from the dogcart. The groom, who had been driving, took away the cart but returned with Ganymede.

"He has been a very good boy your ladyship." He surrendered the puppy to Lady Elizabeth.

The party returned to the house to find Georgiana at the piano and Lydia dancing with an imaginary partner to the music.

Elizabeth and the gentlemen related of their experiences of the day at the gypsy camp.

Most importantly, the gentlemen explained carefully about their cousin, Anne being with the gypsies all the time.

The colonel related the biggest piece of news, "My sister, Anne has married a gypsy and is very happy and looking very well indeed."

For some little time, the company sat silently digesting this information. As the company began to understand the situation, the girls wanted to learn of the gypsy customs. They even expressed a wish to join them at their gypsy evening.

Georgiana was particularly intrigued. "How exciting, real gypsies. Can we come too? I would love to see the gypsies. Do they play violins?"

"Well, one of them plays exceedingly well but have you never heard a violin in your life?"

The colonel joined in. "You can come but on the condition that you do not marry one of them. Anne seems to be very happy with her situation yet one in the family is enough."

Chapter Eleven

A Knight with the Gypsies

The next morning, the entire family residing at Pemberley was experiencing mixed feelings regarding the prospects of their visit to the gypsy camp. Georgiana had little idea of gypsies except that they were dirty and poor people. From the stories Sir Richard, Lady Elizabeth and Colonel Fitzwilliam related, the evening implied promises of an evening of new and exciting experiences. The romantic ideas of the young ladies conjured up handsome men playing violins with a rose between their teeth and women dancing and singing. With these images and furthered by tales from the gentlemen the young ladies were all agog. Their impatience for the afternoon was extreme.

To convey two young ladies to the campsite the party decided it apt for them to travel by donkey, while Elizabeth's preference was for the dogcart. The venison travelled with Elizabeth.

The journey to the campsite took the party past the stallholders and their campsite. Many waved and called out in good humour as the party passed by. On their arrival at the gypsy field, several of the young gypsy boys ran forward to take the venison. While they held it high as they carried the carcass in a triumphant procession to the centre of the camp, women and children were cheering and clapping. After placing the venison on a table, the cooks mounted the body on a spit. Boys rotated it slowly, taking turns with their novel task as a labour of both fun and prestige. Other gypsy children were overjoyed at seeing the donkeys and begged to be able to ride them. Georgiana and Lydia took much pleasure in taking them on donkey rides around the campsite.

Anne and Sacha were eager to be foremost of the welcoming group to introduce their visitors to the festivities. Gypsies, gentlemen and ladies sat around the fire in the customary fashion. At first, the exchanges were jocular but gradually took on a more serious form. Sir Richard was curious to how the gypsies disappeared on their travels to the south for the winter.

Explaining his own worries and the safety of his cousin, he announced, "The military also were concerned for your safety after you were attacked by the French."

Barney replied, "We were also afeared. We always go t'south in t' winter t'escape t' 'ard winters of t'north but we always go south into Wales. So when we turned t'west t' go t' Wales we did so after dark, quiet loike an' with much speed. That way we disappear like t' French when thems run away from us."

This explanation triggered enough laughter to make good the festive atmosphere. Colonel Fitzwilliam turned to Anne to say, "So you have been to Wales?"

Anne smiled back at her brother to reply, "Yes, and what a beautiful country. Can there be anywhere to equal it? Oh, the sights I have seen and the places I have passed through, and people who are so hospitable. Never a cross word and always inviting. Then the magnificent mountain peaks topped with snow and the bays and inlets of the handsome coast. It was on the Welsh coast that Sacha and I were wed."

"Indeed?" Her brother questioned again, "Where exactly?"

"A tiny place on the edge of the world called Llanwynda. We were married in a little old church called, St. Gwyndaf's Chapel. And we may visit each year as we pass by."

Colonel Fitzwilliam, "So you were properly married?"

"Why, yes brother, just as you will be with Lydia."

"Perhaps, but with one difference, my dear Anne. Your mother will be present at our wedding."

Anne became thoughtful to say, "I own to missing many things in my gypsy life. Some things I am glad to miss, while others things I often wish I could have again. I think that must be so with most people, especially after a change of circumstances. We may not have much in worldly wealth but no amount of money can buy the love that I have and the beauty of a gypsy life."

The colonel had never witnessed his sister in a meditative mood. Her experiences had certainly shaped her character into a thoughtful young woman capable of making adjustments to her life.

Colonel Fitzwilliam made an enquiry regarding the marriage ceremonies of the gypsies and how legal were they.

"Dear brother, I am afraid that the ceremonies of the gypsies will not be recognized by the English law. Conversely, the gypsy has no need of English law only his adherence to his duties to his dependents. I have to add that dear Sacha enjoyed our Christian service very much. He took everything very seriously and he thinks that the gypsies should have something similar."

"But consider your mother, Anne. Are you not going to inform your only parent that her only daughter is safe and well?"

"Yes, I must but I do fear greatly her disapprobation. What will happen if I do not tell my mother of my new situation?"

"Your mother may die of a broken heart."

"What will happen if I did tell my mother?"

"Your mother may die of a broken heart."

"Is there nothing that can save me from this division in my life?"

"I cannot imagine."

"I have to say, brother, that while living with my mother, I was very unhappy even though I knew no other life. I yearned for something different. Now that I have found my true love, I am very happy and nothing else in the world is of greater importance. I want no other life."

"I believe your mother demands too much of you. I must warn you also that there are darker intrigues afoot of which you must be aware."

"Oh Brother! What is this? I know of no ill will about."

"Anne, you must know how the French attacked this family of gypsies last summer? They killed two men and ran off with most of the horses."

"I do not know that they were true Frenchmen who did this. I can believe that they were men who happen to be French allies who did this."

"But do you not know that we have been at war with France?"

"Yes . . . but . . . several Frenchmen were at our wedding. They did not kill anyone."

"At your wedding? Frenchmen at your wedding? Dear God, Anne, you must be mistaken."

"No not at all, Brother. They were all very congenial. Their numbers lent a merry mood to the celebrations."

"Where did they come from?"

"Originally, France I presume but they were living quite happily amongst the Welsh people."

Barnie interrupted to add. "We 'ave seen 'em now for two or three years an' mean no 'arm oim sure."

"What were they doing and why were they there?"

"They said that they were waiting for "nos amis a conquirer encore l'Angleterre." The Welsh thought it to be very funny. I too, think they meant no harm."

"Well, well, let us enjoy today and we will think more on this tomorrow."

At this declaration, gypsy women passed mugs of their ale around and the conversation changed to more jolly fancies. The children pulled hot potatoes from the fires, while others passed around plates of sliced venison with aromatic herbs. The whole family gathered round, happy to eat their meat and potatoes. After which, a desert of apples and apricots spread with honey and cream challenged the appetites of even the hungriest of the men. For sometime, they were all content to sit in silence before the warmth of the fire to digest their meal. Just the occasional remark someone would utter between which there was silence or for the odd crackle from the blazing fire. Observations on the meat or the apricots or the fire died away to complete silence for sometime. All around beyond the light of the fire was darkness. Sitting on the embankment surrounding the field, many of the stallholders and others had sat in the darkness watching the gypsy feast.

A very subdued tone, a humming made by gypsy men and women grew gradually louder until a violin joined the harmony. The beautiful, combined effect caused tears to fall down the cheeks of most in the party and the onlookers. The next was a gentle voice singing softly, an accompaniment of lovers' joys and woes. An interwoven mélange of feelings of anguish and love pulled to the uttermost at the heartstrings of everyone present.

The evening became merrier as the hours passed. With dancing and singing and more ale and wines and the fire and everything gypsy, the evening was well spent. Tiredness overcame gypsy and gentleman as they fell one by one into deep slumbers.

Daybreak found the fire cold. The ladies and gentlemen were asleep while gypsies were about their business making preparations for their contribution to the fair. Stalls and marquees were going up here and there. All was activity as preparation for the first official day of the Pemberley Fair. Sir Richard Darcy was to start the proceedings with an official opening speech. In his absence by the cause of being still asleep, Lady Elizabeth took the stand and delivered a few words. Loud cheers followed them from the stallholders and pedestrians.

With no dogcart that the groom had returned to the stables the previous evening, Elizabeth roused all her party for the return to the house. The young ladies took again to their donkeys, while the gentlemen secured their horses. Elizabeth rode behind Sir Richard for their return. As they passed by the fair people, many of them waved, smiling in convivial good cheer.

Chapter Twelve

French Return

For the two days, the Pemberley fair continued without misadventure. The gentlefolk of Pemberley, much distracted by the thoughts of the French in Wales, regarded them still as an enemy. Over the two days, the family discussed little else. Anne had assured everyone that the French, whom she had encountered at Llanwnda, were friendly but perversely pretended the long-term ambition to invade England. Then there were the colonel's dispatches that made a direct threat to Miss Anne de Bourgh's life if he did not release the Frenchman to return safely to France. This information they had not conveyed to Anne and Sacha. The gentlemen were in accord with the need to protect Anne by all possible means. To this end, the colonel sent for a company of dragoons for reassurance. This would allow the release from custody and the escorting of Marcel to Calais under great security. Notwithstanding the soldiers, it must be an extreme perilous adventure still. The vulnerability of the gypsies and Anne could be even more problematic.

The dragoons arrived to make camp on the now vacated site of the fair. The officers were to lodge at Pemberley. The soldiers' behaviour could quickly degenerate if left unoccupied. Colonel Fitzwilliam knew that he must act quickly to keep the dragoons busy to avoid disorderly conduct and to deliver Marcel to Calais.

To escort Marcel to Calais would be an excellent occupation for a detachment of the soldiers; at the same time, secure the safety of his sister, Anne. For the short stay while they prepared for the journey to Calais, the dragoons maintained an orderly company. They divided their occupation between preparations for Calais and satisfying their curiosity of the gypsies.

As the detachment of dragoons moved away from the Pemberley Estate to start their journey to Reading, the gypsies stood watching, waving and cheering to them. The military presence gave the gypsy family a sense of security. The careful selection of several soldiers continued to maintain a deterrent around the estate.

With the absence of most of the dragoons and Colonel Fitzwilliam with them, it was the intention of the gypsies to start their journeying as soon as possible. Preparations continued up until darkness fell. This would allow them to leave the Pemberley Estate safely at day break or earlier.

With the industry of preparations for taking to the road as early as possible, the gypsies had not noticed the absence of their military guards. The soldiers had ventured toward the neighbouring village of Lambton leaving one solitary sentry.

In the early hours of the morning before dawn, a group of men advanced silently towards the gypsy site. Simultaneously, two early rising gypsies were beginning to prepare for their day and departure from Derbyshire. The advancing men dealt with the utmost stealth with the sentry, killing him with a knife delivered from behind.

The gypsies played with the embers of the previous night's fire. They stirred life into them and fed that with more fuel. Quickly a small fire for warmth and cooking was ablaze. One gypsy placed a can of water to make a hot drink, enough for several of his family. The other rolled a cigar and picked up a blazing stick to light it. The low pitch-blackness seems to welcome a minimal light to let the human eye perceive through the gloom. He made out several vague figures approaching in a suspicious manner. It stirred great fear in his mind but he maintained a sober composure. The gypsy lighting his cigar continued with his habit until the cigar was properly alight. He then dowsed the lighted stick. He slowly raised himself from his sitting position, picked up the tin of hot water, and walked slowly towards the nearest caravan. Within a short time a second gypsy appeared. They both made their way towards another caravan. They entered without ceremony to wake a third gypsy.

From there they intended to wake another of their band. As they were proceeding, five of the men advancing quietly emerged from the dark to attack the three gypsies. There was no element of surprise as the attackers had hoped but immediate positive action by the gypsies that included throwing the hot water on two of the men and cudgels at the ready for the rest. The scolded men screamed aloud in French obscenities, disturbing and thus alerting the rest of the camp. More intruders joined the scene with swords drawn and screaming, this time as a battle cry. Gypsies tumbled from their caravans with whatever weapon they could find at hand in haste. The gypsies' numbers began to fall. Women, some half-dressed, made haste from their caravans. While the men engaged French steel with gypsy shillelaghs, the women found an assortment of selected offensive weapons more appropriate to meet the threat. Pitchforks, burning brands, stones and the swords from the fallen French, deployed with little skill but with great effect. The women attacked the enemy from the rear. It was a short bloody battle with many dead and wounded on both sides. The remaining French retreated hastily then fled.

The entire family of the gypsy camp satisfied that the French had withdrawn engaged themselves with the dying, nursing wounded or preparing vitals. Anne knelt beside Sacha. He lay gravely injured on the grass. His blood soaked into the grass and the soil of the Pemberley Estate. Sacha was too weak to speak but he knew that Anne was with him. This was comfort and encouragement to his will as he clung on to his life. Anne was living on a thin sliver of hope for his survival.

The staff of the big house heard the commotion from the direction of the gypsy camp and alerted the stables and the sleeping dragoons. A combined effort brought the soldiers and horses quickly ready to a fighting force. They rode at a gallop towards the gypsy camp. They met with the fleeing French. Within a few minutes, the fresh dragoons dispatched every one of the foreign contingent. The dragoons continued to the gypsy site to discover the tragedy.

A soldier returned to the big house to deliver the news to the master. Sir Richard, already alerted earlier by a servant, was making fast preparations to investigate the disturbance. Hearing the news from the messenger, Sir Richard made haste for the campsite using the soldier's horse. Upon arrival, he looked around trying to assess the gypsy losses.

He saw Barnie lying on the ground. As he knelt down and leaned over him, Sir Richard thought he could see a look of recognition in Barnie's eye before his head fell limp to one side. Sir Richard checked in a desperate hope that there might still be life in the old man still. As the realization began to register, Sir Richard could not help but allow tears to fall shamelessly down his cheeks.

His thought was, "Dear God, why this? Will I ever see his like again?" He stood up from the body with a mixture of sorrow and anger.

Sir Richard called to a soldier and gave him instructions to ride to the big house "Make sure that a doctor is summoned immediately on my orders."

Without as much as an answer, the soldier was galloping away towards Pemberley.

While waiting for professional medical help, fit people employed themselves in the nursing of the injured or a closely related task. Men were still dying even as they worked. Sir Richard eventually found Anne and Sacha. The ashen face bore the omen of mortality of poor Sacha. Sir Richard took his kerchief to Sacha's shoulder. He seemed unconscious but perhaps he could stop the bleeding so that he might survive if only a little longer. Anne returned to her husband with a wooden bowl of soup. There was no acknowledgement between them; they just continued attending to their healing tasks. Sir Richard removed his coat and put it under Sacha's head then propping him up while Anne poured the soup into his mouth.

Two soldiers had constructed a stretcher and they had carried wounded gypsies back to their caravans. They eventually reached Anne and Sacha and laid down the stretcher. However, as they saw Sacha, they readily took him for dead. The soldiers bent down to pick up the stretcher again when Anne called for them to carry Sacha to their caravan.

One of the soldiers said, "I am very sorry ma'am but our instructions are to help the living first."

"He is alive still!" Anne screamed at them.

The soldier looked at the other one who shrugged his shoulders. They replaced the stretcher beside Sacha then rolled him gently onto the stretcher. As the soldiers carried Sacha, Anne walked alongside directing the soldiers towards her caravan. The powerfully built soldiers manipulated the stretcher with its precious load carefully into the caravan to roll the half-dead man onto his bed.

"He'll be alright Mum." The first soldier said.

They picked up their stretcher and left to continue their task of carrying the wounded. Left by herself, with her husband at death's door, Anne felt that she was alone and distraught. She felt the need to do something. She threw Sir Richard's coat over her husband's body to keep him warm.

She emerged from her caravan satisfied that she could do no more for Sacha but might be of help elsewhere. She surveyed the scene of the campsite. It was a picture of carnage. Gypsies and Frenchmen lying lifeless on the ground while wounded gypsy men and women trying to raise themselves; others had given up but all who could give, helped as they could. The dragoon soldiers had assembled seven French prisoners. Some wounded, some fit but dishevelled but all standing.

Anne jumped from her caravan towards a large pitchfork lying on the ground. She picked it up and ran screaming with every ounce of angry energy towards the prisoners. The long spikes of the fork reached out like fingers for death, for revenge. The prisoners stood still watching her advance until so close they realized her full intention. They dispersed in various directions. A dragoon fired into the air but the prisoners did not heed the warning. Anne realized her mission was failing. She stumbled and fell. She let out a shrill and piercing cry of such distress that every gypsy, solder and Frenchman felt shivers of some primeval instinct inside them recoil in horror. Sir Richard ran forward to pick her up and tried to console her. As he lifted her to her feet, he could feel that he was shaking as the result of her scream. Her distress was extreme and he felt it now.

"It was surely because Sacha had not recovered?" He thought.

He spoke softly to his cousin, "Remember, Anne, they are the murderers, not us."

On realizing that the threat had passed, the prisoners stopped running. They turned to to discover the threat had passed. Reluctantly the Frenchmen voluntarily turned back to their allotted posts, as though little boys creeping to school. They knew the dragoon rifles were more deadly than a woman's scream.

Sir Richard accompanied Anne back to her caravan. He helped her up the steps to the inside then lit a candle to see better their patient. "Sacha is still pale but a little back away from death." He thought. Sir Richard looked at Anne. He could see the face of a little girl drowning in a fate of uncertainty with nothing but anguish and sorrows to reach out for life support. Sacha gave a moan and they both looked at him then at each other. Sacha opened his eyes to see Anne and Sir Richard. Sir Richard spoke, "It is alright now, Sacha, you are in good hands. The battle is won and all you have to do . . . ." Sacha smiled, closed his eyes and fell back into a slumber.

"Dear cousin Anne, I am certain that he will recover. He is not badly injured but he has lost a lot of blood. He needs your soup, warmth and rest. I am certain he will recover for you. I most sincerely hope so."

He held her hand as he spoke to reassure her. "Please do not let your family leave the site until the last gypsy is healed and well.

I shall attend to the dragoons. They will stay as long as you wish. Your brother will guarantee that."

She smiled back at him as he spoke. It all seemed so unreal now but she always had the most complete confidence in her cousin and the colonel, her brother.

"It shall be as you advise, Sir Richard."

"Remember that Sacha is now head of the gypsy family and you, as his wife must act for him. Surely the others will do as you decree?"

"They have killed Barnie?" Her face twisted in anguish.

"Yes, Anne. You must be brave to lead the others. The Pemberley Estate will help you with anything. It is the time for all of us to be strong. Raise yourself above all this and look to the future for yourself and all your family."

Chapter Thirteen

The Fate of Marcel

The prisoners would always be a security problem if they thought they were to face retribution. Sir Richard, therefore, gave instructions to the dragoons to treat the prisoners without malice and attend to their needs. Sir Richard explained that their prisoners will be a source of information useful to our officers.

Sir Richard returned to his office to write letters. The first was an express dispatch to Colonel Fitzwilliam at Reading. With the utmost urgency, he had a rider on the road to the South.

Sir Richard's anxiety was to secure the continued detention of Marcel at Reading Prison at all costs. Now that Anne was safe, the Frenchman had no bargaining power. His concern was for the reason the French attacked the gypsies in the hope of finding Anne. The reason for killing Anne before Marcel's release at Calais might be very significant. It would almost certainly, in most cases, lead to vengeance and to the death of Fitzwilliam's prisoner, Marcel, while he was still in prison. Why should the French want their master spy dead? Did Marcel have knowledge of secret military intelligence that the French did not want him to confess? If this was so, where did the order come from to attack the gypsies in the hope of finding Anne?

All this and more Sir Richard conveyed in his letter. He also wanted the colonel to return and take charge of the prisoners in his custody. The military should take responsibility for their prisoners, to confine and interrogate them.

His next letter was to his aunt, Lady Catherine de Bourgh. He was eager to inform her that Anne was safe and well. That she would be staying at Pemberley for a while but will write as soon as she is able. He omitted any mention of gypsies or marriage. Once Lady Catherine becomes content for Anne's safety, she may be more amenable with the life choices that Anne has taken. However, there were grave doubts in his mind if such a change of attitude could happen to his aunt. She is by no means, a lady who one could easily persuade.

—o—

Georgiana and Lydia, at a loss for employment of any kind, descended on Sir Richard in search of amusement.

Lydia spoke first, "We want to make a play but we have no stage. Is it possible that we can have a stage please, Sir Richard?"

The imposition of such frivolities while doing his best to cope with Military affairs affecting the Pemberley Estate, were not the distraction he welcomed. However, the best way to deal with the situation was to respond to it and then return to his more serious business.

"If you think that the blue suite next to the music room will satisfy your purpose, tell Benkison of your plans and he will organize everything you want."

This created great pleasure for the two young ladies. They quickly found the blue suite. An examination of its attributes proved it amply suitable. Some minor alterations Benkinson would necessarily have to make. It was obvious that passed generations used the suite as a theatre before them. It might have been for musical entertainment on a serious scale or acting or both.

For a short time, the two young ladies stood on the stage area and pretended to act and perform orations to an invisible audience. Eventually they became more serious, and more practical with regard to the possible play that they could manage.

Georgiana was the first to observe that their possibilities were limited by their lack of people available to act, "The more numerous our numbers the better our choice of play."

Quickly Lydia responded, "We could ask her ladyship, that is, if she does not feel too grand to humble herself so."

"Oh yes, indeed, and Anne also."

"Let us go now to Elizabeth. She will have ideas of a play. Then we can go to the gypsy camp to find Anne."

"But the gypsies will be moving on soon and Anne will go with them. So she will not be able to join us in a play." Georgiana reasoned.

Lydia confirmed, "That may be so; my sister will tell us all. If we go now, we will have more time to visit Anne this morning."

The two young women located Lady Elizabeth in her private study room.

They gushed out their plans to Elizabeth, including their intended visit to the gypsy camp.

Elizabeth became alarmed at the prospect of unescorted young ladies venturing to the gypsy encampment at such a time. She counselled them not to go but to send a servant to invite their cousin to the house.

Elizabeth added, "Otherwise, if you want to visit the camp, take servants or stable boys with you."

The French offensive on the gypsies was unknown to Georgiana and Lydia. Both Elizabeth and Sir Richard had considered it unwholesome to tell them. The inclement weather prohibited outdoor activities also, there was the fear that French elements may return.

Nobody had therefore considered the possibility that anyone would venture outside. Undeterred, the young ladies made their way to the stables. They explained to the head groom of their wish to visit the gypsy sight. The eager stable boys made themselves busy preparing the dogcart. Each hoped that the head groom would choose him for the outing. The head groom selected two boys to drive them to the gypsies.

The ride was awkward and bumpy. The going was often so bad that the ladies were then obliged to walk while the horse pulled the cart clear of the quaggy grounds. At the campsite, they searched earnestly for Anne and Sacha. After many enquiries, they discovered her to be inside her caravan. As the young ladies approached, they could see through the half-open doorway into the interior where Anne was sitting. They could see just her head above the level of the half door.

Anne heard her cousins calling her. She put her index finger to her lips to indicate that they should not make a noise. The young ladies beckoned enthusiastically at Anne to descend from her caravan. Anne shook her head vigorously to demonstrate her strong objection to leaving the caravan.

Lydia, the more determined and the stronger willed of the two, climbed the steps of the caravan and peered into the gloomy interior. She could see Anne clearly distressed. Sacha lay quite still, even without a breath. Lydia stared for some minutes looking in disbelief at the interior of Anne's home. She noted sadly of the meagre facilities the gypsy life offered then studied the condition of Sacha. His face was ashen. There was no movement at all. Lydia was a young lady but no stranger to the deceased condition of a body. Her personal experience with her husband and the soldiers in the affray at the ball suggested to her that Sacha was just a vacant frame.

Anne turned her tortured face to meet Lydia eyes. Lydia smiled back at her. Anne continued to look or seeming to look at Lydia as though Anne's body too was an empty shell. Tears flowed silently and steadily from Anne's eyes. The realization of something deeply wrong was beginning to register with Lydia. As their eyes continued to meet, one with compassion, the other drained of all sensibility, their emotions fused together. One with the other felt as though someone had turned time inside out. In a moment, a second was eternity and eternity seemed to be passing in a second.

"You alright milady?" the young groom asked of Lydia.

He had intruded into the space of the women to shatter the moment shared. The boy felt concern for his charge.

"Yes, I am composed now. Please take us back to the house."

"Very good milady."

"And as fast as you can."

"Yes, milady."

The return journey to the house demonstrated the skill of the groom. He drove post haste through every kind of dangerous quagmire, skirting at high speed around others but all the time urged on by Lydia to go faster. As they arrived at the house, Lydia begged Georgiana to excuse her for a moment that she might report to Elizabeth.

Lady Elizabeth listened attentively to her youngest sister's account of Anne's disposition and deceased husband. Elizabeth realized that a moment must not be lost. She assured Lydia that action would follow swiftly. Immediately, Elizabeth issued instructions for a physician. "Summon him with all haste." She declared to a servant.

Next, she was relating of the situation to her husband. He took on a very serious turn.

"So the gypsies are leaving." He mused. "I expect they feared further attacks from the French." Sir Richard continued to speak his thoughts, "This is a hapless day indeed. That Barnie should die. That my dear Anne should loose her husband. Her happiness has a habit of deserting her. We must now do all we can for our dear cousin."

"I too love her dearly." Elizabeth added, "Whatever life Anne wishes to pursue now will entail an adjustment. After such a loss, this will be a long and difficult change in her life."

"Thank you for your generosity, my dear Elizabeth. I should never have expected anything less from such a one as you. I think it be unwise for Pemberley to desert her by returning her to Rosings. Anne must stay here."

"But Sir Richard, would that be wise? Does the thought of French intruders not leave you with some fear for more harm to threaten Anne?"

"Why, yes to be sure, again you are quite right. Alternatively, she could go to Matlock Towers. She is, after all, the earl's daughter by way of being the sister of his son, according to Lady Catherine."

On this, they both agreed. Elizabeth decided to inform Anne as soon as she was well enough to bear the news. They agreed also to invite the Bingleys to Pemberley to increase the numbers at the house as Anne was sojourned at Wynnstay Park. Sir Richard confirmed that he should write to Sir Rufus to enlist his assistance with the transfer of Anne to the earl at Matlock Towers.

There were still a number of gypsy caravans left on the vacated site. The invaders having slaughtered the owners while in the defence of their homes and family. Good citizens of Lambton designated a piece of land next to their cemetery for the remains of the fallen gypsy fighting men and women. An acre of land set aside by the citizens but not by way of a Christian burial, because the gypsies had no known faith.

However, special services acknowledged the price the gypsies paid for a fight that was not theirs. Services for the gypsies took place at Lambton and Pemberley.

Stable boys took the caravans from Gypsy Field to store them in the stables. The intention was to return the caravans to the gypsies if or when they returned.

During the following two weeks, the humour of Anne improved enough to agree to take her journey to her paternal home with the earl. She understood that her husband had died but bravely defending his family against the French. She had now to take on the task of deciding what to do with the rest of her life. She needed space and time to help her heal the wounds, both of the mind and body. Anne needed as much space and time again to plan her future. However, first she must lay the past to rest.

Elizabeth took on the task of coordinating Anne's journey with all the parties involved. The plans and scheming advanced to a late stage and preparations began to for Anne's departure. The first stop on the route would be at their neighbours, Sir Rufus and Lady Penelope at Wynnstay House. There she will rest for a week.

From Wynnstay, her journey will take her directly to the earl's guardianship. The plans so well thought through by Sir Richard and Elizabeth meant that Ann would remain at Pemberley until the arrival of Colonel Fitzwilliam.

Although there seemed little fear of a further attack from French assailants, security was Sir Richard's first priority for his cousin. No known spies existed within the vicinity but it was not good prudence to take risks of any sort.

Two parties would assemble, both so similar that it would not be easy to tell them apart.

The plan was for the carriages to leave at intervals of a few minutes so they would never be very far apart on their journey to Wynnstay House.

Shortly after the departure of Anne for Wynnstay, the Bingleys would arrive for their Christmastide visit.

Chapter Fourteen

Anne Leaves Pemberley

On a cold, misty morning, a carriage drew alongside the rear of Pemberley House. Two shadowy figures made their way from the entrance as they said their farewells, then mounted the carriage. With small delays, the carriage pulled slowly away. A hand appeared and waved a handkerchief from a half-open window. Shortly, the handkerchief withdrew and the carriage continued on, gathering pace as it covered the ground towards the open portals.

Following quickly, another carriage drew alongside the place that had been occupied by the first. The same scene of departing and a similar company re-enacted the departure. The horses then made good their speed after the first carriage. Within minutes, they were out of sight. The company, who had wished the travellers a safe journey, slowly withdrew into the interior of the house.

Elizabeth returned to the breakfast room to join her husband at the table. Neither spoke. Both however, had the same thoughts; "Would Anne be safe from marauding Frenchmen?"

Anne chose to travel in one of the two carriages. In the event of a Frenchman being present in the grounds spying on the house, he would be unable to tell if Anne was in either or any coach. This provided some security in addition to the four dragoons who rode between the two carriages.

The dragoons were to return to confirm the safe arrival of Anne to Wynnstay House. Arrivals expected on the same day at Pemberley were Jane and Mr. Bingley and Colonel Fitzwilliam. Elizabeth looked forward to seeing her elder sister again. Jane was closest to Elizabeth's heart but Elizabeth's most eager anticipation was to admire Jane's newly born baby again.

Everyone looked forward to seeing the colonel because he engaged the affections of everyone with his pleasant, natural disposition. On his return journey to Pemberley, the colonel intended to call upon Sir Rufus at Wynnstay House. The Colonel was to take command of and return the dragoons to Pemberley. This would give him the opportunity to see his sister and to be satisfied that she was safe at Wynnstay House.

Anne, two carriages and four dragoons arrived safely at Wynnstay House the same day that they had departed from Pemberley but into a different world. She knew no one, and cared little for the imposition of those formalities that she had left behind at Rosings Park. Behaviour in her gypsy life was always informal but never displeasing. She now found Wynnstay House very old fashion with little to amuse a solitary young woman.

Sir Rufus and Lady Penelope welcomed their young guest and made every effort to indulge her during her short stay with them. Anne, in her turn, tried her own tolerance by doing her best to respond politely to the old fashioned kindnesses offered by her hosts. The day following her arrival, Anne completed a letter to Elizabeth. It went with the morning's post. She wrote of the despair of her state at Wynnstay House and of her eager anticipation of her brother's visit.

He arrived before midday. The household was all excitement of his visit. His hosts engaged him so fully that it was afternoon before she was able to speak with him in private. It was his intention to leave that same day but Anne's indisposition persuaded him to delay his departure until the following day. The colonel gave Instructions to the dragoons to stand down for twenty-four hours and to defer all arrangements. During the early evening, another gentleman arrived. He enjoyed an equal welcome as they had given the colonel. Lady Penelope invited the colonel and Anne to join the company in the lounge before dinner. The company consisted of Sir Rufus, Lady Penelope, and the recent arrival, a tall handsome gentleman. He stood looking at Anne with a slightly serious air. Sir Rufus made the introduction of his son, Rupert to Anne. As he did so Rupert's face lit up with a smile, leaned over to kiss her hand to whisper, "Enchanté Mademoiselle."

All the time he locked his eyes on her eyes. Something affected Anne so that she felt weak. She fought against that which she felt. It seemed to her that this man had thrown a cloak over her to isolate her from the rest of the world, and from her sensibilities and there was this man left and only this man. Anne could hear that Sir Rufus was still saying something but he seemed distant and barely audible.

She did hear, however, "Rupert ask Miss de Bourgh for her choice of drink."

He responded warmly, "May I offer you something, Miss de Bourgh? We have the Christmas punch already for the festive season."

She hesitated just for a moment.

Rupert ready to reassure his guest added, "My mother makes it herself to her own design. You will find it pleasant I assure you."

Upon such an en treaty, Anne felt obliged to sample the punch. The pleasant tasting liquid delighted her palate. Following the second measure of the nectar her senses, which were already disturbed, began a circular journey much as the wind behaves in a maelstrom.

Rupert, seeing that their guest appeared unsteady supported her as the family walked into dinner.

For the rest of the evening, Rupert paid particular respects to Anne, which was the cause of everyone else paying much attention to her. All the time, Anne experienced difficulties responding sensibly to the courtesies of her hosts. However, the party enjoined heartily in conversations and was amused and sometimes charmed by her responses.

The following morning Anne had no recollection of her wit of the evening before. She did remember Rupert. She did remember his blue eyes, his rich brown chestnut hair and his persuasive charm. Anne hurried down to breakfast. To her dismay, she learnt both the colonel and Rupert had breakfasted earlier and left the house.

"Had I known" she thought, "I would have stayed in bed with my head."

She surprised herself with her own pleasantry. While she ate, Anne looked at the unoccupied chair at the table and all the time imagining that Rupert was sitting there.

Upon occupying their usual seats at the breakfast table, her hosts were declared how much pleasure they had with Anne's company the previous evening. Normally they would have played at cards or listened to music. It was Anne and only Anne who provided the entertainment. Anne was all amazed and assured her hosts that any jocularity may have had its source from her ladyship's punch. To which the company laughed immoderately, especially for the breakfast table.

Anne could only groan at their reaction. Soon Sir Rufus and Lady Penelope were pressing Anne to remain at least another week again before travelling on to Matlock Towers.

This was an unexpected but desired option for Anne. The visit to Matlock Towers held no attraction for her. If Matlock Towers was another big house with dreary old occupants with little or no distractions. She would rather be in her caravan and on the road feeling the excited anticipation travelling to the next place. However, for the first time Anne had awoken to the idea that she had a choice. It was for her safety that Pemberley House had planned her transfer to Matlock Towers under guard and with all secrecies. She thought of Rosings Park and her overbearing mother. There was no interest there. To stay with Lady Penelope would be that little more agreeable. Then there was always the chance of seeing *him* again. For sometime, she dwelled on the possibility. She pictured Rupert leaning towards her to kiss her hand. Therefore, Anne pondered over the idea of staying another week again with Lady Penelope. How bored she might be . . . but the idea of the chance of seeing Rupert . . . the very thought of his name was beginning to overtake her. She mentally recomposed herself. The idea that she might see Rupert again might be worth suffering the old-fashioned disposition of Sir Rufus and Lady Penelope for a matter of days. She did not want to venture on to Matlock Towers. Even the name of the place was beginning to offend her senses.

If she stayed at Wynnstay House for two weeks in total and then return to Pemberley House that would fulfill her due courtesies to Lady Penelope.

If there was any hope, "He" would find her "He" would seek her out, in time at not too distance away. The thoughts ran through Anne's imagination and the idea excited Anne. She would stay but make it known to Rupert of her changed circumstances, of her move to Pemberley. She would make it known that she would not continue to Matlock Towers. Thus, Ann had laid her plans.

Anne's first task must be to inform her hosts of her desire to return to Pemberley regardless of the risks. She must further explain to please and not to offend Lady Penelope that she would extend her stay for a further few days.

"Those few days" passed more pleasantly than Anne had expected. Lady Penelope treated Anne with so much affability that she was beginning to feel more at home, more belonging, than she ever did, even with her own mother at Rosings Park. Letters between Pemberley and Wynnstay House exchanged daily. The few days passed into a few more days. The gloss if any, of Wynnstay House was wearing dull. The absence of Rupert continued. Anne did not dare mention his name in case her demeanour should expose her feelings of which Lady Penelope may not approve. Anne was always conscious of her loss of her beloved husband, though now she had her own future to consider. However, others may regard with distaste the lack of grieving for her lately lost partner without considering her personal circumstances. Anne understood that she should act with calculated decorum.

Anne's beliefs that Rupert would return soon to his mother and father faded into a resolution to return to Pemberley. She composed a letter for the afternoon post to inform Elizabeth of her intended arrival at Pemberley the following day. Sadly, Anne placed her letter with the house post waiting collection.

"Perhaps," Anne thought, "It might be for the best. I shall, in time, erase him from my mind."

With this resolution, she returned to her room to sort her clothing for packing. All the time the memory of Rupert kept returning to her mind. She recalled their first encounter.

She thought, "Surely she could not have been mistaken of his meanings, his charm, seemingly levelled at her. Was that mere entertainment? Could he be so cruel? Surely, there was more meaning than an evening's entertainment in his manners?"

Anne found that she was unable to concentrate on her packing and called for a servant. The girl had an obvious skill to pack correctly. Each item she smoothed carefully then folded and arranged with heed in the correct place and position in the trunks. The task was thus time consuming. While the servant girl busied herself with the packing, Anne's mind was still dwelling on alternative possibilities. Anne thought of any further letters she might write. Her active mind sought for some last minute hope. Anne turned her attention to the servant, "You do not have many visitors to the House?"

"No ma'am. But we did have everyone from Pemberley House earlier this year come to our staff ball."

"So few visitors?"

"And then there is Master Rupert, ma'am."

"Am I to understand that Master Rupert visits often? Does he not live somewhere else?"

"We see him but not often. His visits are always very welcome because he is a pleasant young man and he sometimes brings his friends to visit."

"He has many friends?"

"Oh, I think so. His friends are always very jolly young men. We expect him back very soon."

Anne could not have learned better news. She decided now that she must rethink on her plans to return to Pemberley. Her first task was to retrieve her letter to Elizabeth. Upon investigation, Anne learned, to her dismay, that the postman had collected her letter. She was now obliged to write again to Elizabeth. There was also Lady Penelope with whom she needed to make known her revised intentions. Having completed her new letter to Elizabeth, Anne learned from a manservant of the cancellation of the late postal service due to the extreme weather. "Your letter will go in the early morning post ma'am." He assured her.

The inclement weather gave Anne the excuse she needed to prolong her stay yet again. Anne informed Lady Penelope of her concern for the conditions on the roads. Lady Penelope showed much sympathy for Anne and insisted that Anne should delay her departure for as long as she wished.

Lady Penelope replied to her guest, "Why, to be sure you must stay while this foul weather is with us. Now even Rupert, unfortunately, will not be able to return as he had planned. These bad conditions confound everyone."

It was true that Anne did not wish to travel in such bad conditions but her hope was that by delaying her journey home, she might have the opportunity to meet Rupert again. Of course, if she and the post do not travel, neither will Rupert. Now she thought her situation hopeless once more.

The rest of the day passed with few distractions. The following morning the weather had changed for the better. The clouds had gone, the winds had dropped and the sky was blue from horizon to horizon.

Good weather always affects all sensible people for the better. At breakfast, Anne was in good company with lively conversation. During the repast, a manservant entered with a message to the effect that there was a delivery person from the Pemberley Estate. Anne could not help but overhear the servant's conversation with Sir Rufus, especially, "The man awaits your instructions in order to complete his delivery, Sir."

Sir Rufus replied, "Oh, let the man wait while I finish my breakfast."

Anne thought quickly and addressed Sir Rufus, "Sir, might I go with you to enquire of the man, about the roads and the conditions at Pemberley?"

"Why, yes my dear, you may and if that is your wish, we will go at once." Sir Rufus added, "I shall be glad of your company."

Anne did not know what Sir Rufus meant by such a statement. She preferred not to imagine anything into it. It was enough effort and some running to keep up with her host who walked quickly with long strides. The staff was obviously used to his behaviour. She noticed how they anticipated the approach of Sir Rufus by opening doors for him to have free passage and that they were opened with a flourish and in good time for the master. They soon found the carrier from Pemberley sitting patiently on his wagon. Anne recognized Mannings from Pemberley and so did Sir Rufus. They traded conversations for some minutes and since their business concluded, Sir Rufus turned his attentions towards Anne to say to Mannings, "This young lady is Miss Anne de Bourgh and she wishes to know the state of the roads from Pemberley."

After the minimum of courtesies Anne spoke to Mannings, "The road, Mannings, how did you find it?"

"Good and bad milady.

"Tell me of the good and the bad, Mannings"

"Well, yes milady. There is good going on the toll roads but it is the dirt tracks where the horses need to be carefully driven. Otherwise the worst could happen."

Anne needed no further details. She asked for confirmation, "So it is possible for me to return to Pemberley?"

"Yes, but with much providence, milady."

That was all Anne wished to learn. She would now pursue her resolve. She was sure to be back at Pemberley House this very day, among friends and cousins.

Sir Rufus offered his apologies to dismiss himself to return to his breakfast table.

Chapter Fifteen

Halfway Mountain Crag

Anne felt an urgency to return to Pemberley. That was, to escape from Wynnstay House because it held no further interest to her. She had determined in her own mind, not to proceed to Matlock Towers. The experience of Wynnstay House was enough of dusty old houses with a lack of interest for a young lady. Her thoughts of Rosings and Wynnstay House were equally unattractive. Therefore, it was to be Pemberley. The house that her mother anticipated that she would, one day, be the mistress. The thoughts ran through her mind. Something inside her yearned to return to the gypsy life. To imagine such a life without Sacha was not possible for her without some discomfort of the mind. Her resolve therefore, was to return to Pemberley as quickly as possible.

She too dismissed herself curtly from Mannings, to hurry after Sir Rufus. While making good step alongside her host, Anne felt inclined to inform him of her intentions. "I think I might chance the weather and return to Pemberley, Sir Rufus."

His reply was a long way from anything she had expected. "As you wish Miss Anne, as you wish, though my son was looking forward to seeing you again but no matter, no matter. You know best. I will see that there is a carriage made ready for you."

"Your son Rupert, returning to Wynnstay House?"

"Yes, but the storm must have prevented him."

"He will still come will he not?"

"I could not say. The boy is here, there and everywhere all the time. If he could not travel on account of the weather he must have been distracted by other interests."

Anne could not wait for Rupert who may not come anyway. To remain after having stated her intention of leaving for Pemberley might exhibit indecorous behaviour. Her trunks were packed and the carriage would soon be waiting for her. One request before her departure was to use the maid, who packed her trunks, to accompany Ann on her journey. The girl was to return with the carriage the following day.

Sir Rufus and Lady Penelope stood waving to Anne as her carriage pulled away from the house to continue along the drive. Not until the carriage was out of sight did they turn with sad faces, to re-enter their house.

To Anne's satisfaction, the carriage made good headway. This was especially so along the toll roads, as Mannings had promised.

Within a mile or two of halfway to Pemberley, a northerly wind began to make itself felt. The carriage rocked from one side to the other and at times, slowing their way as the carriage threatened to become unstable. The wind grew stronger so that it hindered gravely their progress then, as rain persisted, doubts began to set in the mind of the driver. The horses turned off the road and made for refuge up in the nearby hills. The driver knew of the hollow where it would be safe to shelter. On reaching the hollow, the wind grew stronger and they could still hear it roar but in their refuge they could but barely feel it. They were sheltered too from the rain by an overhang. Their danger had passed while they sheltered in the hollow.

From their elevated situation, the party could look down on the road, now deserted but mercilessly lashed by torrential rain and the ill-tempered winds. For about one-half of an hour the party of Miss Anne, her maid and three liverymen watched the elements do their worst. The weather gave no hint to break off. The angry winds continued to beat the earth with a violent rain.

While the party watched the spectacle of the weather, a lone rider came into view. He strained, doubled forward on his horse, against the hostile wind. His cloak bellowed and waved about behind him while riding as fast as his horse could manage against the wind and the rain. The rider continued his labours against the elements silently, at a distant range. As he came adjacent though still in the distance, to the sheltering party the retinue and the maid called out to him. The rider was unlikely to hear or see them above the wind and the lashing rain and so far off. They continued to shout as he rode on gradually reducing to a dot until he disappeared. Silence returned to the scene as before.

"How brave he must be to battle the weather so." Anne said to the party, "I suppose we shall never know who is. Just a stranger passing silently at a distance and if we did ever meet him we should have nothing to know of him again."

"Not so." Her maid responded, "That was unmistakably young Mr. Rupert riding home to Wynnstay House, begging your pardon Madam."

"Rupert? But why should he be passing this way to Wynnstay House? Surely we are going to Pemberley?"

"It may be that he was visiting Pemberley and with his visit complete is returning home. Yes, that is it I am sure."

Anne returned to the carriage to sit and think. She needed to dwell on this latest change of events. "Will I never find happiness again?"

The party could do little else but wait for the fickle hearted weather of the Derbyshire Hills to change. How Anne was now regretting her impetuous nature. If she had been more cautious, if she had remained at Wynnsty House, she would have been out of danger and she would have had Rupert's company to enjoy. The thought of how stupid she had been and how her impatience had marred her good judgement.

Anne and her maid returned to the shelter of the carriage. The wind gradually dropped but the rain continued, though much restrained. The light was beginning to fade. A cry rose from the men outside. "A rider, a rider again, it is the same one. It must be Rupert!"

Anne called to the men, "Go and fetch the horn." Then as an afterthought she added, "And the blunderbuss under the driver's seat."

Anne called out, "The Gun, the gun, use it now!"

The rider continued his steady pace. The coachman retrieved the horn. Without waiting for further instructions, he blew it loud and long. Then, after a quick breath, blew again short sharp sounds in the hope of attracting the rider's attention. Anne screamed, "The gun man, discharge the gun now!"

Another of the retinue made good timing and fired the blunderbuss at the point where the rider would be nearest to them. A thunderous report echoed around the hills that should have sent dead men running and screaming out of their graves in terror. The rider continued his steady pace. The rider did appear to hear it as he looked round but carefully without compromising his speed or progress. He continued along the road, then around the curve until an overhanging crag blocked their view of the road and the rider. He was gone. The party was silent. The last vestiges of daylight were now fading so that soon, further views of the road would not be possible. They realized that they were to spend the night in this isolated location. The thought of this caused Anne to a shiver throughout her body.

The men searched for anything that would help them keep warm during the night. Every one of the party slowly realized the problems of their predicament. A quick search discovered suitable blankets and heavy outer coats to reduce draughts for the women as they spent the night inside the carriage. The men accepted for granted that they would sleep under the carriage while the lady and her maid would feel most protected and comfortable inside. However, sleeping through the night in similar manner during her gypsy life, taught Anne otherwise.

Anne addressed the men," It is most important, if we are to survive the worst of the weather we may experience during the night, that we all shelter inside the carriage. Also, in the event of more high winds, our combined company will give much extra weight to the carriage. Light the lamps, turn the horses loose and find stones to secure the wheels so that the carriage will remain fast."

While two men worked inside the carriage making it comfortable, the lady and her maid stood outside braving the cold damp night air with the protection of a man's heavy coat. There was still some wind, which carried a chill. The night was dark with no moon or stars. The carriage lights helped the men do their work. They carried out their labours quietly with diligence and all speed.

The men had nearly completed their preparations for the night and were eagerly hoping for a respite. Taking a coat and a blanket one of the men made for the underside of the carriage. Their hopes of a little rest were soon challenged.

The maid screamed, renting the silent night air. The party, having no understanding of the cause, was petrified with alarm. For some moments, no movement came from any of them.

The girl was running to the carriage to throw, without dignity, her terrified body inside. Her voice obviously very much disturbed called out. "There's devils out thar. I'se sores 'em, I sore's 'em. Devils they be."

Anne turned quickly in the direction her maid pointed. At first, she saw only a wall of darkness. She could not make out anything. As her sight gradually grew accustomed to the night's gloom, she could see pairs of eyes reflecting the light of the dim carriage lamps. Pairs of eyes dotted here and there, all suspended, seemingly detached from anything. She continued to stare at the scene as she noticed more appearing. These new eyes randomly emerging must have belonged to those who had been frightened by the girl's screaming.

"If they are frightened of us, why should we be frightened of them?" She tried to persuade herself. Anne became aware that fear had paralyzed her whole body. She struggled to overcome her own feelings of terror.

One of the liverymen approached her. He spoke respectfully in subdued tones, "Beggin' yur pardon m'lady, they are only the old crones who live here ma'am.

Some good local Christian folk brings 'em food and sometimes wood for their fires."

"I wish we had some wood now, to burn." She retorted.

"Aye ma'am and some good Christian folk with food also. We are all hungry and thirsty but we'll 'ave to wait for the morning to 'ave our fill." The man countered.

As the liveryman turned away, a fresh sound, a new haunting sound, of a male voice calling out that sounded that someone else was lost, heralding another soul in distress.

Each of the company turned eyes in the direction from which they thought the voice was calling. They perceived the call was coming first from one direction then another, the wind and the environment of their shelter lent haunting tricks to the ear. The party turned towards pale lights becoming visible, which now gave credence to the direction of the voice. In, apparently, slow motion, human activity emerged from the direction of the craggy overhang that earlier obscured their sight of the horseman. The lights grew stronger as events developed. Two men perceived to be holding their torches aloft. Two men with torches and another man, a tall handsome man leading the way and following were more men besides. There were screams of delight from the two women and hurrahs from the liverymen as they all moved forwards to greet the advancing party.

Anne ran towards the torchbearers. She thought she made out the figure of the tall gentleman as none other than her cousin, Sir Richard. She threw herself at him into his arms, "Oh, Mr. Darcy, you are my hero. Thank you so much for coming. We thought that we would have to stay here all the night . . ."

Sir Richard enjoyed his greeting from Anne but cut her short, "I am sorry to say Anne that we are all obliged to remain here for the night. The men are exhausted and so am I. It has been a long and discouraging climb and we could not find you. We were about to abandon the search but we heard a scream. As you see, we have made our way towards where we thought it came from. We were lucky. The torches will not last much longer. The men will douse one torch and light it again as soon as the first torch is exhausted."

The Sir Richard turned to the company to announce with a raised voice, "Meanwhile, we have brought you all food and wine for your suppers."

This brought much cheer from the tired and hungry people.

Four men had carried two hampers of victuals and demonstrated much relief to be able to discharge themselves of their burden.

As natural as the heather on the hills, the servants and master made separate parties to partake of their provisions. They settled beside what little shelter the carriage offered. Silently, at first, they ate and drank until they became more relaxed. The first torch exhausted before the parties had finished eating. They maintained the second torch as low a light as possible. At this time, the two parties became subdued once more. In the dim light, eating in almost silence, they could easily hear noises coming from the same direction as Sir Richard and his party had arrived. The men, one by one stood up looking in the direction of the noise. All were in wonderment of what it meant.

One of the men whispered, "Douse the light."

Sir Richard ordered, "No, let us see who or what it is first."

One of the servants volunteered, "'T'is only the old crones, I can smell them, they be all 'round us."

Chapter Sixteen

Dangers of the Night

For some minutes, as the party forgot their repast, they stood and waited for some sign of identification of who or what? Each one turned their attention to peer intensely into the dark of the night towards the path that led under the overhanging crag. Faintly, a voice carried loud enough to hear, but too indistinctly for the troubled men and women to recognize. While they waited and wondered, Ann took a step forward as she turned her head to take in the voice better. Then she advanced another step towards the sounds while still listening intently as the plaintive calls continued. She began to advance more quickly until she broke into a run and called out, "Rupert, over here. Do come Rupert, we are all over here."

Hearing her words, the party relaxed and began laughing, clapping, and calling out Rupert's name. Rupert, astride his horse still, though showing signs of extreme exhaustion, was almost falling from his saddle. Anne reached him in time to prevent his fall, encouraging and helping him to descend from the horse to take to foot. Two of the men joined Anne to help the exhausted Rupert to manage the last few steps to meet with the party of lost travellers.

Sir Richard greeted Rupert while all the time Ann stood by the side of the wearied man as they shook hands. Ann spoke the while throwing her words between the two men. Finally, she suggested, "Perhaps Rupert would enjoy some of your fare Sir Richard, if you have the mind?"

Sir Richard responded most enthusiastically in accord so that the greeting broke away. Ann helped Rupert to a sitting position to enjoy a glass of wine and a chicken leg. In a short time, his inclination was to fall on his back to rest, perhaps sleep. Ann took the wineglass from his hand. As she did so, she realized how cold Rupert felt. He was shivering still. In the dim light, she looked more intently at the tired features of his face. He looked not only drained of all energy but also very pale. She left her charge to obtain a heavy coat to throw over his body to keep him warm. Ann felt the cold air pass over her as she shivered. Realizing that she too was in danger of her health breaking, Ann returned to address her cousin, Sir Richard. While shivering, Ann suggested that a fire would provide a welcome respite from the cold night air.

The servants listened to Sir Richard's instructions and then set about to gather combustibles. They collected armfuls of dead vegetation but all of it was too wet to catch alight. The fire needed something more flammable. There was nothing by way of paper or rags. The entire environment could not offer anything that was not wet through by days of rain. The men returned to the master to explain the lack of dry fuel for the fire.

For a few moments, Master and men stood around making noises or activities to manage better the cold. They were searching their minds for a solution to the cold evening air. All were now feeling the cold chill of the night. Sir Richard at length, spoke out, "See what we can take off the carriage to burn. Remove anything detachable that we can use for a fire."

The men set about salvaging parts of the coach in order to build a desperately needed source of warmth. "I am sure that Sir Rufus will not object when he learns of our circumstances." Sir Richard thought.

With the aid of some gunpowder, the men set alight splinters of wood. Quickly they fed the fire with more wood until a blaze was good enough for their comfort. Two men were attempting to dry the bracken the others had collected for additional fuel. One of the men provided a box for Rupert to sit by the fire to warm his cold body. Now and again, he would give a shiver but he was far from the wretched condition in which he arrived. As Ann witnessed Rupert's continuing distress, her thoughts were for his welfare. With that in mind, she sat alongside him on the box. The rest of the party was all in their night quarters, under the carriage or in it, or they were preparing to retire. Ann remained with Rupert sharing his borrowed coat as they sat on the box and enjoying the effects of the fire. They sat close to each other to provide warmth from one to the other. Sir Richard took it on himself to walk around their small encampment to check that all was safe and secure. Before retiring, he approached Ann and Rupert to enquire if they too were ready to join him in the carriage with one of the men and the servant girl.

Ann shook her head, "In a while, later." She assured him.

Sir Richard took a flask from his pocket, "I remembered this. I keep if for just such emergency, would you both like a drop of brandy to keep you warm?"

Again, Ann shook her head then leaned her head over to one side and placed her hands together as though in prayer. Then Anne held her clasped hands against the side of her head to indicate with her eyes that Rupert was asleep.

In the early hours of the following morning, the wind had dropped and the rain had ceased completely. The air was cold but fresh with the promise of a new day. The menservants stirred first. They attended to their tasks and one came to the fire to see if there was still some life in it. He saw that Ann and Rupert were both sitting by the smouldering embers so that he did not wish to disturb them and left the fire until later. The other men collected the horses to bring them to their encampment. Inside the carriage the maid awoke and without a word made haste to attend to her mistress. She was surprised to find Anne by the fire, still. "They must have been there all night." she mused to herself. She approached from the rear and coughed then "Good morning to 'e both. Can I do anything for milady?" There was no reply so she skirted the fire to address them both full face. She looked at the couple huddled up close to each other. They were quite still.

"Them be very still, alike two frozen fishes." She spoke her thoughts to herself. As she continued to peer at the two lovers, the realization was beginning to take and seize her senses. These two, however much their affection, one for the other, were not moving at all. They were not asleep but deathly still. The young girl staggered backwards in horror unable to speak or scream. Incapable as she was of any expression, she fainted to fall on the wet grass.

All hands were busy preparing for the journey home. Each knew that there was no time to lose. Each knew the urgency of their allotted tasks. Not one noticed the heap of human flesh and rags in the wet grass as Rupert and Ann continued seemingly to stare silently into eternity.

Sir Richard, now composed from the night's demands, was making plans for the journey home. He descended from the carriage to espy Rupert and Ann still bonded together, arms around each other. He gave a smile of the scene of young lovers totally absorbed in each other. Sir Richard took a few steps towards Rupert and Ann. A bundle on the ground caught his eye. Looking down at the item, it puzzled him. Gradually his mind and sight synchronized to make out the human shape and to distinguish what he thought were rags but to be the girls clothing.

Fearing her to be deceased, he called out, "Gedolf!"

The man responded immediately, running to Sir Richard who he realized was standing over the petite frame of the servant girl from Wynnstay House.

"She be 'urt, Zur?" The man enquired of the gentleman as he fell to his knees to make a closer examination of the poor soul.

In a few seconds, he turned his head upwards to declare that she was only unconscious. "What t'do Zur?"

Sir Richard asked him if she could stand up. The man tried to rally her senses but the only reaction was a mumbling and the girl pointing her finger with outstretched arm towards the two gentlefolk who were sitting, still, by the spent fire.

The other men had been distracted by the events. All the men watched as Sir Richard turned his head towards the object of the pointed finger. Not understanding or wanting to understand the real significance of the sick girl's gesture, Sir Richard was at a loss for some positive thought or action. Gedolf only, had the presence of mind to take the few steps to the couple. He spoke to the gentleman while the men and master watched with apprehension. They watched as he put his hand on Rupert's shoulder. They watched as he pulled on the shoulder but without very much more force, the body would not move. Gedolf turned his head to look to Sir Richard shaking his head to confirm the worst. Moments passed with no reaction as though this new situation was beyond their comprehension or belief. Sir Richard fell to his knees and this great man broke down. With his head buried in his hands wept out, "My dear, dear cousin." The rest of the party heard and understood him. They took off their hats to show respect.

Some of the men rallied round Gedolf to help him with the task of removing the bodies reverently to the carriage. Rupert was in deep state of rigor mortis while Ann was not. One of the men after checking carefully, called out, "She has a pulse! The lady has a pulse! Thank the Lord, the lady lives!" The men clapped reverently to register their pleasure to the news.

A great wave of relief came across Sir Richard. He was musing on the relating to his Aunt Catherine of the demise of her daughter. What a tragedy for her, also for us all. Now it was only his friend Sir Rufus who he must tell that his first-born had died on the hills of Derbyshire. At the very least, the young man showed much courage to help in the rescue of the party stranded somewhere in the hills and rode to his death in the trying. That courage and spirit in Rupert will be some comfort to his mother and father. Sir Richard thought to himself that he should never forget Rupert. He comforted himself with the thoughts of the safety of Ann. She had much courage and spirit as had Rupert. Perhaps they should have met sooner in their lives and things would have been so different for her.

A servant approached Sir Richard, "We need to keep the lady warm but we have no more fuel for the fire, Sir. With your permission, we could take more wood from the carriage but it will be unusable in such a condition. May I have your permission Sir?"

"Yes, yes, set alight to it. Make warmth as quickly as possible for the life of my cousin."

Shall I send one of the men on horse to Pemberley House Sir?"

"Yes. Do so, do so in all haste. Take Rupert's horse with saddle. And save this poor girl, warm her by the fire."

Quickly salvaging tool pieces and sundries, one man set alight gunpowder, which put the whole carriage structure to flame in minutes. The two women, lady and maid, were put close to the fire for the life-giving warmth needed to sustain them. Meanwhile, the problems of descending the hills with two sick women and a dead body was a problem that he needed to solve. He needed to think quickly if the remaining souls were to survive.

One horse could carry the body of Rupert. Ann could ride the other horse while the maid may be able to sit behind her.

"There is no weight to either of them." He thought.

The remainder, food and sundry items were not worth the salt. They could leave it all to the old crones. His mind dwelt on them for some time thinking what else he might do in thankfulness to the Lord for the saving the life of his dear cousin, Ann.

The men were scavenging in the baskets for any edible remains of their previous night's feast as a final recharge of their constitutions before setting forth homewards.

Sir Richard strolled over to the two women to discover that the maid had just stirred into life. She saw Sir Richard and explained that the heat from the fire was becoming too much for her but Ann would not stir.

Still in a half sleep state she concluded, "In truth, she seemed rather too stiff to move."

Chapter Seventeen

Morning Drama

There remained a silence as Sir Richard stood on the brink of knowing the worst without wanting to believe it. Whispers quickly circulated among the men as an understanding grew of the situation. Their master stood still for several minutes. He was, apparently, insensible to the sounds of human activity and their hailing greetings as they approached but still some distance behind him. The rest of the party turned their heads towards the advancing band of people. Men and women, they waved as they approached and called across to the sojourners of the night. In their turn, Sir Richard's party responded in like but not Sir Richard. He was motionless, oblivious of the activity now surrounding him. Two of his men approached their master. One each side stood by him not knowing what they should do.

One ventured, "Are you alright, Sir?"

The other expanded. We have many people arriving, Sir. They will want to speak to you."

"My cousin, the lady, she is well?"

"Her troubles are over now, Sir. The good Lord has called her home. We will look after what remains, Sir. She looks as though she had a peaceful passing, God be praised."

The man had skilfully phrased his words and they proved some comfort to his master. The new arrivals were now gathering around Sir Richard. Many were throwing questions at him. So many questions upon questions, but Sir Richard was not mentally prepared to talk of the two souls lost sometime during the night.

Sir Rufus arrived with his hand outstretched. Sir Richard took it mechanically but barely responding to the words of greeting.

"We saw the fire and thought someone had lit a beacon to tell us that the French had landed." Then followed in a jovial manner, "We would have seen them off, eh Darcy? Where's my son then? Is he here?"

The sounds of happy voices having discovered the stranded party, were looking around the encampment, some discovered one body while others found the other, which was still lying by the blazing carriage fire. There were screams from several of the ladies. The cries and wailing took the attention away from Sir Rufus's questions.

"Sir Rufus, my dear friend for . . . so many years . . . . yesterday your son braved the elements to search for us, Ann in particular. He found us late last night. He was cold, wet through and exhausted. Ann gave him some victuals and a fire was made to warm him. Ann sat by him by the fire all night . . . . I have the painful . . . duty to inform you that Rupert's condition worsened so that he did not survive the night. Within an hour of the men discovering Rupert, Miss Anne de Bourgh joined him in a better world. We set fire to your carriage to keep Ann warm but like Rupert, she was too far indisposed to continue. Whether it was the cold or the loss of Rupert or a sum of each we may never know but I strongly favour the latter."

"My son, Rupert, died? No! No! It cannot be!"

Sir Rufus turned his head in the direction that the plaintive cries originated.

"There must be some mistake. Good God, there must be some error in this."

Sir Richard relieved to have been able to relate the bad tidings was otherwise distressed and more so now by the discomposure of his friend. There was no way to comfort him. His thoughts turned to Lady Penelope, "She too will be distraught. It will be the least likely intelligence that she will be expecting."

Gedolf approached him on his left side, "We are all ready to leave now sir. Can we go home? The men are eager to go and they will be expecting you back at Pemberley."

The man's words gave rein to his thoughts. "Home." He thought was Pemberley House, "They." His Elizabeth, she would be waiting patiently for him, unaware of the tragedy of the night.

The emotion of the events was catching up with Sir Richard. Tears started to roll down his face. He was unable to speak but just nodded his head. Gedolf waved a hand to the other men of the Pemberley staff. They turned towards the path that lead under the crag and around the hill and then homeward for them. This way took them in the opposite direction from where Ann had originally turned off the road to find shelter. The party from Wynnstay House and the maid went their way, calling back some farewells to their Pemberley counterparts and waving.

Sir Richard took a horse, while the other horses went with Sir Rufus, carrying the bodies. One of the men, being well acquainted with the local topography, led Sir Richard and the others for two hours down the hills to the safety of the north road. The north road would lead them to Pemberley house.

Descending had been much easier than the climb up in the dark with the wind and rain, but not without its own dangers and physical demands. By the time they reached the road, the party, though tired, turned into a more cheerful disposition.

Walking along the road was less challenging than the uneven and angled downward descent of the hills. Though that had taxed their energies, the men now continued along the road with easier hearts. Sir Richard mounted, benefiting by way of a better view of the immediate surroundings. He could see ahead that which the men on foot were unable to see. Sir Richard turned round on his horse, to look at his men. His men he recognized but not the exhausted condition they displayed.

He called out to them, "Stay here . . . rest yourselves."

The men watched him in disbelief as he galloped his horse away at some speed. Their hearts sank, as he grew smaller. They could not see, so were not to know of the carriage standing by the roadside almost a mile further on. The call to "Rest yourselves." was enough to encourage them all to collapse on the banks by the side of the road.

Sir Richard galloped on towards the carriage. As he advanced nearer to the carriage, it grew bigger, so it appeared, and the more real it became. Through a night of cold and discomfort, then a morning of death and misery here was the first promise of civilization and order. When he could see clearly that it was Elizabeth's carriage, he spurred on faster. His thoughts were of Elizabeth and that Elizabeth would be waiting for him. As he approached near the carriage, the liverymen turned round to see who was riding towards them from the rear. One of the men exclaimed, "It's the master, Sir Richard. He is alone."

The attendant staff had voluntarily ventured to search for Sir Richard and his party earlier that same morning. Now their task had its fulfilment. By the time their master approached the carriage; the men had smartened themselves. They were proud to show him of their concern and indulgence. Sir Richard drew alongside the carriage but was now disappointed that Elizabeth was not present.

He called to Harwood, the driver. "The others are a mile further on from you. Bring them home at once."

As an after thought he addressed his men further, "It is good to see you."

Then he rode off without any further word. His only thoughts were of his return to Elizabeth and Pemberley. The road was clear, like the morning air and all of creation that morning seemed blessed by the Heavens.

"Thank God!" His thoughts continued, recalling the night passed.

He was feeling warmer for the exercise. It was a contrast from the cold of the winter's night and the images of the departed Rupert and the final misfortune of Anne's premature call to another world. His thoughts swung backwards and forwards recalling and re-recalling the events. He fell into despair. He cried woefully. His horse, sensing the lack of control from its rider, gave way to a walk until finally came to a standing halt. There was, by purpose or chance, a patch of grass within a potential dining limit. While the horse went about to indulge his nutritional interests, the man slipped away from the saddle to feel the solid ground beneath him. The possible reaction by Elizabeth to the news of the demise of Ann caused him to shake visibly. This adverse news could cause extreme distress and may compromise her present delicate condition. This could damage their yet unborn baby. Then there was Lady Catherine of whom he had the greatest respect and close family ties that made it necessary for him to be the one to tell of the events leading up to the loss of her daughter's life. He must carry out this service, however painful it will be.

The approach of Elizabeth's carriage with his staff expressing their high spirits with singing interrupted Sir Richard's introspections. He re-mounted quickly, dispersing his contemplations to gallop in haste to Pemberley and Elizabeth.

✠

Chapter Eighteen

Good Counsel Has No Price

Sir Richard pressed his horse faster until he reached the first bridge, the small bridge that crossed a brook and was just before a fork in the road. The road to the right of the fork led past cottages of his estate workers and then onward down to the stables. He took the left fork, reined back down to a trot and then a walk. The thoughts of informing Elizabeth of these tragedies and how this news may affect her at this time so close to her confinement, gave him grave doubts of the wisdom of his doing so.

The carriage passed by on the adjacent road but unseen with his men still singing and making innocent merriment. They travelled on the road, down to the stables, shielded from sight but not sound as the road was, by the wooded break between. The noise from Elizabeth's carriage made him suddenly aware of the possible reason for sending the livery for his return. "Why was Elizabeth not with her carriage? Why did she not come too? There must be something wrong here. Elizabeth must have had problems. There must have been complications." He urged his horse on, again at a gallop. His mind in a turmoil now, by the thoughts to what misfortune his dear Elizabeth might have succumbed. How unwise it was of him to leave her so at this time.

He passed through the gates and on to the entrance of Pemberley. He dismounted, jumping off his slowing horse still, to run up the steps to the door, which a servant opened for him.

"Where is Lady Elizabeth?"

"I think you will find her in her rooms, sir."

He made for the stairs at apace rarely practiced by him.

With total disregard for all normal propriety, Sir Richard brought himself with all the utmost haste to Elizabeth's bedside.

She was awake, sitting up and apparently well by all her appearance.

"My dear Elizabeth, you are in good health?"

"Oh, good morning sir. Why thank you, yes I am in as good a health as you saw me just some hours before . . . when you left in haste to Wynnstay House. Has your expedition been fruitful? Did you meet Sir Rufus? Is Ann safe and well?"

Aware, as Sir Richard was, regarding the intimacy between Elizabeth and Anne, he felt it prudent to avoid references to Anne and Rupert and the events in the hills.

"We found the party safe and well . . . but you, you are well?"

"Why, yes sir, I am well, as you see. I am expecting the physician to visit very soon to tell me so." Elizabeth assured him while smiling broadly.

Sir Richard always enjoyed Elizabeth's pleasantries but his concern for her condition was paramount in his considerations. He decided to consult the doctor, secretly upon his arrival, on the wisdom of informing Elizabeth of the fate of her cousin, Anne.

Sir Richard began to feel the effects of the night before and the early morning rise. After which, he descended the hills with his men, then rode hard to Pemberley.

He sank deeply down into a commodious chair beside Elizabeth's bed with his problem unresolved then naturally sinking deeper still into a sleep well earned.

With the peace that returned to Elizabeth's chamber, she called for breakfasts in her chamber as soon as the physician finished his examination.

The clatter of plates and servants going about their tasks disturbed Sir Richard's slumbers. Waking suddenly, he looked round enquiringly, searching for signs of the physician's visit. "Your physician has not yet visited?"

Elizabeth assured him that he had been, had declared her to have excellent humour and joked that I should not be wasting his time. "So you see sir, you need have no concern on my account."

"My dear Elizabeth, you are right of course. I should but express my courtesies to your physician."

Sir Richard signalled to a servant to find the Physician. He then ambled to the door to leave the room. Immediately upon exiting Elizabeth's chamber, he, in great haste hurried after the physician. Sir Richard accosted him as he was preparing to leave the house.

He explained in broad terms his problem with the demise of Ann, and her relationship to the patient. He continued to explain his concern for the welfare of Lady Elizabeth and was dubious about releasing the bad news.

"As your medical adviser, I am unable to say with full certainty, Sir Richard. It may be that your lady would want to know of the news of her friend's fate and she should be strong enough to cope with the tragedy but then she is not in her normal state, thus her ladyship will be more prone to become distressed, perhaps, to a dangerous degree. If you think the risk is worth the penny, as her ladyship's husband, tell her but she may be more grateful to you if she learns after the forth-coming event. I have come to know Lady Elizabeth very well. I would advise, not as a doctor, but as an interested party, take the cautious route, sir, but show no sign of doing so."

"Why, yes, of course. I can understand more clearly now. The distress of the past events and my concern for Lady Elizabeth has clouded my own mind. I will heed your words doctor. I am much indebted to you."

"Tut, tut! Sir Richard, good friendly counsel has no price."

"Thank you doctor. A very good day to you."

Sir Richard returned to Elizabeth's chamber where he discovered, to his delight, Bingley, Jane and their baby girl enjoying their promised visit at this most important time. It reminded him that other members of the family would be joining the party. He must inform the staff of the many guests expected. Strict instructions were given that each guest to be cautioned to remain silent on the fate of Ann and Rupert.

The days following, guests arrived including the whole of the Bennet family, the Colonel Fitzwilliam with Lady Lydia and a certain clergyman from the environs of Rosings Park. Mr. Collins was the most garrulous of all the guests. Sir Richard thought it a matter of urgency to caution Mr. Collins' party. His party included Elizabeth's younger sister Mary, accompanying him to attend to her charge, Mr. Collins's baby daughter. If the parson should make one unguarded word the effect could be injurious to Elizabeth's condition.

Their evenings they spent in convivial games, cards and music. Even Mary excelled with an air of her own composition. Neighbours of nearby estates often visited to join in the distractions of the evenings. By the end of a week, the evening entertainments were wearying for the family and guests. An agreement arose among the company that they should devise a play to stage as a distraction for Elizabeth in her early confinement and for their own inclusion and entertainment.

Chapter Nineteen

The Best of Friends Must Part

The entire family and the guests united in their agreement to act a play. The Colonel and Bingley met in the morning room to discuss the possibilities of which play they should try. The colonel observed, "With many ladies available, a play that would accommodate numerous female parts would be the most likely.

"I fear that is not so," Bingley pointed out that, "There were now only six ladies because my sisters have not yet come. Then, consider, three of these ladies are indisposed. Miss Mary Bennet is nursing Mr. Collins's baby, Jane is nursing her own and Elizabeth is anticipating her event very soon."

"Of course, you are right Bingley, but they will make an excellent audience for our cast to amuse. Do you not think so?"

Lydia, on the excuse of looking for the Colonel, entered the room and was quick to engage in the discussions. "What is it that you think of sir?"

"A play in general, which play specifically and who can take part."

"My sister Mary, writes plays and one especially she likes is very popular with the family. There is just one problem, it does involve extensive piano playing which Mary always insists is her best role. It is so that she is not asked to act. To be sure, her acting cannot be worse than her singing."

"What is this play of your sister, Miss Bennet? Would it be possible to use it for our diversion, do you suppose?"

"Lydia please! Lady if you must. Oh no! That is not what I meant. It is a *deeply* religious play with lots of hidden meanings and unworldly events. Oh, no, not just before Christmas, we should have something more jolly for our entertainment."

At that moment, Mr. Collins entered the room and at once took up the reference to "Christmas" for his consideration. "For this season we should consider a religious theme if only to appear respectable. Consider my most gracious patroness, she should not learn of an imprudent indulgence whilst away from my parish. A Christmas play would be highly commendable. I could count no danger in that."

Lydia feigned a commodious amount of exasperation. The affect on the rest of the company was one of some embarrassment shown by a collective silence. They were, to a degree, all in sympathy with Lydia's feelings but reluctant to show them to be so.

Mr. Bingley was the first to break the silence, "May I suggest something from Shakespeare for our play? Just an excerpt, perhaps from "Twelfth Night"? There is much humour to be enjoyed there and would not give offence to anyone."

If only to conclude a difficult meeting of conflicting views, the company agreed to approach Jane to select extracts from "Twelfth Night" for consideration the following day.

The embryonic impresarios assembled the following morning to learn of Jane's choice of possible scenes.

Jane addressed her fellow thespians, "There is much in "Twelfth Night" to commend it, but it could not be as entertaining as a short excerpt from "A Comedy of Errors." This is much easier to learn and requires little or as much scenery as we wish. Here is something jolly for Christmas entertainment."

The discussions continued across the breakfast table, sometimes heated by controversy, sometimes more pleasantly in accord.

"We could use the part from A Comedy of Errors where Antipholus sends Dromio to deposit his money only to meet up with the other Dromio who swears he knows nothing of the thousand marks and receives such a beating and sends him on another errand. Then later, he meets the other Dromio who swears he knows nothing of the previous altercation. This would require only the basic of scenery or as much as we want."

Only this rudimentary description was enough to cause an infectious good humour amongst the party.

While others considered that the more preparation and much scenery was preferable for the improved distraction this would bring, others were for simplicity. While the discussions continued, they made little progress with the arrangements for the stage, the scenery or costumes. All these considerations besides, the actors were not learning their lines because they had no lines to learn as yet.

With the passing of two more days of discussions, the company continued to make no progress except for some of the cast were learning speeches of Shakespearian origin because they enjoyed the parts. Like cockerels strutting in the fields before their hens, the men would recite passages from Hamlet, Henry V, or King John and such like heroic lines. It was while the preparations had stalled this far from anything conclusive that two visitors arrived at Pemberley.

The family and guests greeted them with enthusiasm and alacrity. The honourable rescuers of the Derbyshire Hills, Sir Rufus and his Lady made their visit without prior notice or appointment.

The greetings from Sir Richard they thankfully received.

Sir Rufus was brisk about their business however, "We bring the most important news, Sir."

Then addressing Sir Richard confidentially continued, "In private if we may."

Surreptitiously Sir Richard ushered the two guests into his personal office.

Sir Rufus spoke in low tones. "We have come in great haste from Rosings Park. We spoke to Lady Catherine about the unfortunate event on the hills."

Sir Rufus stopped and appeared as though he did not know how to proceed. "It was my fault; I had no knowledge of Lady Catherine being in ignorance of the fate of her daughter."

Sir Richard listened to his friends with consternation, only interjecting, "I said nothing to my aunt because I knew you would need to visit her. Thus you would be able to tell Lady Catherine yourself of the unfortunate events leading to the passing of Rupert and Anne."

"Yes, yes, I understood that but our visit went very badly, very ill indeed, Darcy. My news affected her to an extreme. We were in fear of something terrible happening. Lady Catherine broke down with one moment anger and the next in sorrow alternatively until she collapsed. At first, I thought she had expired but we revived her. Then I tried my best to comfort her, to tell her of the love my son and her daughter enjoyed together and that they and we shall have those precious times to share for ever."

"You gave her much comfort then. I must say you managed very well. Is Lady Catherine fully recovered now?"

"Recovered, Darcy? Not a bit of it. The news gets worse."

"Sir Rufus, what could have been worse than the loss of Rupert and her daughter?"

"When I spoke to Lady Catherine, she listened intently. It seemed to settle her. This encouraged me to continue talking to her about Ann. We talked of Ann's friendship with Lady Elizabeth and of the many ways Elizabeth had guided Ann. They were two friends more like sisters. I spoke of her mettle in paring off her son. You know Darcy, the Colonel Fitzwilliam and her daughter? She did the right thing there. I spoke as much as I could, but after exhausting the topic I naturally continued about Ann marring the gypsy fellow, I forgot his name. She seemed puzzled at first but as I went into the details of how happy Ann seemed with the gypsy life Lady Catherine would not have it. I was not aware that she knew nothing of her own daughter's marriage to the gypsy fellow. I did not know that it was not widely understood. As I insisted it was so, she became more and more agitated again. I began to apologize but the more I did, the more she raged until Lady Catherine left her senses utterly. She eventually sank into a faint. The servants took Catherine to her chamber where, sometime during the night, I am so sorry to say, Darcy, she left this world for a better one, perhaps to be with Ann again."

Sir Richard was, at first, dumbfounded without his thoughts being able to take in the whole of the consequences of the events of which Sir Rufus had unfolded.

"Rufus my dear friend, as sorry as I am to learn of these events, you must not hint at this to anyone who might relay the tragedy to Elizabeth. She is very vulnerable in her present condition. If she should learn of this, the intelligence will naturally lead her to discover of the fate of Ann and Rupert. To learn of this triple tragedy I fear could seriously affect her well being."

"You have my word, Darcy. She shall not hear of it from my lips. For now, I shall return home where our secret will remain for the time being. Might I suggest you tell of this to the Colonel? He is an interested party as possibly now, the only heir to Rosings Park, I understand. We will leave you now to return to Wynnstay. I hope all goes well with Lady Elizabeth at this time."

Sir and Lady Rufus left without ceremony asking Sir Richard to tender his apologies to his guests. The reason to offer was that they had been away from home and had much in the way of affairs requiring their attention. They again assured Sir Richard that other persons should not hear of these events from their lips.

It was for Sir Richard to tender his apologies to his guests for their sudden departure.

Sir Richard singled aside his cousin the Colonel, to inform him of the events that had passed at Rosings. He also hinted, as the sole remaining off-spring of Lady Catherine, he would the most likely to inherit the entire estate of Rosings Park and that he and Lydia should make all haste to their new home to secure the house and the contents from outside interference.

With a little formality and hasty packing of trunks, the couple was soon ensconced in a carriage and ready to leave Pemberley for the journey to Rosings Park.

Sir Richard said his farewells and regrets of their leaving Pemberley and added, "We have a lawyer in the family in London who will do everything to assist you in the transfer. You can trust him. I have written down his details here, his name is Mr. Gardiner. I will write now and inform him of the events."

The colonel took the details with thanks. They shook hands through the open window. The colonel could say, only "The best of friends must part."

Sir Richard could add no more. They continued their farewells as the carriage drew away.

The loss of the Colonel and Lydia made a serious shortage to the players. Lydia's absence reduced the company to two able women, Georgiana and Kitty.

Returning to his guests, Sir Richard realized that the news from Rosings of the demise of his esteemed patroness must be of some importance to Mr. Collins. His duty must be to inform Mr. Collins of the broad outline of the situation and not omitting that Lydia would now be his patroness and hopefully live up to her predecessor's affability and condescension.

Chapter Twenty

Christmas Day

No man feels happy away from home when events affecting him there are unfolding. Upon learning confidentially from Sir Richard of the accounts of the demise of his patroness, Mr. Collins and his party, hastily took their leave of Sir Richard; then made their way to their carriage for a return journey to The Parsonage.

The loss therefore, of Miss Mary Bennet, reduced the troupe to three or perhaps four ladies and three gentlemen. The participation of the fourth lady, Jane, depended on her availability and the demands of her baby. The third member of the troupe, being Mrs Bennet was apt to forget her lines or mix them so that nobody could understand her. Georgiana laughed and giggled as the play turned into a pantomime of forgotten lines and missing actors.

During the following two weeks, four members of the troupe worked diligently with their parts. All the while, men from the estate volunteered for the necessary carpentry and women for the costumes. In spite of the many involved, they all managed the events in various ways to maintain a cloak of secrecy from the rest of the household.

Even Mrs Bennet remained so silent that neither Elizabeth, nor anyone unconnected with the production, suspected they were preparing a play in the blue suite. Excuses made to the Pemberley staff for the irregular activities were always convincing. Even before the carpenters had completed their work, the cast were rehearsing their parts on the stage.

By the end of the second week, shortly before Christmas day, the stage, thespians, costumes and scenery were ready for the final rehearsal.

During this time of rehearsals and the many preparations, Mrs Bennet summoned the physician at intervals to Elizabeth on the anticipation that her time was immediate. Each call proved to be a false anxiety of Mrs Bennet's judgement. The doctor took each mistaken intelligence with politeness and as preferred prudence.

With the complete success of the final rehearsal, the cast and helpers felt confident to offer Lady Elizabeth their performance on Christmas Day.

The company assigned to Jane the pleasure to inform her sister of the proceedings that would take place on Christmas day in the blue suite in her honour.

The thought of the enjoyment the play would bring Elizabeth and at such a time, filled Jane with excitement. The distraction of a play and poetry would bring to her younger sister the best of the season's joys and comforts during her present circumstances. The cast universally agreed that Jane should be the best member of the family to take the news to Elizabeth.

Jane became excited in the thoughts of how Elizabeth would delight in her announcement of their play for Christmas day. With this inspiring her thoughts, Jane entered Elizabeth's chambers. The two sisters embraced as best they could while Elizabeth was recumbent in her bed and so near to her delivery. With the customary courtesies completed, Jane was in such high spirits that it was not difficult for Elizabeth to conclude that it was not without some worthy reason. Elizabeth enquired of Jane for the reason of her sprightliness.

"I have an announcement to make which I know will please. You cannot guess, so I will tell you, dear Elizabeth. These last weeks we have been rehearsing in the blue suite to make a play for your enjoyment on Christmas day. There! Does this not excite you? Will this not help your confinement to pass more quickly?"

"Sweet Jane, you must know that the biggest event is due any day shortly. I could not possible chance the journey to the blue suite or anywhere. I prefer to remain here where I can be safe and secure. The housekeeper, Mrs Reynolds, told me that the staff has arranged sacred songs to sing to me on Christmas morning. The choir will be coming here, to me, into my own bedchamber. I feel very sorry but thank you Jane, for your good intentions"

Jane felt a sudden drop in her good composure. Having hoped for a joyful response to the news of a happy distraction, this unexpected news caused Jane, to shed tears involuntarily. Not only the disappointment of not pleasing Elizabeth, which was foremost, but for hard work of the troupe who now have to suffer the disappointment. Further, more, it rests on her to make the pronouncement to the players.

Jane with good pretence put on a cheerful countenance to make her withdrawal from her sister's bedchamber.

— o —

In the early hours of Christmas morning, Sir Richard's valet had to work hard to awaken his master. The late night before, in the company of his relatives and following into later hours of the night with Elizabeth, did not make for an easy awakening. Daylight had not yet fully dawned.

"Good morning sir, are you awake?"

"What is it man? Good God, it is not yet light. What is amiss? Have the French invaded?"

"Not to my knowledge sir. Lady Elizabeth asked me to summon you to her chambers. Your good lady has something to show you that you have been expecting for some months."

"Are you sure? I have not been expecting anything, nothing at all!"

"I am quite sure, Sir Richard, that is, I think she would like to show you her new baby."

"Good grief man, why did you not say so. Fetch my breeches quickly."

With the minimum delay, Sir Richard, wearing one brown shoe and one black shoe, with his attire in some disarray, was hurrying towards Lady Elizabeth's chambers.

Meanwhile, the staff heard of the fulfilment of the expected event. Therefore, they had made their way to Elizabeth's Chambers to welcome the newly born to this world on Christmas morning with their compilation of seasonal hymns.

As Sir Richard hurried along the corridor in the early hours at a time quietness was normal, he could hear the gentle choral harmony of the singers in Elizabeth's chambers. In the morning air and the stillness that persists before the day begins, Sir Richard could hear the singers. The choir sang softly, sweetly in perfect harmony to a tiny mite to welcome it into this world. Sir Richard arrived at the door, pushed it gently open, just a little, to peep cautiously into his lady's chambers. He slowly approached Elizabeth's bed while the harmony continued. Rarely had he heard such quality of voice or so moving a chorus. The singing continued.

"Elizabeth, how are you?"

In the subdued light, for a while, he could make out Elizabeth's face only. Continuing to peer into the shadows, Sir Richard's eyes fell upon a face alongside Elizabeth. This was another face but which he had never seen before. It was a tiny face on a tiny head, which must have been on a tiny body. The face spoke without words. Spoke of perfection, innocence and everything good. Inside Sir Richard must have felt the same as any new father does on those precious minutes of seeing his first newly born child for the first time.

Elizabeth whispered, "Our baby is sleeping."

For a few minutes neither parent spoke. No words could frame the moment. The only sound was the gentle harmony of the choir. For those few holy minutes, it seemed time did not belong but just was.

Sir Richard leaned over the bed to be close enough to whisper to his lady.

"Tell me, dear Elizabeth, am I a father to a little boy or a little girl?"

Elizabeth beamed.

Sir Richard thought he could detect amusement in that smile "Yes."

He smiled back for the humour that was ever Elizabeth it seemed.

He leaned over further across the sleeping babe to kiss Elizabeth on her forehead and whispered, "Dearest . . . Loveliest . . . Elizabeth . . . mine."

✥

The End of Volume Three

TO BE CONTINUED